INTERPRETING SCRIPTURE
across CULTURES

INTERPRETING SCRIPTURE
across CULTURES

An Introduction to Cross-Cultural Hermeneutics

WILL BROOKS

WIPF & STOCK · Eugene, Oregon

INTERPRETING SCRIPTURE ACROSS CULTURES
An Introduction to Cross-Cultural Hermeneutics

Copyright © 2022 Will Brooks. All rights reserved. Except for brief quotations in critical publications or reviews, no part of this book may be reproduced in any manner without prior written permission from the publisher. Write: Permissions, Wipf and Stock Publishers, 199 W. 8th Ave., Suite 3, Eugene, OR 97401.

Wipf & Stock
An Imprint of Wipf and Stock Publishers
199 W. 8th Ave., Suite 3
Eugene, OR 97401

www.wipfandstock.com

PAPERBACK ISBN: 978-1-6667-0748-9
HARDCOVER ISBN: 978-1-6667-0749-6
EBOOK ISBN: 978-1-6667-0750-2

JUNE 10, 2022 8:29 AM

Scripture quotations are from the ESV® Bible (The Holy Bible, English Standard Version®), copyright © 2001 by Crossway, a publishing ministry of Good News Publishers. Used by permission. All rights reserved.

Some of the material in chapter 10 is adapted from Will Brooks, "Grammatical-Historical Exegesis and World Mission," in *World Mission* (Lexham, 2019). Used with permission.

Some of the material in the introduction and conclusion first appeared in my article "Hermeneutics for Healthy Churches." EMQ (January 2017). The current copyright holder is *Missio Nexus*. Used with permission.

For my parents, Randy and Debby Brooks,
who have always loved and supported me

Contents

Acknowledgements | ix

Introduction | 1

SECTION 1

    Section 1 | 11

1   The Challenge of Context | 13

2   The Challenge of Pursuing the Author through the Text | 27

3   The Challenge of Self-Theologizing | 40

4   The Challenge of Contextualization | 52

SECTION 2

    Section 2 | 67

5   Postcolonial Hermeneutics | 69

6   Cross-Textual Hermeneutics | 79

7   Rhetorical-Interactive Hermeneutics | 83

8   Ethnohermeneutics | 95

9   Other Models | 110

SECTION 3

      Section 3 | 123

10   Principles for a Cross-Cultural Author-Oriented Approach | 125

11   Applying the Model in Various Contexts | 148

12   Applying the Model Among Oral Learners | 170

Conclusion: Importance of Hermeneutics in Missions Contexts | 184

Bibliography | 189

Acknowledgments

THE WORK OF A SEMINARY PROFESSOR is often a bit lonely—toiling away by oneself reading, writing, or preparing lecture content. Perhaps that's why so many of us are introverted. I would include myself in that list of those who are introverted and who enjoy being alone with our books. But I say that with a caveat, namely that I often learn best in community. While I do need time to think and reflect, I also find I make great strides in thinking about some topic when I have a lively discussion or debate with colleagues or students. These times in the learning community often encourage me to consider a topic from a new perspective.

To that point, I'm thankful to so many people who helped me in the process of writing this book and who took the time to think through and discuss the content with me. Of course, I started thinking about this topic during my first semester as an MDiv student when I took both Hermeneutics and Intro to Missions. And then later I focused on the integration of these topics during my PhD studies. During those years I was blessed with so many conversations with professors and classmates who challenged me and sharpened my thinking on this topic.

In recent years, I've enjoyed numerous conversations with colleagues on this and related topics. Fellow professors Vincent Ooi, J. C. Chua, Wendel Sun, Scott Callaham, Chris Santiago, Kyle Essary, Chris Abner, Phil Barnes, Kevin Rodgers, and Mark Johnson have all helped me with conversations related to topics like cross-cultural hermeneutics, theological education in the Majority World, contextualization, etc. Ben Rainey and Trip Whalen also helped me considerably in thinking through the chapter on oral hermeneutics. In addition to these coworkers, I bounced many ideas off Preston Pearce. He read several editions of the manuscript and gave me valuable input, especially on chapter 2.

Acknowledgments

I've also had the privilege of teaching a course on this and several related topics. I'm thankful to ICTS and MBTS for the opportunities to teach these courses, mostly because these were opportunities to interact with so many gifted students—more than I could begin to mention here. Conversations with Lee and Miki Lo strengthened my understanding of interpreting in the East Asian context. In terms of the manuscript itself, Melanie Lim read a few chapters, and C. J. Ng read an early version of the entire manuscript. Both gave valuable insight into how to improve it. C. J. also helped track down and summarize many resources related to ancestor veneration and other material in chapters 10–11.

Most importantly, this book would not exist were it not for the support of my family. This book is dedicated to my parents, who have always supported and encouraged even though obeying God's call took us all so far from them. My kids prayed regularly for me as I tried to finish this project, and one son helped me scan through the manuscript looking for certain errors, in exchange for Starbucks, of course! My wife Winnie made countless sacrifices to free me up and give me more time to work. She made many of these sacrifices while she was finishing her own MA. It is no exaggeration to say I would never have finished this project, or many other ones, were it not for her faithful support.

Introduction

ON A DIRT ROAD somewhere in the Middle East, a missionary walks alone. As he walks, he wonders what work God might be leading him to do that day, and then, seemingly out of nowhere, a man appears on the horizon. He approaches the man and notices he is intently reading some document. Filled with boldness and sensing God's leadership, the missionary draws near and asks the man what he is reading. The man replies that he is reading a curious document written by someone named Isaiah. Sensing a God-ordained gospel-sharing opportunity, the missionary asks him if he understands what he is reading. The man's reply is illuminating: "How can I unless someone guides me?"

Perceptive readers have already realized that this historically accurate event did not take place in a contemporary setting, but was recorded in Acts 8:26–40, when Philip encountered the Ethiopian eunuch. That said, don't miss the missiological significance of the event—the eunuch had a portion of the Scriptures in a language he could understand, and yet he still needed someone to help him understand it. This event helps us see the vital connection between missions and hermeneutics.

The task of missions is not complete when a few are converted, when an initial church is planted, or even when many churches are planted among a people group. A critical aspect of the missionary task is the training and equipping of believers—the "teaching them to obey all things" aspect of the Great Commission. The goal of the Great Commission is not merely the existence of a church but the existence of a healthy, vibrant, growing church.

So, then, what makes a healthy church? Missionaries who consider such a question are often plagued with tunnel vision. Rightly loving and laboring to see the advance of the gospel into new areas, they define church health solely in terms of the church's ability to start new churches. Self-propagation, then, becomes the sole defining metric of church health.

In reality, many other components should be included in a discussion of church health, and, to be fair, most of those components are not easily quantifiable.

The reality is that, like the Ethiopian eunuch, every church needs guides—guides who will lead the church to interpret Scripture in a way that is faithful to the original author's intent. This fundamental need is the reason why Paul commanded Timothy to labor to become "a worker who has no need to be ashamed, rightly handling the Word of truth" (2 Tim 2:15).

Biblical interpretation is so critical to the overall health of a local church that it is fair to say that it affects every single area of church health. For example, biblical preaching and teaching is without a doubt a key aspect of church health, but it's hard to imagine a church having healthy biblical teaching without healthy biblical interpretation. Likewise, a church would not have biblically healthy evangelistic and missiological practices without faithful exegesis of the Scriptures, which teach us the correct way to think about God, his nature, and his heart for the nations.

More specifically, consider the issue of prayer. Most would agree that prayer is an essential aspect of church health, but few consider how much biblical interpretation influences the way a church prays. A church that places little importance on understanding the truths of God's word will pray little or will repeat the same phrases again and again. But the church that loves the word, rightly understands the word, and rightly applies the word to their lives will pray in accordance with those truths.[1] When they read in Psalm 31 of the testimony of the Psalmist who took refuge in God, cried out to him, and found him faithful, they will praise God for his faithfulness and say, "Be faithful to me, O God, and help me to take refuge in you and not in the things of this world."[2] Or when they see Daniel pray and say, "We have sinned and done wrong and acted wickedly and rebelled" (Dan 9:5), being able to read this text and understand it in its original context will inform their own prayers of confession. Healthy biblical interpretation leads to healthy prayer.

The Scriptures naturally stand at the center of all that a local church is and does, and thus biblical interpretation is critical to every area of church health. In fact, it is so important that one could make the argument that if a local church has healthy biblical interpretation, they will naturally be

---

1. Leeman, *Word Centered Church*, 149–158, esp. 150.

2. I learned this method of praying the Psalms from Don Whitney, and he explains his approach in Whitney, *Praying the Bible*.

healthy in every other area. Mark Dever explains it this way: "If you establish the priority of the Word, then you have in place the single most important aspect of the church's life, and growing health is virtually assured, because God has decided to act by his Spirit through his Word."[3] In other words, if a church gets this right, everything else will fall into place.

We might ask, then, how does a church get there? How does a church grow in this area, or how does a church learn or implement the type of healthy biblical interpretation that influences every other area of church health? We can take the conversation one step further and connect it to the work of missionaries, who go to other contexts for the sole purpose of seeing a healthy, vibrant church planted in those locations. In some ways, the key question of this book is: *How does a missionary plant a church in a context formerly untouched by the gospel and do it in a way that ensures the church will be able to interpret the Bible faithfully?*

Biblical Interpretation in Intercultural Contexts

In that sense, we can ask: what happens when biblical interpretation is done in missiological contexts? In other words, what happens when people from two different cultural contexts attempt to interpret the Bible together? In what ways do their differing cultural contexts affect the process of interpreting Scripture? Are there principles that can be utilized in any cultural context that can aid the interpretive process? Is it paternalistic to think that believers in other cultural contexts should interpret the Bible using so-called "traditional" methods of biblical interpretation?

To illustrate the complex nature of these questions, imagine a scenario in which a missionary from a Western context begins to study the Bible with a group of new believers in an Asian context. As they begin to look at a specific text together, these Asian believers explain that their method for interpreting any sacred text is allegory. The Western believer, steeped in the heritage of the Reformation, finds allegorical interpretation of the Bible unacceptable. How should he respond? Is it arrogant for the missionary to tell believers from another cultural context that their methods of interpretation are incorrect?

Or we can consider a couple specific texts. Many people memorize John 3:16 as children, since they consider it a clear, concise summary of the gospel. If read in a Hindu context, however, some might interpret the

3. Dever, *Nine Marks of a Healthy Church*, 43.

verse's emphasis on eternal life as teaching reincarnation. In this case, the gospel would seem unattractive, since Hindus are trying to avoid *samsara*, the endless cycle of reincarnation, and enter *nirvana*. It is easy to see how that cultural context complicates the process of interpretation.

Romans 3:23 is another verse that is often used in gospel presentations, where Paul wrote that "all have sinned and fall short of the glory of God." When interpreting this verse, a Western believer might focus in on sin and the resultant guilt all have before God. Many Asian believers, though, would emphasize the falling short of God's glory and interpret that phrase within an honor-and-shame perspective. Is one perspective more correct than the other? Are both aspects of the gospel message equal and valid?

Presenting the gospel in new cultural contexts can be challenging. At the same time, interpreting Scripture in those contexts *after* people become believers can be even more complex. For example, many Asian cultures practice ancestor veneration. Even after their conversion to Christ, some new believers wrestle with how they should understand these traditional aspects of their cultures, especially since these activities are woven into the fabric of every tradition, festival, and family gathering.

To apply just one text to this situation, the missionary may point to the First Commandment in Exodus 20:3 and argue that we should not worship ancestors since God commands us to worship no other gods except him. The Asian believers might respond, though, with the Fifth Commandment in Exodus 20:12, explaining that these practices are simply a way of honoring their parents and the memory of already-deceased relatives. And while many of these practices are "worship" of the spirits of deceased ancestors, Western missionaries will be surprised to find out that some of the activities deemed "ancestor worship" *are* actually only means of honoring their memory. What initially seemed like an easy question to answer suddenly becomes much more complicated.

At this point my purpose is simply to illustrate the complexity of interpreting the Bible when multiple cultures are involved. We often don't realize how our own cultural lens affects how we interpret Scripture. To give a couple other examples, it is easy to see how someone from America, with its cultural emphasis on individuality and historical rejection of the monarchy, would overlook aspects of Scripture that emphasize the sovereign rule of God. Or we could consider someone who comes to Christ in a context that is highly animistic. The cultural emphasis on power and the

Introduction

need to manipulate and control the spirit world might make it difficult for this person to understand aspects of Scripture like the nature of prayer or the purpose of miracles. There is no pure reading of Scripture, but in every case, the interpreter must work to overcome his or her own cultural biases.

The Need for a Cross-Cultural Model

In this discussion, it is important to note the meaning of a few words. The use of "cross-cultural" envisions those aspects of culture that are similar or can be reproduced from culture to culture. "Intercultural," on the other hand, has in view the interaction that takes place when people from two separate and distinct cultures communicate.

In terms of the importance or the application of this book, then, we can envision three "contexts." These include:

- Intercultural contexts.
- Multicultural contexts.
- Cross-cultural contexts.

With intercultural contexts, we might consider a missionary from one cultural context who is teaching or studying the word alongside those from a different context. In multicultural contexts, we might envision a situation where people from multiple cultural contexts are studying the word together. Such an event might even take place in a regular worship service, thus the pastor or speaker needs to consider how to explain and apply the text to a variety of cultural perspectives.

While some answers have been given for how to interpret the Bible in intercultural contexts, the purpose of this book is to provide a cross-cultural model for biblical interpretation that upholds authorial intent. That is to say that I hope to present some principles for interpretation that can be used in any cultural context, including intercultural and multicultural contexts. I will discuss the fact that the author is the determiner of meaning, and thus the goal of biblical interpretation is to determine the original author's meaning. We will also see how the grammatical-historical method of exegesis can and should be utilized in different cultural contexts.

There are several reasons why the issue of cross-cultural biblical interpretation demands consideration. First, the biblical model of church planting displayed by the apostle Paul includes a commitment to teach and to train native leaders.[4] It is imperative that missionaries continue to consider not only the best ways to communicate the gospel but also the best ways to train indigenous leaders. Questions related to the appropriateness of the extent and use of culturally-sensitive and receptor-oriented hermeneutical methods fall within this discussion. Considering this issue will aid missionaries as they seek to be faithful in discipling those whom they lead to Christ.

A second reason this issue is important is because one of the primary tasks of theological education is to prepare ministers to handle the word correctly. As Larry Caldwell explains, "Interpreting God's Word for others, as well as training others to correctly interpret God's Word, is the heart of theological education."[5] The difficulty in this task increases when, as in many mission contexts around the world, the trainer and the trainee have different cultural backgrounds. The trainer must take into consideration the biblical context, the trainee's context, and his own context.[6]

To help us understand the complexity, we can imagine a scenario where someone from Indonesia travels to Sweden. How does she explain an item from her culture, for example a coconut, that doesn't exist in the new culture? Not only are there no words for that object, but nothing similar exists. Even more complex, imagine if the Swedes have never heard of the Bible. This sister from Indonesia has to explain a third culture to them. Three cultural categories are involved when someone seeks to communicate biblical truth in a new context.

As this example shows, intercultural communication in missionary contexts is quite complex. So, when a missionary trains believers to interpret the word, they must know the biblical culture but must also evaluate the ways their own cultural background influences their understanding of the text. They then must commit time to studying the trainee's cultural background and his worldview. On this last component, missionaries often have difficulty understanding the meaning behind the forms of a culture, that is, what certain cultural norms actually mean to people in that culture or why they do those things. This lack of understanding makes the

---

4. Schnabel, *Paul the Missionary*, 236–41.

5. Caldwell, "Towards an Ethnohermeneutical Model for a Lowland Filipino Context," 22.

6. For further discussion on these issues, see Grunlan and Mayers, *Cultural Anthropology*, 269–70; Hesselgrave, *Communicating Christ Cross-Culturally*, 108. Hesselgrave's model is adapted from Nida, *Message and Mission*, 52–53.

application of God's word, and the training of others in how to apply God's word, difficult in cross-cultural contexts.

Third, Caldwell is again correct in recognizing that although numerous resources exist to aid in the process of biblical interpretation, "few directly address the complexities of interpreting the Bible in multicultural contexts."[7] Along the same lines, Timothy Tennent in his work *Theology in the Context of World Christianity* explains that despite the growth of the church in the Majority World, the pressing theological issues of the Majority World are largely absent from theological discourse and publications in the West.[8] Although the task of training indigenous leaders is an important and painstaking process, it has not been given enough attention. Scholars need to write more about these issues if indigenous leaders are to interpret Scripture in a way that they are able to apply what the Bible teaches to the pressing practical and theological issues of their own contexts.

Fourth, this issue is important because there is a strong connection between the authority of Scripture and the methods used in interpreting it. No one has made this clearer than J. I. Packer, who, in the midst of the battle for inerrancy, wrote, "Biblical authority is an empty notion unless we know how to determine what the Bible means."[9] In other words, if the methods one uses to interpret the Bible undercut the truth intention of the original author, the nerve of evangelical commitment to the authority of Scripture is severed. Thus, it's important for us to consider the best ways to train national partners how to faithfully interpret Scripture in their contexts.

Looking Forward

In discussing the issue of cross-cultural biblical interpretation, this book will proceed along the following lines. Section 1 considers the challenges, specifically why interpretation is more difficult when done in intercultural contexts. And this challenge must not only be faced by missionaries but, given issues like globalization, in today's world all interpreters must consider that their hearers may have a different worldview than they have. This section will also consider issues of indigenization and contextualization and will show that raising up indigenous interpreters of Scripture who

---

7. Caldwell, "Towards the New Discipline of Ethnohermeneutics," 23.
8. Tennent, *Theology in the Context of World Christianity*, 11–12.
9. Radmacher, "Introduction," xi.

can apply the Bible's teaching to their contexts is the goal of cross-cultural hermeneutics.

In this section we will also consider the importance of authorial intent to biblical interpretation while also considering the challenges related to pursuing the author's meaning. Is it possible for interpreters today to understand the biblical authors when we are separated from them by two thousand years? Is it possible to reproduce their intended meaning? We will consider these and other questions as we consider the need for an author-oriented approach to interpretation.

Section 2 provides an evaluation of intercultural and cross-cultural theories of interpretation. In these chapters we will examine postcolonial hermeneutics, cross-textual hermeneutics, rhetorical-interactive hermeneutics, ethnohermeneutics, and several other models. We will summarize the main aspects of each view and state both the positive and negative aspects of view.

Section 3 starts by providing principles for interpretation that can be utilized in any cultural context. Then it considers the practical implications of how to apply the model. These chapters examine several specific biblical texts and the difficulties that arise when interpreting these texts in various cultural contexts. This section will also examine the issue of oral learners and propose a strategy for how oral learners can faithfully interpret Scripture.

With this direction in mind, we turn attention to the first section of the book. What historical events and discussions shaped scholarship in the areas of hermeneutics, indigenization, and contextualization? What challenges do missionaries and believers in intercultural contexts continue to face today? To these questions and others we now turn.

SECTION 1

Section 1

I LOVE TO RUN. In fact, my students often joke with me that my commitment to running, especially running long distances in difficult terrain, is something of an obsession. In late 2021, with little training and on something of a whim, I ran eighty kilometers (fifty miles) around the island where I live in Southeast Asia. I had trouble walking for a few days after that. Several times I've completed the Spartan Ultra, a grueling fifty-kilometer (thirty-mile) obstacle course on rugged terrain with elevation and more than sixty obstacles. Preparing to run that distance on trails with elevation while stopping every half mile to carry a heavy object or jump over a wall is not easy.

My friends often ask me why I keep signing up for races like these, and the truth is, I like the challenge. I enjoy the mental challenge of figuring out the best way to train and prepare, how to combine endurance running with speedwork, elevation gain, strength training, and the right nutrition plan. Of course, the race day has its own challenges. But success on race day often happens because of the hours of preparing and training.

Truth be told, whenever I commit to a new challenge, I feel a sense of excitement. At some point, though, reality sets in, and I realize that it's going to be hard. This is true not just in exercise-related pursuits but also in other areas of life. Sometimes I consider teaching or writing on a subject, and I think, "It'll be fun to wrestle with that topic." Then I start to actually look at it, and I wonder, "Why did I choose such a difficult topic?" By the end, though, I may not have completely overcome the challenge or found "the answer," but my understanding has grown and improved.

The same can be said about the topic of cross-cultural hermeneutics. Several challenges confront us as we seek to interpret Scripture in a way that recognizes the ways our own culture influences our reading of Scripture, while at the same time we seek to apply its truth to the context where we live. As we saw in the introduction, making this more complex is the fact that we are often interpreting Scripture alongside those who have a different cultural perspective than we do.

In this section, we want to look at a series of challenges related to cross-cultural hermeneutics. Each challenge touches on the subject from a slightly different perspective, and each one adds another layer of complexity. As with all challenges, though, by the end we'll be in a better place of understanding how to move forward in interpreting Scripture in the multicultural world we live in.

1

The Challenge of Context

Before I attended seminary, I spent several years in a cross-cultural setting in East Asia. At first, the missionary task seemed easy to me: share the gospel, and if people showed interest, get them reading the Bible. It *was* easy for a while—that is, until I had people who started reading the Bible. What happened when they started to read? They had lots of questions. Some of them were difficult to answer because I was still growing in my ability to communicate in the local dialect. But some of their questions were difficult for a different reason—they were questions that arose from their context, and they were questions that had never crossed my mind before.

On one occasion these very young believers who were reading through Luke came to Luke 8:21, where Jesus refused to see his mother and brothers and instead said, "My mother and brothers are those who hear the word of God and do it." Given their Confucian upbringing that placed emphasis on filial piety, they could not understand why Jesus would disrespect his mother in such away. Not having great interpretation skills myself and knowing even less about their background and context, I was at a loss as to how to answer this question.

A few weeks later, they had read through Luke 11, where Jesus explains why he is able to cast out demons (11:17–23), and they had even *more* questions. They had specific questions about how to interact with demon-possessed people. Having grown up in the West, I had never encountered such a person and assumed, like many others, that such events only happened in Jesus' day. They also had questions about the unclean spirits of 11:24–26 and wanted to know how it related to the spirit world.

Again, having grown up in the West and having never read about Hiebert's excluded middle,[1] I was clueless as to how to answer their questions. I didn't even know what the spirit world was!

The point here is that these questions grew out of their context. They interpreted mother-son relationships through the lens of their context. They considered implications of exorcism according to experiences from their context. They read Jesus' teaching about the spirit world and assumed that his words confirmed aspects of their worldview. They did what we all do—they read Scripture through the lens of their context. Their context influenced and affected the ways they approached, interpreted, and applied Scripture.

The point for us is to realize that our contexts influence our reading of Scripture more than most of us realize. In this book I argue that the goal of biblical interpretation in any context is to understand the original author's meaning. But we can't escape the fact that sometimes our context helps us in that pursuit (when our context is similar to the biblical one), and yet sometimes it hinders us (when our context is different from the biblical one). We also can't escape the fact that everyone seeks to understand the original author's meaning *so that* they can apply that meaning to the contemporary world. So, when we think about the challenge of context, we also absolutely must consider the challenge of how we determine the implications and applications of words written two thousand years ago.

To better understand the challenge of context when interpreting Scripture, I want to consider four questions in this chapter. The first question attempts to define the idea of culture and explain the ways it influences how people think. The second explores the complexity of interpreting the Bible when people from multiple cultural contexts are involved. The third question builds on the second one by considering why all interpreters in any context need to consider these challenges. Then, the final question examines some practical applications and insights in light of these challenges.

What Is Culture?

The opening illustrations display some of the ways that our own cultural contexts influence how we approach and read Scripture. Perhaps before moving forward it is necessary for us to stop here and ask a more fundamental question: What is culture? This is a word we often use in casual

---

1. See Hiebert, "The Flaw of the Excluded Middle."

conversations. For example, I recently read a critique of sports team that they were losing because the program didn't have the right "culture." Though we're familiar with this term, we rarely define it.

Paul Hiebert explained culture as "the more or less integrated systems of ideas, beliefs, and values and their associated patterns of behavior and products shared by a people who organize and regulate what they think, feel, and do."[2] Diagram 1 helps us to visually understand the relationships among these concepts. In his definition, ideas, beliefs, and values serve as the foundation of culture. We might also describe these as the internal aspects of culture which are always there and which affect everything but are not likely to be seen. These aspects of culture are much harder to learn as an outsider because they function more like assumptions or presuppositions rather than being directly stated concepts.

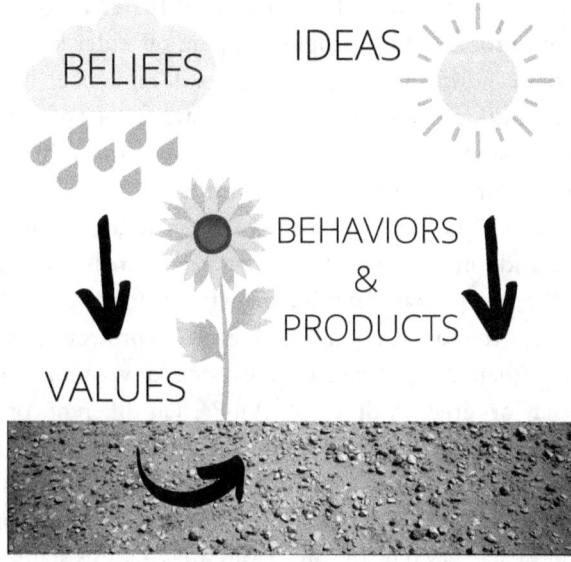

Diagram 1: Culture "Cycle"

The diagram also helps us to see that the second part of Hiebert's definition, that of shared behaviors and products, is "created" by the first. If we were walking along the road in the diagram, our eyes would naturally fix on the flower. We might notice the uniqueness of its colors or shape. We might also recognize other details that differentiate this flower from those in our

2. Hiebert, *Anthropological Insights for Missionaries*, 30.

home context. It would be much harder for us to see that the uniqueness of this flower is a product of the combination of rain, sun, and soil in this specific environment.

In other words, when it comes to culture, the internal ideas, beliefs, and values shape, inform, and "produce" the group's actions and lifestyle. This aspect of culture is more external and is much easier for an outsider to observe and evaluate. When someone enters a new cultural context, they often immediately notice the different ways that people dress, the different foods they eat, or even the unique ways that they communicate and interact. It will be much harder and take much more time, though, for them to understand the specific ideas, beliefs, and values that have shaped those behaviors.

It might help to consider an example of this internal/external dynamic. Imagine it's summertime and you're making your annual journey to the beach. What do you find when you get there? If you're in the US or Europe, you probably find people stripping off outer layers of clothes, laying prostrate, and trying to "get a tan." I still remember living in Massachusetts in middle school, and we were always jealous of the kids whose families traveled south during any break. They were the only ones who had a tan during the dark and dreary days of winter.

But if you're in Asia and you make your way to the beach during summertime, you find something very different. People are not laying out under the sun, but they are probably putting on extra layers to *cover* their arms or neck. Or perhaps they are carrying an umbrella to protect themselves from the sun. Same situation—people go to the beach for vacation—but their actions and behaviors are very different. Why? Their different conceptions of beauty (internal aspect of culture) affect their behaviors (external aspect).

To give one more example, in many places around the world specific locations have a unique "staple food" like rice, noodles, or some type of bread that they eat every day. In some cases, they eat this staple food at every meal, and only the other dishes change. When I was living in East Asia, my friends used to compare what the staple food was in their hometown. And of course they would ask me what the staple food was in America. These conversations always confused me for several reasons. I didn't know what a staple food was, and even after I learned what it was, I never knew how to answer their question about my staple food, since we didn't think or talk about food in that way.

The Challenge of Context

These conversations relate to how people organize and regulate information. Again, we may be able to immediately recognize that some group of people always eat rice or always eat *naan* with every meal. The reason they have the external behavior is because of an internal aspect of their cultural perspective, namely that they organize their knowledge about food in this way. By way of contrast, growing up in the US, we always organized our knowledge about food in a different way. We learned that healthy meals had components of all the necessary food groups: vegetable, fruit, dairy, wheat/grains, and meat.

The point here is not to say that one perspective is correct and one incorrect. The point here is simply to recognize that these two ways of organizing or thinking about food are *different*. And not only do these differences lead to different practices, but they can also lead to miscommunication. When someone (me) who has always organized his knowledge about food into distinct food groups interacts with others (my friends) who organize their knowledge about food in terms of the need for one single staple food, the question, "What is your staple food?" results in miscommunication and confusion. Even when I knew what they were asking, there was no easy way to answer the question.

Other scholars help us to think about the differences in cultures by focusing on different cultural values. In their book, Lingenfelter and Mayers point to several systems of contrasting values, like time versus event orientation.[3] One type of culture values the precise management of time, and all events must start and finish according to the clock. But the contrasting approach is to value the event itself, and in these cultures, people don't worry so much about when the event starts or finishes. Or another value system is task versus person orientation. Some cultures value finishing tasks, and they organize their values around completing a certain number of tasks each day. Other cultures place the value on relationships.

In her book *Foreign to Familiar*, Sarah Lanier argues that these different values are directly related to the climate in that location.[4] So, in places where the climate is warmer, people tend to be more relationship-oriented. They seem more relaxed and have more casual conversations. But in colder climates, people are more task-oriented. Perhaps because the weather is so cold, they don't have time to stand around and chat.

---

3. Lingenfelter and Mayers, *Ministering Cross-Culturally*.
4. Lanier, *Foreign to Familiar*.

She also gives a few other cultural value paradigms.[5] These include direct versus indirect communication styles and individual versus group orientation. She argues that locations with colder climates tend to be more direct in stating what their purpose is, but that warmer-climate cultures are more indirect in the way they state their purpose. In the same way some cultures—she argues these are the colder ones—emphasize the individual and individual choice. In contrast, the warmer-climate cultures emphasize the whole group and are often called collectivistic cultures.

Our point here is not to stereotype people in a certain cultural context, but simply to recognize the different value systems that a group of people have in common. This is why in his definition Hiebert explained that these concepts are "shared by a people who organize and regulate what they think, feel, and do."[6] In other words, when we describe cultures in this way, we are not seeking to pigeonhole people into always responding the same way in certain situations. What we are trying to do is evaluate and discern shared patterns of thought or shared values among some group of people. Understanding these different values or ways of organizing information will help us as we think through the challenges of interpreting Scripture in different cultural contexts.

Why Is Interpretation Harder in Intercultural Contexts?

Now that we've taken some time to define and understand culture, we can begin to consider why interpreting Scripture is harder in intercultural contexts. That is, why would culture and the existence of people from two different cultural backgrounds make it harder to interpret the Bible? The opening illustrations gave some picture of the difficulty. And in the section on culture, I hinted at the miscommunication that can occur when different cultural values or ways of organizing information are brought into conversation. Now let's briefly consider how these issues affect interpretation.

In the previous section we considered the different value system of individualism versus collectivism. Now we can also consider how these contrasting values might affect the interpretation of Scripture. For example, if we look at Acts 16:25–34, we see the story of the Philippian jailer and the miraculous events that led to his family coming to Christ. Someone from an individualistic cultural context might pay closer attention to verse 30,

---

5. Lanier, *Foreign to Familiar*, 31–40, 41–54.
6. Hiebert, *Anthropological Insights for Missionaries*, 30.

where the jailer asks, "What must *I* do to be saved?" In contrast, someone from a collectivistic background might point to verse 31, where Paul responds, "Believe in the Lord Jesus, and you will be saved, *you and all your household.*"[7]

We see the same dynamic in Acts 10 when Cornelius's whole family gathers to hear the word. To decide what actually took place in terms of individual versus group decisions, we would need more detailed analysis of the text. At first glance, however, we notice some individualistic aspects, for example, when Peter says that "any*one* who fears him and does what is right is acceptable to him" (10:35). At the same time, though, we see the Spirit falling on "*all* who heard the Word" (10:44).

The point here is not to alleviate the difference and state that one perspective is correct and the other wrong. My point is just to make us all aware of the difficulty. Our own cultural perspectives resonate with certain aspects of the text. We focus on certain details in the text and often miss those details that don't support or confirm our own cultural values. Most Westerners scoff at the idea of group conversion because we have always made and will always make decisions as individuals. To be honest, as a Westerner, the idea of group conversion makes me uncomfortable, but I've lived in Asia long enough to know that it doesn't make those from collectivistic backgrounds uncomfortable. In fact, they *tend* to read the text that way.

In their book *Misreading Scripture with Western Eyes*, Richards and O'Brien have a section on collectivism, in which they focus on the theme of family and the idea that becoming a Christian meant entry into the group.[8] This aspect in the New Testament of the church as the family of God is often lost on Westerners because of their individualistic cultural perspective. It also doesn't help that English has no way of distinguishing between second person singular and plural; thus many miss the fact that so many New Testament commands are directed to the church as a whole and not just to individuals. For example, in 1 Peter 1:3–9, Peter writes of salvation and uses phrases like "In this *you* rejoice," "the tested genuineness of *your* faith," and "obtaining the outcome of *your* faith, the salvation of *your* souls." All of these statements on salvation and the results of salvation are plural and are directed to the church as a whole.

---

7. Richards and O'Brien also give Acts 16 as example of a whole household coming to faith together: Richards and O'Brien, *Misreading Scripture with Western Eyes*, 130.

8. Richards and O'Brien, *Misreading Scripture with Western Eyes*, 133–35.

My point here is not to introduce subjectivity into the process of interpretation. Every culture does not have the freedom to interpret the text in any way they see fit or in any way that supports their existing cultural values. As interpreters, though, we do need to wrestle with the fact that people from different cultural contexts will focus on different details in the text and will end up in different places than we do. And when we interpret the Bible together with them, we need to be aware of such complexity and need to be prepared for dialogue about such issues.

To illustrate this complexity, we can consider Diagram 2. Following Hiebert's definition of culture, every culture has certain ideas (I), beliefs (B), and values (V) that lead to specific behaviors (B) and products (P). When we come to the Bible, it also presents specific ideas about issues like who God is, how the world was created it, etc. In many places it also points to values in terms of standards for righteousness and holy living. These biblical ideas, beliefs, and values also lead to specific behaviors, namely in the commands of Scripture. An example would be in Ephesians where chapters 1–3 use indicative verbs to help believers understand their position in Christ, and chapters 4–6 build on that foundation by using imperatives to command specific gospel-centered behaviors.

Diagram 2: Interaction Between Culture and Scripture

When any one person interprets Scripture, their own cultural ideas, beliefs, and values either resonate with or contradict the ideas, beliefs, and values in Scripture. As in the examples above, sometimes this cultural preunderstanding helps them to better grasp certain details, and at other times it hinders the interpreter. As the diagram shows, though, this process is not a one-way street. Scripture is the final authority. And while every

The Challenge of Context

interpreter has some level of cultural preunderstanding, the ideas, beliefs, and values of Scripture should ultimately influence and inform the interpreter's perspective.

Of course, for our purposes here, we not only need to note the complexity of this process for any single interpreter, but we also must recognize the added complexity when interpreters from two different cultural backgrounds study Scripture together. In that case, we have two contrasting and possibly contradicting sets of "I, B, V" on the left side of the diagram, which influence how each interpreter engages the "I, B, V" of the biblical text and affect their communication with one another. This situation is familiar to missionaries. They must lay aside their own "I, B, V" and study the "I, B, V" of the local believers to better communicate the biblical truth to them.

To illustrate this idea, consider an experience of one of my students. He was reflecting on the difficulty of interpreting Habakkuk 1 with a people group that live in an isolated, mountainous area. This people group has been oppressed and persecuted over the years, and as a result they had gradually retreated into the mountains. Outsiders often refer to them as "savages," but this people feels like they are the ones who have been treated savagely. In this sense, they can relate to Habakkuk's questions about the problem of evil, and their history and culture of skepticism to the outside world enables them to understand the questions the prophet raises.

At the same time, though, their view of God is highly animistic, so teaching about Habakkuk's questions and God's answer could lead to significant confusion and misunderstanding. This student recognized that the details in this text had some aspects that were similar to their worldview and some aspects that were significantly different. These differences created challenges for him in interpreting the passage and communicating it with them. In order to effectively communicate with them, he needed to know their culture and worldview.

In this sense, we can see that in any cultural context certain details of the text will resonate with aspects of the culture, while other details will confront or challenge aspects of the culture. When we interpret Scripture alongside those who have a different cultural perspective than we do and we are not aware and informed of their cultural perspective, we may not understand the issues that support or contradict their perspective. Even if we are aware of these differences, it can be time-consuming and complicated to work through them together. The existence of multiple cultural perspectives makes intercultural interpretation much more complex and challenging—and rewarding!

Why Does Everyone Need to Consider This Issue?

Now that we're beginning to understand the complexity of interpreting Scripture in intercultural contexts, it's important for us to consider how this issue relates to all of us. Some readers may already be involved in the kinds of ministries where they are daily and intentionally interacting with those of other cultural backgrounds for the sake of the gospel. The relevance of this discussion will be immediately clear to them. But for others, they may be wondering why they need to consider such issues. Let me give you a couple reasons.

First, in today's world, there's a sense in which all of us are living in multicultural contexts. We interact with and encounter those of differing cultural backgrounds far more often than we realize. Many readers will be familiar with the influence the West has on the rest of the world. For example, recent years have seen an increase in the export of not only Western foods and businesses but also movies and other products. While Starbucks only opened its first store outside of the US in 1996 and its first in China in 1999, in 2020 it had over 4700 in China alone.[9] When the movie *Avengers: Endgame* debuted in 2019, it had the largest grossing opening weekend ever, making $1.2 billion. But $850 million of that total was made outside the US.[10]

What scholars have given less attention to is the missiological implication of the ways Western ideals and values that are inherent in these movies, businesses, and music are influencing culture in other parts of the world. For example, in the Avengers movies, Ironman personifies many Western stereotypes of masculinity: he is individualistic, self-sufficient to the point of selfishness, takes advantage of women, and is often quite arrogant. And yet, in the movies, not only does he make these characteristics look "cool," but he also becomes the hero. Imagine the contrast for kids growing up in cultures that emphasize a quiet strength that places the needs of the community above the needs of self.

One recent missiological study examined this very issue and found that because of globalization youth in Nepal often face identity confusion

9. Blazyte, "Number of Starbucks Stores in China."
10. Abad-Santos, "Avengers."

since they identify more with Western guilt and innocence concepts as opposed to the traditional honor/shame values of their parents.[11] On a similar note in the field of business, Inun Jariya explores how Western management practices can affect the workplace.[12] For example, he notes that individualism would lead human resources to evaluate candidates and provide training based on individual achievement, when in fact success in non-Western societies is based on personal relationship and group interaction.[13] This is but one example of many he gives that shows how detrimental these supposed "universal" business practices can be in non-Western contexts.

At the same time, we also see increasing influence in the other direction, for example, of the East on the West. I experienced this reality when I pastored a church in rural Kentucky. An evaluation we did of our community showed that it was 98 percent Caucasian. Our county was not diverse, and in no sense was it "globalized." And yet there were still people from Japan and China with whom my church members came into contact. Several of my church members asked me for training or for resources that would help them communicate with and potentially share the gospel with people of different cultural backgrounds. In the same way, recent years have shown much more influence of Eastern thought on Westerners. You might watch a baseball game, see a player struggling, and hear the commentator say, "He must have angered the baseball gods!" Such a statement is classic animism.[14]

Additionally, the church in the West must consider this issue given issues of global migration.[15] From 2000 to 2020 the percentage of the global population that is migrants went up slightly from 2.8 percent to 3.5 percent. The number of refugees went up from 14 million to 25.9 million. The primary destination for these migrants in 2020? The United States, with nearly 50 million resident migrants compared to Germany, with 18 million in second place. And since more than 40 percent of all global migrants were born in Asia, this means more and more people in the West are having intercultural interactions on a daily basis.

---

11. Kaptain, "Globalization Acculturation in Honor Shame Contexts."

12. Jariya, "Western Cultural Values and Its Implications on Management Practices," 66–67.

13. Jariya, "Western Cultural Values and Its Implications on Management Practices," 66–67.

14. Van Rheenen, *Communicating Christ in Animistic Contexts*.

15. These statistics are from Edmond, "Global Migration by the Numbers."

The point here is to recognize that in today's world, whenever we interpret Scripture, we are doing so in a diverse and multicultural context. With globalization and increased interaction between, for example, Eastern and Western cultures, every pastor and church leader needs to be prepared to think through how to interpret the Bible in communion with those from different cultural backgrounds. They all need to be equipped to think through the challenges and complexities of intercultural interpretation. And more to the specific purpose of this book, they need to be equipped with specific skills that they can use to interpret the Bible in any context.

Another reason we need to think through this issue is because interpreting the Bible with those of different cultural backgrounds makes us better interpreters of Scripture. As we've already seen, having a different cultural perspective enables someone to recognize certain details more easily in the text. Interacting and communicating with those of a different cultural background, like the example of my student, force us to consider how the text interacts with their history and context.

For example, we can consider the idea of direct versus indirect communication. In Genesis 23, Sarah dies, and in verses 10–16 there's a confusing interaction between Abraham and Ephron about a burial place. What's confusing about their interaction is the fact that Abraham offers to buy the field, to which Ephron answers, "I give you the field." Sounds like the deal is done, but Abraham continues to press the issue in verses 12–13 by bowing and then again offering to pay for the field. To which Ephron replies in verse 15, "My lord, listen to me: a piece of land worth four hundred shekels of silver, what is that between you and me?"

To direct communicators (like me), it sounds like Ephron is again saying that he desires to give the land to Abraham, and he doesn't need to pay the price of the land. In the next verse, though, it says, "Abraham listened to Ephron, and Abraham weighed out for Ephron the silver that he had named." This is a clear case of indirect communication, where Ephron shows respect to Abraham and subtly tells him the price of the land. Abraham recognizes what Ephron is doing, and thus asks for the price of the land multiple times.

For a long time, the communication in this passage was confusing to me, until I lived in a context where people communicate like this everyday. Living among or interacting with those who have a different cultural background than we do can make us better interpreters of Scripture. Interpreting Scripture alongside others in the global church broadens our horizons, makes us aware of different ways of thinking, and enables us to recognize and understand aspects of Scripture that we normally overlook.

What Should We Do in Light of This Reality?

Now that we've seen some of the challenges of and some of the reasons for intercultural interpretation, we turn in this last section to one final question. Based on all that we've seen, what should we do? We will give more attention to this question in the rest of the book, but for now, we can make some simple observations. First, we interpret with humility. Now more than ever, we must recognize that we are part of a global church and that those in other cultural contexts may have insights that we never considered before.

Second, and along the same lines, we must dialogue with those of other cultural backgrounds. Part of the problem here is that although more believers exist today in the Global South, the majority of theological resources are produced by theologians in the West. With more and more theologians being trained in South America, Africa, and Asia, the global church needs to hear more from these voices. These theologians have insights into the text that benefit us all.

Another point of application, especially for missionaries, is that they must train and equip indigenous interpreters. As missionaries share the gospel and plant churches, they must recognize that those churches need leaders who have the ability to interpret Scripture and apply it to the pressing needs of their context. Missionaries must not teach new believers in a way in which they say, "Here are all the theological answers you need to know." Instead, they must lead them to the Scriptures and equip them with the exegetical skills to interpret on their own. This issue is one to which we will return in chapter 3.

In that sense, missionaries themselves need solid biblical interpretation skills. If they are to interpret Scripture alongside brothers and sisters in a new cultural context, if they are going to help those believers navigate their own cultural influences, and if they are they going to equip them to apply Scripture to their own context, they themselves must be experts in interpretation. Unfortunately, the conversation surrounding missionaries is often focused on whether they need theological training *at all*. If all they need to do is share the gospel, why do they need to attend seminary? But this is a nearsighted perspective of the missionary task. Missionaries must not only have the ability to interpret the Bible, but they must also know the best ways to *teach others how* to interpret. This is a key aspect of the missionary task.

But what does it mean to interpret Scripture well? What are some basic guidelines we should follow when we interpret the Bible? We'll seek to answer these questions in chapter 2.

2

THE CHALLENGE OF PURSUING THE AUTHOR THROUGH THE TEXT

EARLIER I MENTIONED HOW much I enjoy running, especially running on trails. Running on a trail is so much different than running on the road because the trail will wind around, go up and down, and, depending on the terrain, the runner needs to climb over fallen trees or large boulders. Especially in longer races when one is out on the trails for hours at a time, the mind begins to wander and focus on the goal—finishing. It is easy to question, "Am I really making progress?" "Am I getting any closer to the finish?" Occasionally it seems like the answer is no because what seems like a straight path suddenly turns in a different direction or winds upward on a long, slow climb.

At times, we may have the same attitude toward interpretation. In the last chapter we considered how what initially seemed an easy task—just read the Bible and apply it to your life—becomes much more complicated when we factor in the way culture affects the details and ideas in the text to which we pay attention. Considering and focusing on these issues may seem like running up a long, winding trail with endless fallen trees to climb over. We're not moving in a straight line but are constantly having to divert our attention to what may seem like nonessential issues.

This issue gets to the question this chapter attempts to answer, namely, what is the goal in interpretation? In other words, in the last chapter we examined the challenge of context and considered how our culture and worldview affect understanding of the text, both in terms of how our cultural perspective helps and hinders us. At this point we can reflect on the process of interpretation a bit more as we consider what exactly we are trying to accomplish when we interact with any specific text. So while in the last chapter we considered the ways in which culture affects the interpreter, this chapter argues that the goal of interpretation is to understand the intention of the original author as he has communicated it through the text.

With that goal in mind, we will first examine what an author-oriented approach actually is by considering two important topics: determinacy and reproducibility. In the process we will examine some criticisms of this perspective and consider the implications for cross-cultural hermeneutics.

What Is an Author-Oriented Approach?

Every written act of communication contains three elements: the author, the text, and the reader. Robert Stein explains that of these three elements, the traditional understanding of interpretation viewed the author as the determiner of meaning:

> Who or what determines the meaning of a text, code, message, or writing? At the beginning of the twentieth century the general assumption was that the author was the determiner of a text's meaning. The text meant what the author of the text consciously willed to convey by the words he or she had written. Texts were understood as a form of communication, and in communication we seek to understand what the author of that communication seeks to convey. Thus, if in a Bible study we were engaged in a study of Paul's letter to the Romans, and by some miracle the apostle Paul entered the room and explained what he meant by the passage under consideration, this would settle the issue. Our goal was to understand what the author, that is, Paul, meant by this passage, and we now know what he meant.[1]

This traditional view of the author as determiner of meaning was largely under attack through the twentieth century. At the same time, though, this view has not been without contemporary proponents. For example, E. D. Hirsch refers to this traditional view of interpretation as a "sensible belief"[2] and states that when this view was rejected, "no adequate principle existed for judging the validity of interpretation."[3]

---

1. Stein, "The Benefits of an Author-Oriented Approach to Hermeneutics," 451.
2. Hirsch, *Validity in Interpretation*, 1.
3. Hirsch, *Validity in Interpretation*, 3.

The Challenge of Pursuing the Author through the Text

If the author's intent drives our interpretation, we must be able to determine what the author intended and reproduce that meaning (i.e., derive the author's content in our context) for ourselves and our hearers.[4] But are these goals realistic, or even possible for us?

Determinacy of an Author's Meaning

We can in fact identify the author's meaning because in the process of writing virtually every author submits himself to the norms of language. Hirsch explains that "the norms of language exert a powerful influence and impose an unavoidable limitation on the wills of both the author and interpreter."[5] Words cannot mean anything that an author or interpreter desires them to mean. Thus, what the author is able to communicate is determined and controlled by the use of language. In the same way, the interpreter is also bound by those same constraints of language when he engages the text. Words, then, also provide a common ground of communication by placing those same boundaries on both the author and the recipient.

Hirsch likewise explains that the determinacy of verbal meaning requires authorial intent. Words do not mean anything in and of themselves, but it takes some intelligent will, what Hirsch calls a "discriminating force," to make it mean one thing and not mean something else. He writes, "That discriminating force must involve an act of will, since unless one particular complex of meaning is willed (no matter how 'rich' and 'various' it might be), there would be no distinction between what an author does mean by a word sequence and what he could mean. Determinacy of verbal meaning requires an act of will."[6]

We can also expect to find the author's intent because the choice and arrangement of words are not random. This unique choice and arrangement of words is purely a result of the will of the author, who intended that each word contribute to a particular meaning determined by him. This is also true of the biblical authors. When the biblical authors wrote, they were limited by the standards of the languages they used. At the same time, though, they were cognitively involved in the writing process. They made

---

4. Hirsch, *Validity in Interpretation*, 27. For further explanation of this aspect of Hirsch's argument, see also Vanhoozer, *Is There a Meaning in This Text?*, 74–75; Blue, "The Hermeneutic of E. D. Hirsch Jr. and Its Impact on Expository Preaching," 255.

5. Hirsch, *Validity in Interpretation*, 27.

6. Hirsch, *Validity in Interpretation*, 47.

conscious decisions to use specific words and specific grammatical constructions. This act of will in arranging and organizing their material in a certain way is what we speak of when we discuss authorial intent.

Diagram 3 attempts to put this concept into visual form. In this diagram, the linguistic norms of any given language provide some boundaries and place some limitations on the author. Still, even as he/she follows those standards, the author exercises his/her will in writing.

Diagram 3: Determinacy of Language

Some have pushed back on this concept of author's intent, saying that determining the author's meaning requires that we climb back into his mind to determine his thoughts; and even if this were possible, it would place emphasis upon the author rather than on the text. This in effect makes interpretation a psychological study rather than a textual one.[7]

Stein responds to this criticism by stating that it is true that no one can climb back into the mind of the author, but a psychological analysis of the author is not the goal of an author-oriented hermeneutic.[8] As a result, Stein differentiates between the "mental acts" of the author, which he defines as

---

7. Wimsatt and Beardsley, "The Intentional Fallacy," 471–74, 477–82.

8. Stein, "The Benefits of an Author-Oriented Approach to Hermeneutics," 456. The psychological analysis of the author was an important component to Schleiermacher's hermeneutic system, but Grant Osborne distinguishes Schleiermacher's approach from the one currently being argued for by referring to Schleiermacher's as an "author-centered approach" (Osborne, *The Hermeneutical Spiral*, 468).

the "experiences the author went through when he wrote,"[9] with the "meaning" of the author, which he consciously willed through his words in the text.[10]

Stein also explains the fact that a text can *convey* meaning, but it cannot *produce* meaning.[11] Texts are simply word groups of symbols organized together on a page, but the organization of the symbols into a specific message requires the conscious will of an intelligent being. The production of meaning, then, requires the intelligent thought of an author. Thus, an author-oriented hermeneutic is a study of the internal evidence of the text; more specifically, it is a study of what message the author sought to convey through his organization of the words in that text.

Behind this question lies a deeper issue related to interpretation: who assigns meaning to a text—the author or the reader/interpreter? Some argue for public consensus—the meaning of a text is not what the author intended but what the public understands. But the text is the product of the author's intelligent thought and conscious choice, so it is the study of that text that enables interpreters to understand the author's intent.[12]

On this point, Jeannine Brown provides the helpful affirmation that "meaning is author-derived but textually communicated."[13] As a result of this dynamic she continues, "Meaning can be helpfully understood as communicative intention."[14] She goes on to explain that "a communicative model emphasizes the artificiality of separating authors from their texts."[15] As interpreters we study the text because it is the means by which the author is able to communicate with us. This communicative model helps us to see this relationship, that the author communicates meaning through the

---

9. Stein, *A Basic Guide to Interpreting the Bible*, 52.

10. Stein, "The Benefits of an Author-Oriented Approach to Hermeneutics," 456. Stein goes on to explain why it is important to speak of the author's "conscious" determination of meaning. He explains, "It should be noted that the term 'consciously' is used to describe the meaning that the author wished to convey. This is to distinguish our definition from those views that seek to demythologize the myth that the author has written and to find out the subconscious meaning of the author that lies behind the myth. It also distinguishes our definition from such views that reject the surface-level meaning and seek to discover the substructural meaning of a text" (Stein, "The Benefits of an Author-Oriented Approach to Hermeneutics," 457–58).

11. Stein, *A Basic Guide to Interpreting the Bible*, 19.

12. Hirsch, *Validity in Interpretation*, 13.

13. Brown, *Scripture as Communication*, 89.

14. Brown, *Scripture as Communication*, 89.

15. Brown, *Scripture as Communication*, 71.

text, which is then understood by the hearer. The text has meaning because of the author's intelligent will, and the interpreter is able to understand that author's message because it was inscribed in the text.

Another important factor related to author's intent is that specific genres of literature contain certain rules of interpretation. So, when authors write a piece of literature in a certain style, they expect readers to interpret their words according to the norms of that type of literature. Hirsch explains, "The norms of language are neither uniform nor stable but vary with the particular sort of utterance that is to be interpreted."[16]

Stein explains this concept with the phrase "playing by the rules."[17] He states that a soccer ("football" to everyone except Americans) fan attending his first American football or basketball game would be confused unless someone explained to him the rules of the game. He then states how this analogy applies to biblical interpretation:

> In a similar way there are different "game" rules involved in the interpretation of the different kinds of biblical literature. The author has played his "game," has sought to convey his meaning, under the rules covering the particular literary form he used. Unless we know those rules, we will almost certainly misinterpret his meaning. If we interpret a parable as if it were a narrative, or if we interpret poetry as if it were narrative, we will err. Similarly, if we interpret a narrative such as the resurrection of Jesus as a parable, we will also err.[18]

These genre-specific "rules" confine both author and interpreter.

Hirsch writes that the important point here is the *shareability* of these norms of language.[19] The fact that these norms of language are shared between author and interpreter provides some common ground, or a mutual playing field in Stein's analogy, which enables them to communicate. It is the shareability of these norms of language, given their determinate nature, that provides any sort of validity and objectivity in the process of interpretation. Due to its shareability, then, authorial intent is the ground of interpretation.[20] In other words, because interpreters are bound by and follow

---

16. Hirsch, *Validity in Interpretation*, 31.
17. Stein, *A Basic Guide to Interpreting the Bible*, 75–76.
18. Stein, *A Basic Guide to Interpreting the Bible*, 76.
19. Hirsch, *Validity in Interpretation*, 31.
20. Vanhoozer, *Is There a Meaning in This Text?*, 74–75. Vanhoozer here is explaining Hirsch's arguments for authorial intent as the guiding principle for how one should

The Challenge of Pursuing the Author through the Text

the same predetermined linguistic standards, they are able to understand the meaning communicated by the author.

Reproducing the Author's Meaning

Up until this point, we've focused mostly on the author, the norms of language he followed, and his will which produced the text. But in order for a text to communicate, we as interpreters must be able to reproduce the author's intent. Hirsch writes, "Reproducibility is a quality of verbal meaning that makes interpretation possible: if meaning were not reproducible, it could not be actualized by someone else and therefore could not be understood or interpreted."[21] In other words, the goal of interpreters is not only to understand the meaning that an author willed but also to reproduce that meaning. Although Hirsch recognizes that reproducing the author's meaning is not always easy, he argues that it is possible, and thus it provides objectivity to interpretation.[22]

Kevin Vanhoozer explains the concept of reproducibility by describing it as the goal of interpretation. He writes, "An interpreter grasps the meaning of a text when he or she experiences sameness of content (or object) despite differences of context."[23] Hirsch states in a similar way, "All valid interpretation of every sort is founded on the re-cognition of what an author meant."[24] In this sense, we can see that the reproduction of the author's meaning is the goal of the interpretive process.

But is any of this possible as interpreters of the biblical text? Practically speaking, do contemporary interpreters really have the same linguistic or cultural norms as the biblical authors, since we are separated by two thousand years? Moreover, is it actually possible to grasp or reproduce what an author meant, since those authors are no longer living and are unable to verify that our interpretation is correct? The first question gets to the importance of the topic of chapter 1—that is, understanding the ways our own cultural perspectives and those that we interpret alongside affect the ways we approach the text. Good interpreters recognize their own preunderstanding, and they also become students of the word in such a way that

---

define meaning.
21. Hirsch, *Validity in Interpretation*, 44.
22. Hirsch, *Validity in Interpretation*, 235–36.
23. Vanhoozer, *Is There a Meaning in This Text?*, 76.
24. Hirsch, *Validity in Interpretation*, 126.

they seek to gain an ever-deepening grasp of the historical context of the original authors of Scripture.

For the second question, interpreters must recognize their own limitations. This is why in chapter 1 I mentioned the importance of interpreting with a level of humility. While our goal is to reproduce the author's meaning, we must recognize that, first, our ability to verify our own interpretation is limited since the author is no longer alive to verify our articulation of his meaning. And second, we also realize that our understanding of the meaning of a text, how it relates to the original author's historical situation, and how it relates to the broader context of the passage is always growing.

In this sense, Grant Osborne's hermeneutical spiral is a helpful concept that portrays the process interpreters go through as they interact with the text.[25] The interpreter approaches the text with questions, and then the study of the text addresses issues in the interpreter's context. Each time interpreters return to the text for further study, they grow deeper in their understanding of the text (including original context, word usage, grammar, theology, relation to the broader context, etc.). Thus, with each "loop" of the spiral, the interpreter moves closer to the intended meaning of the original author.

Diagram 4: Hermeneutical Spiral

---

25. Osborne, *The Hermeneutical Spiral*, 417–19. Osborne's diagram is actually more of a circle. I've adjusted it so that the spiral moves to a point, thus indicating how we move closer to the author's meaning as we move through each loop.

The Challenge of Pursuing the Author through the Text

Important here is the place of the text itself. It is *through the text* that interpreters can ascertain the original author's intention. Following the standards and rules of the language, authors put their meaning into the text, and thus the text is intimately related to the author's intention. In the same way, readers pursue the author's meaning through their intentional and directed study of the text. And it is though the text that authors and readers can have effective and meaningful interaction.

Brown has a helpful assertion here that "meaning is imperfectly accessed by readers, both individual readers and readers in community."[26] Similar to Osborne's spiral, Brown recognizes that limitations exist in our ability to understand the original author. Each time we read a text we may consider aspects of it we never considered before, thus deepening our understanding of the author's intention. She explains, "The complexity of meaning implies that readers will struggle to 'get it right' and will fall short of 'getting it fully.' Yet even as we acknowledge that readers access meaning imperfectly, we need not give up on the goal of reaching meaning."[27]

Nonetheless, Robert Stein explains that communication between two people cannot take place unless the reader assumes that the meaning of a text is what the author intended it to mean:

> One cannot have a meaningful conversation or even a serious debate about this issue without assuming [that an author determines the meaning of a text]. During the present reading of this article, you, the reader, have been seeking to understand what I, the author, meant by the words I have written. Probably it has not even entered into your mind that the words I have written should be treated independently of my intention or that you should give your own meaning to these words. Communication between two people can only take place if both parties seek to understand what the other person means by their words.[28]

For meaningful communication to take place between two parties, the author must be the determiner of meaning.

Robert Plummer gives an example of what would happen if an author no longer determined the meaning of what he has written or said:

> If your friend says, "I would like a hamburger for lunch," and you respond, "Why is it that you hate Caucasians?" the person would

---

26. Brown, *Scripture as Communication*, 78.
27. Brown, *Scripture as Communication*, 78.
28. Stein, "The Benefits of an Author-Oriented Approach to Hermeneutics," 455.

rightly respond, "Are you crazy? Did you not hear what I said?" Any act of communication can progress only on the assumption that someone is trying to convey meaning to us and we then respond to that meaning intended by the speaker or writer.[29]

When this principle is rejected, the process of communication between the author and the reader breaks down.

Implications for Cross-Cultural Hermeneutics

After this brief survey of issues surrounding the pursuit of the author as the goal of hermeneutics, what implications are there for us as we seek to develop a cross-cultural model of biblical interpretation? First, it is important that we recognize the author as the one who determines the meaning of a text, and thus, no matter which cultural context we are in, the goal is the pursuit of the original author. In the last chapter we saw that culture often influences the way an interpreter approaches Scripture. When people from two different cultural backgrounds study the text together, they may pay attention to or focus on different details in the text.

The question interpreters in any context should be asking, though, is not "Which parts of the text are most similar to my cultural perspective?" or "Which parts are most interesting to me?" Instead, interpreters should be asking what the original author meant. Of course, as we'll see in the following chapters, this process can be a complicated one, especially when interpreters from multiple cultural backgrounds are studying the text together. Nonetheless, it should be the goal to consider what the original author was seeking to communicate with his original audience.

Of course, some may ask whether "correct" interpretation is possible or even necessary. Daniel Espiritu considers a similar question when he writes that contemporary reader-driven or culturally-driven methods of interpretation are "a manifestation of the spirit of the age"—the spirit of postmodernism.[30] He goes on to state that the evangelical presupposition concerning the nature of truth, namely that it is objective, requires evangelical interpreters not to "engage in an 'endless play' with the biblical texts."[31] Instead, they must utilize methods that enable them to determine

---

29. Plummer, *40 Questions about Interpreting the Bible*, 130.
30. Espiritu, "Ethnohermeneutics or Oikohermeneutics," 272.
31. Espiritu, "Ethnohermeneutics or Oikohermeneutics," 278.

The Challenge of Pursuing the Author through the Text

God's message that he communicated through the human authors in the words they chose.

While a recognition of the author as determiner of meaning is important for communication to take place, we may also add a note about the serious nature of the interpretive enterprise. Since Scripture is God's word, the eternal consequences of misinterpretation are devastating and potentially eternal. That doesn't mean that any one person's interpretation of a given text is infallible. It does mean, though, that since God's word is communicated through the intention of the original author, the church must take interpretation seriously.

Thus, as we construct a model of interpretation that could help people in any cultural context that helps people navigate the challenges of their cultural presuppositions, we must always emphasize the pursuit of the original author. Our goal in interpretation is not to fuse the horizon of contemporary context with the original context or to simply find commonalities. Our goal is to understand what the author meant by his choice of words in his historical context.

Second, we recognize that the means by which anyone in any cultural context can ascertain the author's meaning is through the study of the text. Thus, the church, missionaries, seminaries, etc. should always promote the faithful study of the text. Church leaders need to demonstrate and model sound biblical interpretation as they preach and teach. Seminaries should likewise train emerging leaders with the knowledge of the historical and cultural context of the original writers and should also equip their students with the skills and abilities to interact with the text. Missionaries should do the same. As they enter a place that has had little or no contact with the gospel, they should plant a church there in such a way that they teach new believers faithful exposition of the text.

At the same time, especially given some of the issues raised in the previous chapter, we recognize that some challenges exist in pursuing the author's meaning through the text. One challenge that the previous chapter addressed was that our own worldview influences how we approach the text and affects what details we pay more attention to in the text. This "preunderstanding," as Schleiermacher called it, helps us in situations where similarities between our context and the original context exist. At other times, though, it hinders us. Part of becoming a faithful interpreter is utilizing those aspects of our culture that aid in interpretation while simultaneously allowing Scripture to critique the aspects of our culture that are unbiblical.

Another challenge with which those in the West may be somewhat unfamiliar with is that of orality. Some 70 percent of the world's people are either primary oral learners or prefer to learn through oral methods.[32] While this number of primary oral learners includes many in parts of the world where languages have no literate form, the number of preferred oral learners is likely growing due to people gaining more and more information through digital media services like YouTube, podcasts, Twitter, etc. How does the church train people to pay attention to grammar and syntax either when no written form of the language exists or when people prefer not to read at all? It is possible, and we will return to this challenge in chapter 12.

Even when a written form of some language is available and the Bible has been translated into that language, it can still be a challenge to teach others how to study the text in pursuit of the author's meaning. One needs considerable time to learn about the historical context of the first-century world, and one likewise needs time to learn how to pay attention to certain grammatical and syntactical details to make an informed decision about the author's meaning. In the best of cases, this means an opportunity to study the original languages, but in many parts of the world these opportunities are not available. In fact, in Asia, original language teachers are so sparse that accreditation agencies don't require the languages for MDiv programs. Larry Caldwell, whose views we will examine in chapter 8, brings up the issue of lack of resources in the Majority World.[33] In many places, Bible study tools and resources aren't available or are simply too expensive for most church leaders.

All of these issues are significant challenges to pursuing the meaning of the original author through the text. Nonetheless, it is possible, and the church in every location needs faithful expositors who are able to study the text and apply its meaning to the pressing issues of their context. And as we saw in the last chapter, as these indigenous interpreters bring the text of Scripture to bear on their context, the global church benefits through the new and unique insights they have into the text. In that sense, Osborne's hermeneutical spiral is not just about one interpreter in one context studying the text, but it is about a global community of interpreters studying the text, sharing their insights, and learning from one another. And as that process continues, the church in every location moves closer and closer to the original author's meaning.

---

32. International Orality Network, *Making Disciples of Oral Learners*, 3.
33. Caldwell, *Doing Bible Interpretation!*, 11–14.

The Challenge of Pursuing the Author through the Text

Again, Jeannine Brown is helpful here:

> If it is the case that we lack the ability to access Scripture perfectly because of both our inherent finitude and the effects of sin, how should we proceed in interpretation? An important initial response would be acknowledgement of these realities. Humility would be the order of the day. Yet our limited perspective does not require giving up the goal of understanding the text. If God has chosen to speak through Scripture, we can trust that the capacity to understand has been built into us, however finitely and imperfectly. If the author is not obsolete or lost forever, but has communicated in and through the text, then meaning is *in theory* attainable. What we ought always to remember, however, is that when we do access textual meaning, we do so in less-than-complete ways. This condition provides great encouragement to read carefully, with an awareness of what we bring to the hermeneutical process, and to read in community. If my access to meaning is partial at best, then I need you to read with me. I can learn from what others see when reading Scripture. Reading with and across communities, intentionally and humbly, in one way of expanding our limited horizons. Hearing from others, especially from voices that have not been at the center of interpretive conversations, can help us to perceive better our own interpretive blind spots.[34]

But as missionaries enter a new location, how do they raise up indigenous interpreters? Why is it important for them to consider the church's need for interpreters in that context? We'll consider those and other questions in chapter 3.

---

34. Brown, *Scripture as Communication*, chapter 4, section 4, para. 5.

3

The Challenge of Self-Theologizing

In the movie *The Matrix* (1999), the main character, Neo, spends his entire life plugged into a computer system called the matrix, oblivious to the true makeup of the world. Then he meets Morpheus and takes a red pill, which frees his mind and allows him to see the world as it really is. Taking the pill changes everything for Neo. His mind and body are both released from the oppressive structure of the matrix computer system, and he realizes that his preexisting worldview was incomplete and inadequate. He must learn to think in new ways.

The picture of Neo embracing and adapting to a new world is similar to those who hear and accept the gospel message for the first time. They learn about how sin has affected their thinking and clouded their judgment. They come to a realization that only Christ has the power and authority to redeem them. These and other biblical truths affect their lives in profound ways.

For starters, these new believers must learn to think theologically about the world around them. But the doing theology in this new context—especially since it will be done by relatively new believers—is a tricky process. In this chapter, in an attempt to better understand the challenge of self-theologizing, we will consider the history of the indigenization movement, how that led to the discussion of self-theology, and then we will make several summary statements.

The Challenge of Self-Theologizing

History of the Indigenization Movement

Throughout much of what is known as "The Great Century" (1792–1910), the two major aims of the mission enterprise were evangelization and civilization.¹ In the midst of several revivals in Europe and America, significant missionary fervor was released into the world, and that fervor helped characterize missions in this century by its "rapid geographical expansion of the work."² At the same time, though, missions was also characterized by its spread of Western civilization to the rest of the world. David Bosch explains that in America "it was increasingly thought that the overseas mission of the American churches consisted in sharing the benefits of the American civilization and way of life with the deprived peoples of the world."³

The relationship between the competing aims of evangelization and civilization was a complex one. In some cases, the expansion of the colonial powers opened new fields of service for missionaries.⁴ In other cases, the presence of the British Empire closed doors to missionaries.⁵ In still other cases, it was the missionary expansion of the church that aided the global expansion of the state.⁶ To summarize this difficult relationship, many have pointed to the statement made by one who was a victim of colonial rule: "First they had the Bible and we had the land; now we have the Bible and they have the land."⁷

---

1. Beaver, "Introduction," 13. The term "The Great Century" was first coined by Kenneth Scott Latourette in his seven-volume classic on the history of Christian missions, *A History of the Expansion of Christianity*.

2. Neill, *A History of Christian Missions*, 215.

3. Bosch, *Transforming Mission*, 283.

4. In 1842 the treaty following the Opium War ceded Hong Kong and five other ports to the British for trading and residence. Several years later, in 1854, then, when Hudson Taylor first sailed for missionary service in China, he was able to freely enter Shanghai, which was one of the ports opened to foreigners. For information on Taylor's story, see Taylor, *Hudson Taylor's Spiritual Secret*.

5. William Carey, considered by many to be the father of the modern missionary movement, is one of the missionaries who experienced this impact of colonial expansion. At the time of his service, the British East India Company was afraid that the evangelization of the native population would hinder their economic interests. He was forced out of Calcutta and ultimately found an opening for ministry in the Danish colony of Serampore, where he spent the rest of his life. For a brief overview of Carey's life see Anderson, "The Great Century and Beyond"; for a more extensive treatment, see George, *Faithful Witness*.

6. Porter, "An Overview, 1700–1914," 47.

7. Cited in Etherington, "Introduction," 3.

In the middle of the nineteenth century, the indigenization movement developed in reaction to many of the excesses of this period. Missionaries and organizations began to realize that they had not placed enough emphasis on ensuring that the types of churches they planted looked like they belonged in that context. Too often they looked like they actually belonged in England or the US, and not in the location where the missionaries were serving. In the same way, they realized they had also not placed enough emphasis on raising up leaders. Two leaders who helped the mission world to begin to consider these issues were Venn and Anderson.

Venn

Henry Venn (1796–1873) was general secretary of the Church Missionary Society (CMS) in London from 1841 to 1872.[8] His life was guided by a passion to see the gospel extend into new harvest fields. During his leadership of the CMS, he placed an emphasis on planting native churches and raising up native leaders. To this end, he developed the three-self formula for indigenous churches—that they should be self-governing, self-supporting, and self-extending.

Venn argued that an essential step in the founding of an indigenous church was for that church to be self-supporting. He wrote that "a second step in the organization of the Native Church will be taken when one or more congregations are formed into a Native Pastorate, under an ordained native, paid by the Native Church Fund."[9] For a church to be indigenous, it must be led to support its own ministries.

Venn also argued for an indigenous church to be self-governing. Responding to critics who claimed his approach to government was too European, Venn explained the need for a cautious transition of the leadership responsibilities:

> Though, in the first instance, and while the tentative and transition stage lasts, it may be advisable to give a preponderating influence to European Missionaries, yet as the Native Councilors become efficient, and as the native contributors enlarge, and the Society's

---

8. This biographical information is from Warren, "Introduction: Henry Venn," 18–25; see also Anderson, "The Great Century and Beyond," 208–09.

9. Venn, *To Apply the Gospel*, 70; see also Venn, "On Steps Towards Helping a Native Church to Become Self-Supporting, Self-Governing, and Self-Extending," 243–49; Venn, "Three-Self Principles," 207–09.

The Challenge of Self-Theologizing

grant in aid is diminished, the European element will be gradually withdrawn, until the Native Church becomes wholly free and independent.[10]

In addition to the need for indigenous churches to be self-supporting and self-governing, Venn added self-extending to his formula. He wrote of an exciting missionary spirit among the native church:

> The case needs to be stated to exhibit the warning and the duty that every convert should be instructed from his conversion in the duty of laboring for his self-support, and for the support of Missions to his Countrymen, and to lay himself out as a Missionary among his relationship and friends to bring them to the truth.[11]

He went on to write that passing on a missionary spirit to the native church would open the door to a new day of missionary effectiveness in which the native converts led their fellow countrymen to Christ. He wrote that a missionary spirit "will often give a reality, a vigor, an independence to native Christianity which it now wants [i.e., lacks] . . . and above all the work would spread as we may say of itself, and such an extension would soon appear, as we have hitherto almost ceased to expect."[12]

Arguing for his three-self formula, Venn explained the limitations of missionary-led churches.[13] He wrote that when missionary-led or missionary-supported churches are planted, the missionary's hands become full, and he focuses less and less of his attention on the unsaved. The converts, then, become dependent on the missionary, and the missionary society invests its resources in ground already gained instead of focusing on "the regions beyond."[14]

To support this formula, Venn explained the importance of training leaders. He wrote,

> Missionaries should remember that it is upon the training up and location of such Native Pastors as we have described that their own labors and the resources of the Society will be best economized;

---

10. Venn, *To Apply the Gospel*, 76–77.
11. Venn, *To Apply the Gospel*, 64.
12. Venn, *To Apply the Gospel*, 64.
13. Venn, *To Apply the Gospel*, 67.
14. Venn, *To Apply the Gospel*, 67.

and that a preparation will be made for the transfer of Missionary labors to the surrounding heathen.[15]

Missionaries become good stewards of their organization's resources by focusing on training leaders. Focusing their time and energy in this way enables them to raise up more laborers capable of shepherding the flock and of reaching the harvest fields.

Venn also wrote of the "euthanasia of mission,"[16] where the missionary cautiously removes himself from the leading of the mission and begins to focus on new fields. He taught missionaries to keep in view the time when

> the missionary is surrounded by well-trained Native congregations under Native Pastors, when he gradually and wisely abridges his own labors, and relaxes his superintendence over the Pastors till they are able to sustain their own Christian ordinances, and the District ceases to be a Missionary field, and passes into Christian parishes under the constituted ecclesiastical authorities.[17]

Working to that end, Venn argued would lead to a time of great growth and expansion of the indigenous church, similar to the time when "the flowers of a fertile field multiply under the showers and warmth of summer."[18]

Anderson

A contemporary of Henry Venn and another scholar who wrote on indigenization was Rufus Anderson (1796–1880). Anderson was the senior secretary for the American Board of Commissioners for Foreign Missions (ABCFM) from 1832 to 1866.[19] Under his leadership, the ABFCM grew to support twelve hundred missionaries and focused more attention on evangelism and the training of native pastors.

Like Venn, Anderson developed his philosophy of missions in reaction to the dual emphasis on evangelization and civilization. He believed that the primary work of missions was the evangelizing of the lost in places where churches did not exist. To that end, he wrote, "Education, schools,

15. Venn, *To Apply the Gospel*, 63.
16. Venn, *To Apply the Gospel*, 63.
17. Venn, *To Apply the Gospel*, 63.
18. Venn, *To Apply the Gospel*, 71.

19. Biographical information is from Beaver, "Introduction," 10–12; see also Anderson, "The Great Century and Beyond," 208–09.

the press, and whatever else goes to make up the working system, are held in strict subordination to the planting and building up of effective working churches."[20] He continued, "The governing object to be always aimed at is self-reliant, effective churches—churches that are purely native."[21]

Anderson looked to Paul as the missionary par excellence. He explained the mission work of the apostle through five qualities: the aim was to save men; the means employed was the gospel; the power relied upon was the Holy Spirit; the success was in the middle and poorer classes; and the result was the planting of churches and the ordaining of leaders.[22] He then argued that if these were the attributes of Paul's missionary work, they ought to be the attributes of contemporary missionaries. In a separate article, he wrote of Paul, "His manner of treating the native pastors and churches is a model for missionaries and their supporters in our day."[23]

Anderson argued that missionaries should never seek to become the pastor of a church they plant. As a result, he argued for the importance of investing resources in training native pastors. He wrote, "Without education, it is not possible for mission churches to be in any proper sense self-governed; nor, without it, will they be self-supported, and much less self-propagating."[24] He argued that focusing on training leaders saves time and resources by raising up more leaders:

> The cost of a ten-year course of education for five natives of India, would not be more than the outfit and passage of one married missionary to that country. And when a company of missionaries is upon the ground, it costs at least five times as much to support them, as it would to support the same number of native preachers . . . The cost of educating a thousand youth in India, from whom preachers might be obtained, and afterwards of supporting two hundred native preachers and their families, would be only about $25,000; which is but little more than the average expense in that country of twenty-five missionaries and families.[25]

---

20. Anderson, *To Advance the Gospel*, 99.

21. Anderson, *To Advance the Gospel*, 99.

22. Anderson, "Principles and Methods of Modern Missions," 251; Anderson, *To Advance the Gospel*, 97–98; Beaver, "Introduction," 14–16.

23. Anderson, *To Advance the Gospel*, 94–95.

24. Anderson, *To Advance the Gospel*, 99.

25. Anderson, *To Advance the Gospel*, 105.

Missionary organizations, Anderson argued, are better stewards if they train pastors and church leaders rather than allowing Europeans to fill those positions.

Nevius, Allen, and Hodges

In addition to Venn and Anderson, John Nevius and Roland Allen also contributed to the missiological discussion related to indigenization. Nevius (1829–93) was a missionary to China with the American Presbyterian Board.[26] His writings focus particularly on the concept of self-support. Roland Allen (1868–1947) focused on the apostle Paul as the exemplary missionary. His books *Missionary Methods: St. Paul's or Ours?*[27] and *The Spontaneous Expansion of the Church*[28] addressed the need for missionaries to return to apostolic church planting pattern by planting self-sufficient churches and relying on the Holy Spirit.

Melvin Hodges (1909–86) was an Assemblies of God missionary in Central America for eighteen years, and while he was influenced by Roland Allen, he sought to blend the three-self principles with his own Pentecostal theology.[29] His work, *The Indigenous Church*, focused especially on the issue of self-governing, which he argued was the most difficult to accomplish.[30] Within the subset of self-governing, Hodges devoted an entire chapter in his book to the issue of training leaders. Among other concepts, he argued that one key issue of training leaders is the main topic we want to address in this chapter—self-theologizing.

Self-Theologizing

Melvin Hodges was one of the first to devote time to the issue of self-theologizing. He wrote that "there must be a standard of doctrine and conduct

---

26. The biographical information in this paragraph is from DuBose, "John L. Nevius: Introduction," 256–57. For a fuller treatment of his life, see Nevius, *The Life of John Livingston Nevius*.

27. Allen, *Missionary Methods*.

28. Allen, *The Spontaneous Expansion of the Church*.

29. Hodges, *The Indigenous Church*, 131–34. See also Hodges, "Why Indigenous Church Principles," 8.

30. Hodges, *The Indigenous Church*, 22.

The Challenge of Self-Theologizing

accepted in common by the believers."[31] He went on to state, "One point here deserves special emphasis. The standard of doctrine and conduct must be an expression of the convert's own concept of the Christian life as they find it in the Scriptures."[32] Hodges argued that the missionary can help with this process, but ultimately the native believers must make these decisions for themselves. These new believers must learn to do theology on their own, apart from the missionary's leading.

Charles Brock built on Hodges's ideas, mentioning the concepts "self-teaching" and "self-expressing" alongside the traditional three.[33] For self-teaching, Brock looked to Paul's letters in Romans 15:14; 1 Corinthians 14:26, 31; and 1 Timothy 4:13, where Paul commanded these churches to be faithful in teaching its members the word. An indigenous church must do the same. For self-expressing, Brock explained that an indigenous church must be free to express itself in culturally appropriate ways during worship. All of these are an outgrowth of the indigenous church having the ability to think theologically.

Charles Kraft encouraged the development of indigenous theologies through a process he refers to as "dynamic-equivalence theologizing."[34] He explained this process in stating, "Dynamic-equivalence theologizing is the reproduction in contemporary cultural contexts of the theologizing process that Paul and the other scriptural authors exemplify."[35] Essentially, Kraft is saying that Paul and the other authors of Scripture conveyed truths about God by communicating them through culturally bound theological statements. The indigenous church must utilize its cultural norms and practices to convey the same truths about God in culturally appropriate ways.

Kraft explained that in order to convey the theological truths in culturally appropriate ways, they must be presented using receptor-oriented methods:

---

31. Hodges, *The Indigenous Church*, 26.
32. Hodges, *The Indigenous Church*, 27.
33. Brock, *Indigenous Church Planting*, 92–94.
34. Kraft, *Christianity in Culture*. For a discussion of "dynamic-equivalence theologizing," see Kraft, *Christianity in Culture*, 228–44. For his discussion of "ethnotheologies," which is similar to Hiebert's "transcultural theology," see Kraft, *Christianity in Culture*, 10, 94, 230–33, 305–06, 314; and Kraft, "Toward a Christian Ethnotheology." For a discussion of how this issue relates to the three-self principles, see Kraft, *Christianity in Culture*, 247–56, or Kraft, "Dynamic Equivalence Churches," 39–57.
35. Kraft, *Christianity in Culture*, 228.

> Theological truth must be re-created like a dynamic-equivalence translation or transculturation within the language and accompanying conceptual framework of the hearers if its true relevance is to be properly perceived by them. Theologizing, like all Christian communication, must be directed to someone if it is to serve its purpose.[36]

Kraft explained that for theological truth to be accepted and embraced, it must be presented in relevant terms. Kraft went on to argue that the indigenous church should not simply embrace theology in Western terms, but it must use its emic cultural perspective to explain its own ethnic understanding of God's unchanging truth, which he referred to as "ethnic theologies."

In order for the indigenous church to develop an ethnic theology, Kraft encouraged the adoption of an ethnotheological or supracultural hermeneutical perspective.[37] He explained that Bible interpreters typically utilize culturally conditioned methods of interpretation when interacting with Scripture. While the knowledge of God that is uncovered by these culturally determined methods is adequate, it is not absolute. Kraft explained, then, that to uncover supracultural truth about God that lies beneath the surface of Scripture's culturally specific commands, the interpreter must go beyond his culturally conditioned interpretational reflexes (for Westerners, the grammatical-historical method of exegesis) to an ethnolinguistic or ethnohermeneutic approach.

While several others discussed the concept, it was Hiebert who coined the term "fourth self."[38] When Hiebert wrote *Anthropological Insights for Missionaries*, he explained, "Every church must make theology its own concern, for it must face the challenges of faith raised by its culture."[39] In other words, a legitimate function of an indigenous church is to develop theologies that speak to the relevant issues in their specific cultural context.

---

36. Kraft, *Christianity in Culture*, 233.

37. Kraft, *Christianity in Culture*, 100–108. Kraft himself acknowledged the massive implications that *Christianity and Culture* has on biblical hermeneutics and the cross-cultural transmission of the gospel when he states on page 102, "There is a sense in which a new or deepened approach to hermeneutics is the major subject of this whole book." More than any other person, it is Kraft's student, Larry W. Caldwell, who has fleshed out many of those implications. I will examine and critique this view in chapter 8.

38. Hiebert, *Anthropological Insights for Missionaries*, 193–224. Also see Whiteman, "Anthropological Reflections on Contextualizing Theology in a Global World," 60–61. For an explanation of how Hiebert's view differs from Kraft's, see Nishioka, "Worldview Methodology in Mission Theology," 468–69.

39. Hiebert, *Anthropological Insights for Missionaries*, 214.

The Challenge of Self-Theologizing

He stated that the most pressing missiological issues of the time were related to how an indigenous church should be planted. Two of the crucial questions with which missionaries were wrestling and which Hiebert sought to answer were: "Should [the native believers] be encouraged to develop their own theologies?" and "What should the missionaries do when these theologies seem to be going astray?"[40]

Answering those questions, he explained that everyone's cultural background influences his theology: "We think that our studies of the Bible are unbiased, that our own interpretations of the Scriptures are the only true ones. It disturbs us, therefore, when we begin to discover that theologies are influenced by culture."[41] He continued, "The fact is, all theologies developed by human beings are shaped by their particular historical and cultural contexts—by the language they use and the questions they ask."[42]

Hiebert then challenged missionaries to teach new Christians to not just teach the people the Scriptures, but also to teach the people *how to study* the Scriptures.[43] He wrote, "It is essential that we train leaders who can wrestle with the theological issues that emerge within their cultural context."[44] As new believers grow in their faith, they learn how to apply the Scriptures to the pressing religious and social issues of their day.

That said, Hiebert displayed balance on this issue by noting, "Although they have a right to interpret the Bible for their particular contexts, they have a responsibility to listen to the greater church of which they are a part."[45] He referred to this dynamic as a "transcultural theology."[46] A transcultural theology is formed when each individual culture understands how Scripture speaks to the issues of its day, and then the various cultural perspectives are compared and explored to determine the biblical universals. As this global-level hermeneutical community forms, cultural biases and areas of syncretism are uncovered, and ultimately the church grows to understand God more clearly.

---

40. Hiebert, *Anthropological Insights for Missionaries*, 193.
41. Hiebert, *Anthropological Insights for Missionaries*, 198.
42. Hiebert, *Anthropological Insights for Missionaries*, 198.
43. Hiebert, *Anthropological Insights for Missionaries*, 215–16.
44. Hiebert, *Anthropological Insights for Missionaries*, 215.
45. Hiebert, *Anthropological Insights for Missionaries*, 217.
46. Hiebert, *Anthropological Insights for Missionaries*, 216–19.

Summary

What can we learn from the insights of these scholars? First, based on the historical development of this discussion, we can see the importance of self-theologizing. As missionaries carry the gospel into new areas and plant churches there, they must give considerable thought to how to plant an indigenous church. Missionaries must resist the temptation to plant a church in the new cultural context that would look exactly the same as a church in the context they've been sent out from.

This process of indigenization includes theology. The conversation on self-theologizing is helpful on two levels. It reminds us that the church needs theologians. It needs leaders who can think theologically long after the missionary is no longer with them. This point is critical when we consider the apostolic nature of the missionary task, that the goal of missionaries is to equip the local church, to help the local church develop, and then, eventually, to leave. A key component of how a missionary disciples these new Christians is the process of training them to think theologically.

At the same time, this conversation is helpful because it reminds us that the leaders of the local church need to do theology in their own context. Because this newly planted church is in a unique cultural context, issues exist in that context for which no one has ever given any serious theological reflection. For a number of reasons, the leaders of this church must have the theological acumen to think clearly and biblically about these unique cultural issues. These issues may include cultural perspectives like a certain type of collectivism, polygamy, or being a matriarchal society. They may also be more theologically inclined concepts like views of the afterlife.

Believers in this context must be able to evaluate their own existing cultural norms and patterns to determine which aspects are biblical and permissible and which aspects are not. At the same time, they must recognize the ways in which their own worldview and cultural ways of thinking affect the way they interpret Scripture. This aspect of preunderstanding can cloud the judgment of every interpreter in any context, and thus all interpreters must be aware of their own cultural perspectives and how it affects them.

From a positive and perhaps more controversial perspective, being able to self-theologize means that the believers in the new context may have insights into the text of Scripture that others (even those who brought the gospel to them) may not have considered before. This reflection may happen not only as they consider unique challenges that arise in their cultural

The Challenge of Self-Theologizing

context, but also as they reflect on key doctrines of the faith. For example, Jackson Wu has written of how prevalent honor-and-shame dynamics are in the book of Romans.[47] Why have these insights often been neglected by Western scholars? Because Westerners don't have those concepts in their worldview, and thus, it has taken Asian scholars looking at the text from a slightly different perspective to bring out this aspect of the text.

A second insight from this discussion is the complexity of self-theologizing. Hiebert's comments are helpful here that yes, the new church must self-theologize, but at the same time this new church has a responsibility to listen to the global church as well. How does the new church think theologically in culturally appropriate ways while at the same time remaining orthodox? This is the great challenge of self-theology.

Thus, this discussion of self-theology leads us back to the main topic of this book—hermeneutics. As Hiebert said, to find the correct balance here, the new church must be taught how to interpret Scripture. These believers must be able to go to the Scriptures for themselves, to read and apply it to their own context. To be clear, to think well theologically, they must learn in other areas as well—biblical theology, historical theology, etc. But biblical interpretation is fundamental to being able both to theologize and to evaluate potential theologies.

---

47. Wu, *Reading Romans with Eastern Eyes*.

4

The Challenge of Contextualization

A few years ago, I was teaching a doctoral course in the local language of the country where I live. As part of the course, we read some local theologies—books and articles written in the local language using indigenous thought patterns. In these articles, scholars tried to examine cultural issues in a biblical way, and in some they attempted to show that these common cultural ways of thinking were part of the teaching of Scripture, even though the ideas were largely rejected by Western theologians.

The class was made of students who had read widely in their field, but the majority of their studies had focused on books written in the West and only later translated into the local language. Reading these contextual theologies was a new experience for them, and their response was split. Three fourths of the class said they had never read anything like this before, but the reading was thought-provoking. "I need more time to reflect on these ideas," was the response from this group. And while this was the response from most of them, several others in the group were dead set against the articles, calling them heresy.

This scenario displays the difficulty of contextualization. On this topic we can reflect on questions like, How do we think about the gospel in culturally relevant ways without losing the gospel? And what about after people become Christians? How can we help them to become a church that looks like it belongs in the culture while at the same time not abandoning the core truths about what it means to be church?

To put this chapter in the context of the whole book, we can reflect back on the fact that in chapter 1 we considered the ways our own cultural perspectives help or hinder us when we approach the text. In chapter 2 we examined the need, regardless of our cultural background, to focus on the text and to seek the original author's meaning. In this chapter we want to reflect on the challenge of what we do once we begin to understand what the original author meant. How do we take the truth intention of the original author and apply it or flesh it out in terms that are understandable in this local context?

With this broad structure in mind, we will consider a brief survey of contextualization, looking at the various discussions that have taken place historically. As we reflect on some of the ways contextualization has been done in the past, we will consider the difficulties and then examine why it is critical for biblical interpretation to drive the contextualization process.

A Brief History of Contextualization

In the 1970s, the discussion of contextualization largely replaced the discussion concerning indigenization principles. The term was formally introduced in a 1972 report by the Theological Education Fund of the World Council of Churches.[1] Norman Thomas noted that the term was introduced in response to an ecumenical frustration with the indigenization movement. He explained, "Whereas indigenization referred often to relating the gospel to traditional cultures, contextualization was used in relation to cultures undergoing rapid social change. It implied taking into account the processes of secularity, technology, and the struggles for human justice being expressed by peoples of the Third World."[2]

Despite the term's ecumenical roots, Evangelicals adopted "contextualization" and sought to redefine it. In one of the early attempts to redefine contextualization, Byang Kato explained that contextualization deals with the relevance of the unchanging gospel message:

> We understand the term to mean making concepts or ideals relevant in a given situation. In reference to Christian practices, it is an effort to express the never changing Word of God in ever changing

---

1. A portion of this report is included in World Council of Churches, "From Indigenization to Contextualization," 175–76. See also Bosch, *Transforming Mission*, 420–21; Hesselgrave and Rommen, *Contextualization*, 28–29; Hesselgrave, "Contextualization That Is Authentic and Relevant," 115; Kwan, "From Indigenization to Contextualization," 237–38.

2. World Council of Churches, "From Indigenization to Contextualization," 175.

modes for relevance. Since the gospel message is inspired but the mode of its expression is not, contextualization of the modes of expression is not only right but necessary.³

Kato went on to state that this type of process "can take place in the area of liturgy, dress, language, church service, and any other form of expression of the gospel truth."⁴

Another author who has dealt extensively with contextualization is David Hesselgrave. Early on in this discussion, Hesselgrave gave a broad, inclusive definition of contextualization when he wrote, "Contextualization is the process whereby representatives of a religious faith adapt the forms and content of that faith in such a way as to communicate and (usually) commend it to the minds and hearts of a new generation within their own changing culture or to people with other cultural backgrounds."⁵ For Hesselgrave, the mission of the church and the desire to take the gospel from one cultural context and implant it in another makes the contextualization process a necessary one.

In a book that Hesselgrave later cowrote with Edward Rommen, Hesselgrave defined contextualization narrowly as "the attempt to communicate the message of the person, works, Word, and will of God in a way that is faithful to God's revelation, especially as it is put forth in the teachings of Holy Scripture, and that is meaningful to respondents in their respective cultural and existential contexts."⁶ This definition helps to envision a marriage between faithfulness to Scripture and sensitivity to culture.

Enoch Wan presented a similar view when he defined contextualization as "the efforts of formulating, presenting and practicing the Christian faith in such a way that is relevant to the cultural context of the target group in terms of conceptualization, expression and application; yet maintaining theological coherence, biblical integrity and theoretical consistency."⁷ Again, inherent in the contextualization process is a commitment to both faithfulness to Scripture and sensitivity to culture.

---

3. Kato, "The Gospel, Cultural Context, and Religious Syncretism," 1217.
4. Kato, "The Gospel, Cultural Context, and Religious Syncretism," 1217.
5. Hesselgrave, "Contextualization and Revelational Epistemology," 694.
6. Hesselgrave and Rommen, *Contextualization*, 200; Hesselgrave, "Contextualization That Is Authentic and Relevant," 115.
7. Wan, "Critiquing the Method of Traditional Western Theology and Calling for Sino-Theology."

The Challenge of Contextualization

While these statements are helpful in terms of defining what contextualization should be, in practice Evangelicals have noted the difficulty of maintaining such a balance. D. A. Carson explained,

> Broadly speaking there are two brands of contextualization. The first assigns control to the context; the operative term is praxis, which serves as a controlling grid to determine the meaning of Scripture. The second assigns the control to Scripture, but cherishes the "contextualization" rubric because it reminds us the Bible must be thought about, translated into, and preached in categories relevant to the particular cultural context.[8]

Missionaries and missiologists have tended to emphasize either Scripture or culture and have struggled to find proper balance between the two.

Paul Hiebert examined historical approaches to contextualization and considered the various types of responses to the question, "How did, and how should, missionaries who bring a new gospel respond to the old one?"[9] There have been three periods of missionary activity in which the church has answered this question differently. These periods include the era of non-contextualization, the era of emerging contextualization, and the era of over-contextualization.[10]

The Era of Non-Contextualization

Although earlier periods of missionary activity contained an emphasis on cultural study and gospel contextualization, the modern missions era that began with William Carey in 1792 was initially an era of non-contextualization. Mission efforts during this period were guided by the desire for the evangelization *and* civilization of the target peoples.

---

8. Carson, "Church and Mission: Reflections on Contextualization and the Third Horizon," 220.

9. Hiebert, "Critical Contextualization," 104. See also Hiebert, *Anthropological Reflections on Missiological Issues*, 75. For an excellent treatment of the life and legacy of Paul Hiebert, see Barnes, "Missiology Meets Cultural Anthropology."

10. Hiebert gives two eras: the era of noncontextualization and the case for contextualization. He then proposes critical contextualization as a means of finding the proper balance between Scripture and culture. In a later article, Hiebert used minimal contextualization, uncritical contextualization, and critical contextualization. I have modified his breakdown to give some attention to the over-contextualization that has been influential in the period since he first wrote. For Hiebert's later article, see Hiebert, "The Gospel in Human Contexts: Changing Perceptions of Contextualization," 84–94.

One of the reasons that this era was guided by non-contextualization was the influence of colonialism on missions.[11] Hiebert explained the attitudes of many Western missionaries during this period:

> Colonialism proved to the West its cultural superiority. Western civilization had triumphed. It was the task, therefore, of the West to bring the benefits of this civilization to the world. Old medical systems were seen as witchcraft and hocus-pocus and had to be stamped out. Old governments were seen as feudalistic and had to be replaced by modern, national governments.[12]

Not only did the Western world consider colonialism necessary because of the superiority of Western civilization, but they also understood the spread of colonialism as an act of divine providence.[13]

Along the same lines, this era was also guided by an attitude of cultural evolution.[14] People in the West considered Western culture superior and of a higher order than non-Western cultures. This perspective is seen in many of the missiological writings of that day. One missionary whose writings display this attitude is John Philip, who was a missionary in South Africa in the 1820s. He argued that "permanent societies of Christians can never be maintained among an uncivilized people without imparting to them the arts and habits of a civilized life."[15] During this period missionaries practiced non-contextualization because they believed that non-Westerners were "uncivilized" and their cultural settings were so inferior that churches could not be maintained in them.

Hiebert explained that these attitudes had two consequences during this period of missions.[16] First, since missionaries grouped the aims of evangelization and civilization together, Christianity was typically seen as a foreign religion. Non-Westerners identified Christianity as a Western religion, and this perspective became a barrier to the gospel for many people.

A second impact of this period of non-contextualization was syncretism. Since missionaries did not contextualize the message of the gospel or the forms of Christian worship, those who became Christians adopted Christian beliefs and practices only on the surface level. This dynamic has

---

11. Hiebert, "Critical Contextualization," 104.
12. Hiebert, "Critical Contextualization," 104.
13. Etherington, "Introduction," 6.
14. Hiebert, "Critical Contextualization," 105.
15. Porter, "An Overview," 52.
16. These two consequences are found in Hiebert, "Critical Contextualization," 106.

The Challenge of Contextualization

become known as "surface accommodation."[17] Converts did not give up their native beliefs and religious practices; they simply gave their native practices Christian names, or they placed Christian modes of worship on top of their existing belief system. Hiebert explained, "Amulets were hidden under shirts, and Christians did not admit to Christian doctors that they were also going to the village shaman."[18]

The Era of Emerging Contextualization

While the era of non-contextualization merged evangelization and civilization, in the twentieth century, this situation began to change. The two major developments of this period were the decline of colonial rule and the rise of anthropological theory.[19] In missions theory, the previous chapter has already noted the impact of Venn and Anderson's focus on the three-selfs of an indigenous church. The indigenization movement in missions revealed a growing dissatisfaction with colonialism. The recognition that churches should be self-governed was coupled with the idea that nations as a whole should be self-governed.

The emphasis on education during the colonial period also played a part in the end of the colonial period.[20] The effectiveness of the education systems implemented by the colonial powers created a new group of potential leaders who had learned from Westerners and had the ability to govern their own people. These educational institutions turned out to be, especially in Africa, the birthplace of democracy for many British colonies.[21]

Around the same time, the world experienced two world wars, which shattered many concepts of Western cultural superiority. People considered the technological and scientific advancements Western nations made in the nineteenth and early twentieth centuries and believed that society was evolving and advancing to a create a better world. In the course of the evolution process, Western nations were more advanced, and by extension they needed to civilize the rest of the world. When those same advancements were used for destruction and the unimaginable horrors of

---

17. Van Rheenen, *Communicating Christ in Animistic Contexts*, 63.
18. Van Rheenen, *Communicating Christ in Animistic Contexts*, 63.
19. Van Rheenen, *Communicating Christ in Animistic Contexts*, 63.
20. Hiebert, "Critical Contextualization," 106.
21. Maxwell, "Decolonization," 289.

the Jewish Holocaust, though, it put to rest any notion of Western cultural superiority.

After World War II (1939–45), Western nations were more focused and interested in other cultures and languages.[22] At this time the United States was involved in rebuilding much of Europe and Japan, as well as directing projects aimed at the development of Third World nations. In spite of the fact that technology was advanced and potentially beneficial to the people, most of these projects failed due to the way technology was implemented. The US representatives failed to learn the language or study the cultural setting, and as a result, when they implemented the technology, they overlooked key cultural considerations. In light of these failures, more attention was given to scholarly research in areas like linguistics and cultural anthropology.

The consequences of these developments on missions were far reaching. The death of Western attitudes of cultural superiority meant that Christianity would no longer be seen as a foreign religion.[23] In most cases, missionaries no longer lived in isolated compounds but among the people, and they likewise embraced the lifestyles of the people. As a result, the gospel was not seen as message in which one had to become westernized in order to believe it, but the gospel was clothed in cultural terms that the people could understand and appreciate.

The developments of this period led to attitudes of cultural relativity in which all cultures were valued and considered worthy of study.[24] As a result, missionaries placed more emphasis on cultural acquisition and language learning. This renewed emphasis on cultural anthropology created more interest in presenting the gospel in culturally appropriate terms. These studies also helped missionaries to prevent and avoid syncretistic practices.

---

22. The information in this paragraph is from Rogers and Steinfatt, *Intercultural Communication*, 59–66; Hiebert, "Critical Contextualization," 108.

23. Hiebert, "Critical Contextualization," 108.

24. Cultural relativity is the belief that all cultures are true and no one culture can judge another. I am aware that extreme cultural relativity leads to pluralistic attitudes in which all aspects of culture are acceptable and beyond critique. If the extreme position is avoided, cultural relativity helps missionaries recognize that some aspects of culture like language, food, communication methods, or any aspect that Scripture does not address are amoral and can be different from culture to culture. The challenge for Evangelicals is to combine cultural relativity with biblical authority.

Another result of this period was the development of the people group approach to missions. It was amidst this period of emerging contextualization with its renewed emphasis on linguistic and cultural anthropology that Donald McGavran and Cameron Townsend developed the missiological concepts that led to the understanding of people groups.[25] Ralph Winter then took those concepts and presented them at the 1974 Lausanne Congress on World Evangelization, challenging missionary leaders to focus on reaching these unreached people groups.[26] This emphasis on people groups, with their unique cultural and linguistic settings, opened the door for the contextualization discussion.

The Era of Over-Contextualization

With the emergence of the contextualization discussion in the 1970s and 1980s, scholars focused much attention on defining contextualization and measuring its appropriate limits. Some considered certain missiological practices to be "over-contextualization." It is helpful to remember Carson's explanation of the two strands of contextualization—one puts the emphasis on Scripture as authoritative, and the other puts the emphasis on culture as normative.[27] Those who over-contextualized sided with culture. There were several developments that led to this over-contextualization.

One of the trends of this era was the postmodern turn. Myron Penner explains, "I want to suggest that the postmodern turn is best understood when one resists the temptation to define it categorically, as either a field of beliefs or a set of philosophical theses—except in the most general way."[28] Penner's resistance to defining postmodernism reveals something about postmodernism itself—its rejection of absolutes. Postmodernism calls into question the validity of all ideologies by examining the subjective nature of human knowledge.[29]

---

25. Winter, "Four Men, Three Eras, Two Transitions: Modern Missions," 260.

26. Winter, "The Highest Priority: Cross-Cultural Evangelism," 213–41.

27. Carson, "Church and Mission: Reflections on Contextualization and the Third Horizon," 220.

28. Penner, "Introduction," 16.

29. Vanhoozer, "Pilgrim's Digress: Christian Thinking on and about the Post/Modern Way," 80–81; Hiebert, "Critical Contextualization," 108.

Postmodern thought is an attempt to think when absolute certainty or absolute truth no longer exists.[30] The problem with this mentality from an evangelical perspective is that absolute truth is the foundation of the Christian faith, and the exclusivity of Christ is the core of the gospel.[31] Hiebert echoed this concern when he wrote that "the denial of absolutes and of 'truth' itself runs counter to the core Christian claims about the truth of the gospel and the uniqueness of Christ. Moreover, if the gospel is contextualized, what are the checks against biblical and theological distortion?"[32]

Hiebert's fears over how the rejection of absolute truth would affect the contextualization process were realized with the onset of over-contextualization. The subjectivity of postmodernism combined with the growing cultural relativity displayed in the era of emerging contextualization to create an environment in which culture, not Scripture, drove the contextualization process.

Perhaps the greatest example of over-contextualization is the paradigm seen in insider movements.[33] In its simplest form, an insider movement is a movement of people coming to faith in Christ that intentionally keeps people inside their networks of relationships after they become believers.[34] At face value, keeping believers "inside" their networks of relationships is a helpful missiological principle. The problem and overall critique of insider movements is that keeping believers inside those networks, and not scriptural considerations, becomes the driving issue in evangelism. In terms of contextualization, it is cultural considerations, namely what is culturally appropriate or not appropriate to keep people relationally connected, that controls the contextualization process.

---

30. Penner, "Introduction," 25.

31. Todd Miles explains exclusivism as the position that "conscious faith in the gospel, defined as the good news of the life, death, and resurrection of Jesus Christ as anticipated, developed, and presented in the Holy Scripture, is necessary for salvation" (Miles, *A God of Many Understandings?*, 3). Some Evangelicals, referred to as "inclusivists," hold that some inherit salvation without conscious knowledge in this life of the saving work of Christ. The clear teaching of Scripture, contrary to the inclusivist position, is that conscious faith in Christ is necessary for salvation.

32. Hiebert, "Critical Contextualization," 108.

33. For an excellent treatment of insider movements, see Wolfe, "Insider Movements."

34. Lewis, "Promoting Movements to Christ within Natural Connections," 75; Higgins, "The Key to Insider Movements," 156.

The Challenge of Contextualization

One example of an insider movement is the proposed C5 level of contextualization among Muslims.[35] At C5 on the contextualization spectrum, Muslims who accept Jesus continue to refer to themselves as Muslims. They seek to share their faith with unsaved Muslims, but they also seek to "remain legally and socially within the community of Islam."[36] Some Christian missionaries are even willing to *begin* referring to themselves as Muslims for the sake of reaching potential C5 believers.[37]

In one specific example of C5 evangelism in South Asia, missionaries, for the sake of creating an insider movement, would not baptize an individual until the head of his family became a believer.[38] Following the pattern of ethnic Jews who come to faith in Jesus as the Messiah, these Muslims refer to themselves as "completed Muslims."[39]

In 1998, Phil Parshall led a group of researchers to study a C5 movement.[40] The encouraging signs of the study included the participants' beliefs in Jesus as the only Savior, in God's forgiveness through Jesus' death for them, and in the importance of regular Christian worship. At the same time, though, these same participants also believed that "there are four holy books, of which the Qur'an is the greatest. Nearly half continue to go to the traditional mosque on Friday where they participate in the standard Islamic prayers which affirm Muhammed as a prophet of God. And nearly half do not affirm the Trinity."[41]

In a similar study among Hindus and Muslims in Southern India, Herbert Hoefer examined a group of 200,000 "non-baptized believers."[42] Since public baptism would signify a departure from their religious and cultural setting and in fear of being cut off from family and other relationships, these believers had never been baptized.[43] Hoefer commended this practice as a successful contextualization of Christianity in India, despite

---

35. For an explanation of the C1 to C6 contextualization spectrum, see Travis, "The C1 to C6 Spectrum."

36. Travis, "The C1 to C6 Spectrum," 210.

37. Travis, "Must all Muslims Leave 'Islam' to Follow Jesus?," 412.

38. Ali and Woodberry, "South Asia," 681.

39. Ali and Woodberry, "South Asia," 682.

40. Parshall, "Danger! New Directions in Contextualization," 405; Parshall, *Muslim Evangelism*, 68.

41. Parshall, "Danger! New Directions in Contextualization," 405.

42. Hoefer, *Churchless Christianity*.

43. Hoefer, *Churchless Christianity*, 8.

the fact that many of these non-baptized believers "tended to carry on with their worship of Christ in the same manner as they had previously worshipped their other gods."[44]

These practices do not pose a problem for Hoefer, who wrote, "We do not want to change the culture or the religious genius of India. We simply want to bring Christ and his gospel into the center of it."[45] As a result, he argues that baptism should not be seen as a movement away from one's cultural and religious background, but it should be understood as a "sacrament of fulfillment."[46] It is fulfillment of one's indigenous religious system through the person and work of Jesus Christ.

Numerous attempts have been made to give a biblical foundation for insider movements,[47] but others have pointed out the hermeneutical weaknesses of those arguments.[48] The bottom line for adherents of insider movements is that the question they are asking is not "How can a convert be faithful to the Scriptures?" but "How can one become a Christian and not leave his culture?" While scriptural considerations are important, culture is ultimately driving the practices of C5 insider movements.

The era of over-contextualization is an important consideration for this study because it is the era in which many scholars began to develop various theories for intercultural and cross-cultural interpretation. For some, it was the desire to be receptor-oriented in communication and contextualization of the gospel that fueled their desire to develop culturally appropriate methods of interpretation.

Summary

As we've seen, the problem with over-contextualization is that culture drives the process—not Scripture. In chapter 1 we saw that our worldview is part of our preunderstanding anytime we study Scripture, but chapter

44. Hoefer, *Churchless Christianity*, 199.
45. Hoefer, *Churchless Christianity*, 201.
46. Hoefer, *Churchless Christianity*, 199.
47. Higgins, "The Key to Insider Movements," 155–66; Woodbery, "To the Muslim I Became a Muslim?," 23–28; Higgins, "Acts 15 and Insider Movements among Muslims," 29–40; Ridgway, "Insider Movements in the Gospels and Acts," 77–86. See the responses to Corwin's questions, especially numbers 3, 4, and 8 in Corwin et al., "A Humble Appeal to C5/Insider Movement Muslim Ministry Advocates to Consider Ten Questions," 5–20.
48. Waterman, "Do the Roots Affect the Fruits," 57–64; Corwin, "A Response to My Respondents," 53–56.

2 reminded us that the goal of our study of Scripture is not to reinforce or find justification for our preconceived ways of thinking. It is for this reason that faithful contextualization starts with understanding the text of Scripture and the meaning of the original authors.

Of course, to say that contextualization "starts" with Scripture fails to take into account the ways culture affects our reading of Scripture. Thus, faithful exegetes will study their own cultural perspective so they can be aware of the ways it affects their exegesis. In the same way, we must be aware of the target culture and its cultural categories even as we study the text of Scripture so that we can best know how to flesh out the truth intention of the original author in the local context.

Despite the excesses of over-contextualization, many positive examples of healthy contextualization exist today. In chapter 9 we look in a bit more detail at Paul Hiebert's approach of critical contextualization, which is essentially his response to the historical developments we just looked at. In that process, he encourages: 1) examining a specific cultural practice, 2) interpreting biblical texts that relate to that practice, and 3) adjusting the practice so that it conforms to biblical teaching.[49]

Another healthy model comes from Jackson Wu.[50] He approaches the process of contextualization through the lens of biblical theology and relates the themes of the biblical story with the "themes" of the culture. He then provides a four-step process where we: 1) identify the biblical themes, 2) interconnect the cultural themes, 3) interpret biblical meaning, and 4) infer cultural significance. He then provides a couple caveats:

> The above definition of contextualization suggests a center and a context. The Bible is the centerpiece of contextualization. Biblically faithful contextualization always acknowledges the Bible's authority over any particular culture. Additionally, Christians want to see aspects of contemporary culture ultimately transformed to reflect the biblical vision for the world. From beginning to end, the Bible should be the ground and the goal of contextualization.[51]

Lest we think that contextualization is simply a study of the text only, Wu continues, "On the other hand, our model recognizes that contextualization never happens in a cultural vacuum. Even if Christians focus their

---

49. Hiebert, "Critical Contextualization," 109.
50. Wu, *One Gospel for All Nations*, esp. 87–111.
51. Wu, *One Gospel for All Nations*, 109.

attention on the Bible, they always do so from within a social context."[52] Thus, even though our aim is to study Scripture and understand the meaning intended by the original author, our cultural perspective affects the way we approach the text. In addition, we must have a deep grasp of the culture if we hope to implant the truth of Scripture in that context.

Matthew Kim makes a similar point when he writes, "To contextualize God's word, as we understand it, is not to alter the meaning of the text, but rather to interpret it in such a way that hearers can understand and grapple with its meaning and apply it in a relevant way."[53] Contextualization is especially interesting when we consider multicultural contexts, such as Kim's exploration of Asian North Americans who often have a fusion of cultural influences. He explains that preachers must "explore and evaluate their listeners' ethnic and cultural identities and identify the complexities that arise from living in two or more discrete cultures."[54]

Thus, we see that in some ways the idea of contextualization is synonymous with the idea of application. When we consider contextualization, we examine the ways that the message of Scripture can be explained, understood, or lived out in a specific context. The process can be complex and complicated, but we can see the importance that the word takes in this process. As we discussed in chapter 2, the goal is to understand the meaning of the original author and then communicate that truth or live out that truth in culturally appropriate ways. In the next section, we will look at several proposals for how we should handle the text in a way that does that.

---

52. Wu, *One Gospel For All Nations*, 109.
53. Kim and Wong, *Finding Our Voice*, chapter 2, section 5, para. 3.
54. Kim and Wong, *Finding Our Voice*, chapter 2, section 5, para. 4.

SECTION 2

Section 2

In 2016 I was teaching a seminary course on missions. A coworker of mine who had been in South Asia for two years was not in the course, but I invited him to attend one of the sessions. It just so happened that when he attended we were talking about the range of theological views as they relate to key aspects of the missionary task. For example, we discussed the continuum between prioritism, which sees evangelism as the primary focus, and holism, which emphasizes an approach that meets both physical and spiritual needs.[1]

Of course, I was willing to share what my view was on the variety of issues we discussed, but the primary goal of the lecture was to give students a framework for understanding the range of views which people hold. Recognizing this continuum can help them not only decide what their view is, but it can also help them understand how they relate to other views.

My friend who attended the class already had two years of missions experience in a difficult place. After attending the session, though, he said that studying the various positions helped him make sense of many of his experiences. He said that when he was in South Asia, he saw some missionaries focusing only on evangelism even though they were surrounded by devastating poverty. On the other extreme, some missionaries spent all their time on social projects. He often wondered why they utilized such different approaches, but it was only after studying the variety of views that he realized it was because these missionaries emphasized different aspects of biblical teaching and ended up in different places on the continuum.

It's important, then, for all of us to study and understand the variety of views and approaches related to some specific topic. The same is true

---

1. For those interested in study some of these issues, see Hesselgrave, *Paradigms in Conflict*.

when it comes to cross-cultural hermeneutics. So, in this section we will consider a range of views and approaches related to interpreting Scripture in intercultural and multicultural contexts. Examining these views and considering their strengths and weaknesses will give us a broad perspective of those who have written on this topic.

5

Postcolonial Hermeneutics

Travel throughout the Majority World, and you'll still see vestiges of the colonial era. In fact, from my balcony where I sit writing this book, I can see an old colonial home next to a modern highrise. Around the corner from that is a traditional temple. In many parts of the world Christians seek to navigate these various aspects of their history: the traditional, the contemporary, and the colonial. Given that Christianity entered many of these countries during the colonial period, a period in which those from the West often took advantage of local resources and looked down on the local population, complicates the situation. Postcolonial hermeneutics seeks to make sense of this complicated perspective of Christians today by providing a way forward.

One of the primary proponents of this approach to hermeneutics is R. S. Sugirtharajah. Sugirtharajah is a Sri Lankan theologian and a professor of biblical hermeneutics at the University of Birmingham in the United Kingdom. He has written extensively on issues related to indigenous hermeneutic systems. His works focus on Third World contextual theologies, hermeneutic methods during the colonial and postcolonial period, and Asian understandings of Scripture. The distinguishing marks of his works include a denial of biblical absolutism, a denial of the exclusivity of Christ, an approval of vernacular readings of Scripture, and an approval of postcolonial rereading of Scripture.

Denial of Biblical Absolutism

One of the features of Sugirtharajah's system is a denial of biblical absolutism. He argues that the Bible is not the sole provider of information concerning God's revelation of himself. He explains, "What postcolonialism attempts to do is to demonstrate that the Bible itself is part of the conundrum rather than a panacea for all ills of the postmodern/postcolonial world."[1] He goes on to refer to the position that the Bible provides the answers to life's questions as an "illusion."[2]

As a result, Sugirtharajah proposes that indigenous hermeneutical systems must include the use of indigenous sacred texts. He writes, "The Christian Bible's place amidst the other sacred writings depends on the acknowledgement that no scripture conveys the full divine experience, and that any scripture can help us to see the traces of that experience, if one approaches the sacred writings with openness and sensitivity."[3] For effective cross-cultural hermeneutics, Sugirtharajah argues, the Bible should be seen as one text among many.

He states that the faith experience one has through the Scriptures is analogous to the encounters of others. The Bible is not unparalleled in its nature or unique in its place as provider of information about God's character.[4] The claims of the Bible, in his view, are not competing claims against the sacred texts of a people but are complementary.

Inherent in Sugirtharajah's understanding of Scripture and his hermeneutical system as a whole is a rejection of the original author as the determiner of meaning. He argues that "the author as a readily recognizable figure who approves and supervises the exact and intended meaning of a text is no longer tenable."[5] To point to the author as the determiner of meaning is colonial and, in his mind, hegemonic and outdated.[6]

Modern biblical interpreters, he argues, must move beyond the fascination with the author to embrace interpretation as "reading encounters."[7]

1. Sugirtharajah, *Postcolonial Criticism and Biblical Interpretation*, 100.
2. Sugirtharajah, *Postcolonial Criticism and Biblical Interpretation*, 102.
3. Sugirtharajah, "Bible: Introduction," 14–15.
4. Sugirtharajah, *Postcolonial Criticism and Biblical Interpretation*, 205.
5. Sugirtharajah, *Troublesome Texts*, 32.
6. Sugirtharajah, *The Bible and the Third World*, 61–73, 110, 116; Sugirtharajah, *Postcolonial Criticism and Biblical Interpretation*, 202–203; Sugirtharajah, *Troublesome Texts*, 32.
7. Sugirtharajah, *Troublesome Texts*, 32.

Doing so means interpreters must also recognize that texts have multiple meanings, and they must be open to alternative meanings to biblical texts.[8] Understanding texts as only having one meaning, he argues, is a feature of historical criticism and is a mode of interpretation for a bygone era.[9]

To display his own system, Sugirtharajah examines the Johannine letters. He rejects the aspects of the letters which confront heretical, divisive theological positions and those aspects that project an imperial Christ because at those points the intention of the author is colonialistic.[10] Postcolonial interpreters, he argues, should focus on the aspects of the letter that focus on truth, justice, and love as they seek to be ethically involved in their own communities.[11] At the same time, he contends that the Epistles were influenced more by Buddhist thought than by Judaic or Hellenistic categories, and thus it is clear from the letters that "sacred texts are textual coalitions."[12] He argues that postcolonial interpreters should not be ashamed, then, to utilize indigenous sacred texts as they develop new meanings for biblical texts.

Denial of Exclusivity of Christ

For Sugirtharajah, just as the Bible is not the absolute and final word from God, Jesus Christ is not the sole means of salvation for men. He explains,

> In a multireligious context like ours, the real contest is not between Jesus and other savior figures like Buddha or Krishna, or religious leaders like Mohammed, as advocates of the "Decade of Evangelism" want us to believe, it is between mammon and Satan on the one side, and Jesus, Buddha, Krishna, and Mohammed on the other ... The question then is whether these religious figures offer us any clue to challenge these forces, or simply help to perpetuate

---

8. Sugirtharajah, *Troublesome Texts*, 32–33; Sugirtharajah, *Postcolonial Criticism and Biblical Interpretation*, 202–03.

9. Sugirtharajah, *Troublesome Texts*, 129.

10. Sugirtharajah, *Troublesome Texts*, 33–35.

11. Sugirtharajah, *Troublesome Texts*, 40–41.

12. Sugirtharajah, *Troublesome Texts*, 39, 42. Sugirtharajah claims that in John's writings "God does not do anything but is called light (1 John 1:5), love (1 John 4:8, 16) and, in the Gospel, spirit (John 4:24) as a result of the actions of human beings." He goes on to state that "It is the act of love which makes the presence of God real" (Sugirtharajah, *Troublesome Texts*, 39). For him, the presence of this theme is a result of Buddhistic influence on John.

them, and how the continuities rather than contrasts among these savior figures may be experienced and expressed.[13]

In today's globalized world, he argues, what benefits society most is not competing claims between different religions and their salvific figures but mutual harmony and a conscientious effort to confront the social evils of society.

As a result, Sugirtharajah encourages Majority World theologians to utilize hermeneutic techniques that "integrate, synthesize, and interconnect" their indigenous religious systems with the gospel in order to refashion it in Asian terms.[14] He explains that Asian theologians are going beyond contextualization in their reformulation of the gospel: "The task is seen not as adapting the Christian gospel in Asian idioms, but as reconceptualizing the basic tenets of the Christian faith in the light of Asian realities. The new mood is not to assume the superiority of Christian revelation but to seek life-enhancing potentialities also in the divine manifestations of Asia."[15]

Christ, in Sugirtharajah's view, is not the sole mediator of salvation for all cultures for all time. He is simply one option among many. In his treatment of the supposed missionary claims of John 14:6, Acts 4:12, 1 Timothy 2:5, and similar passages, he argues that the unbiased stance of postcolonial biblical hermeneutics enables interpreters to see that early Christian literature is confessional rather than missionary in nature. He explains that these passages

> Should be seen in the light of the constituency of intended readers, the narrative setting of these sayings, and, more importantly, as supportive of internal theological positions within the early Christian communities. In other words, they are not to be seen as statements made with Hindus, Buddhists, Sikhs, and countless indigenous people in mind. These assertions, if we read them with the above-mentioned perspectives, look much less triumphalistic.[16]

Recognizing that these claims were made to people who were already Christians, he argues, helps interpreters to understand that Jesus did not make these statements to exclude from salvation people of other faith traditions.

---

13. Sugirtharajah, *Asian Biblical Hermeneutics and Postcolonialism*, 119.
14. Sugirtharajah, "Introduction," 5.
15. Sugirtharajah, "Introduction," 5.
16. Sugirtharajah, *Postcolonial Criticism and Biblical Interpretation*, 98.

In a work that Sugirtharajah edited, *Asian Faces of Jesus*, various Asian theologians present their indigenous perspectives of Jesus. Sugirtharajah introduced the project by explaining that these views of Jesus "counteract this imperial, supremacist, and absolutist understanding of Jesus."[17] He then explains two of the common themes of these articles, and of Asian understandings of Jesus in general: "They fiercely resist any attempts to apply well-established and timeless truth about Jesus . . . They demonstrate that perceptions of Jesus are not validated by their timeless claims or by their dogmatic soundness, but by the appropriateness of the image to a specific context."[18]

A second theme is similar: "Their Christological constructions demonstrate that one need not necessarily appeal to precedents or paradigms enshrined in the gospel or other early Christian works, nor have these constructions necessarily been based on or legitimized by canonical writings."[19] For Sugirtharajah, then, contemporary Christians need not utilize traditional Christian hermeneutical methods; nor do they need to conceive of Christ in traditional Christian terms or even consult the Bible to gain an understanding of Christ. The issue for him is not whether a conception of Christ conforms to the Christ of the Scriptures, but whether it conforms to the Asian context.

Approval of Vernacular Readings

Sugirtharajah explains that one helpful hermeneutical model for Majority World Christians is what he refers to as vernacular hermeneutics. He states that vernacular biblical hermeneutics "is an attempt to go 'home.' It is a call to self-awareness, aimed at creating an awakening among people to their indigenous literary, cultural, and religious heritage."[20] This method attempts to recover the indigenous aspects of the culture that were oppressed during the colonial period of missions.

Sugirtharajah states that since the biblical text is culturally far from these indigenous peoples, the stories of Scripture are often difficult for them to understand and grasp. It is at this point that he views vernacular hermeneutics as helpful. He explains,

17. Sugirtharajah, "Prologue and Perspective," ix.
18. Sugirtharajah, "Prologue and Perspective," ix.
19. Sugirtharajah, "Prologue and Perspective," ix.
20. Sugirtharajah, *The Bible and the Third World*, 177.

> Vernacular interpretation seeks to overcome the remoteness and strangeness of these biblical texts by trying to make links across the cultural divides, by employing the reader's own cultural resources and social experiences to illuminate the biblical narratives. It is about making hermeneutical sense of texts and concepts imported across time and space by means of one's own indigenous texts and concepts.[21]

In this process, indigenous beliefs are used to help make the biblical text more understandable.

Sugirtharajah states three methods, or modes, for implementing vernacular hermeneutics. He calls the first mode conceptual correspondences. Utilizing this mode, the interpreter seeks parallels between the indigenous sacred texts and the biblical text,[22] and he looks for textual analogies that can elucidate the foreignness of biblical concepts and terms. Sugirtharajah gives numerous examples of this process: Indian believers using Vedic texts to explain creation and the fall, Tamil converts using Tamil poems explaining one's love for his beloved to explain the death of Christ, Chinese believers using Confucian concepts to explain the Holy Spirit, and South Africans using the concept of *ubuntu*[23] to explain the Joseph narrative.[24]

The second mode of vernacular hermeneutics is narratival enrichments. This mode seeks to "re-employ some of the popular folk tales, legends, riddles, plays, proverbs, and poems that are part of the common heritage of the people and place them vividly alongside biblical materials, in order to draw out their hermeneutical implications."[25] Sugirtharajah explains that an example of this mode is Peter Lee's juxtaposition of the drama *The Injustice Done to Tou Ngo* with the book of Ruth.[26] Although the two stories are quite different, they are both set within paternalistic societies and both portray a daughter-in-law's devotion to her mother-in-law.[27]

---

21. Sugirtharajah, *The Bible and the Third World*, 182.

22. Sugirtharajah, *The Bible and the Third World*, 182.

23. "Ubuntu refers to behaving well towards others or acting in ways that benefit the community. Such acts could be as simple as helping a stranger in need, or much more complex ways of relating with others. A person who behaves in these ways *has* ubuntu. He or she is a full person" (Thompsell, Get the Definition of Ubuntu").

24. Sugirtharajah, *The Bible and the Third World*, 184–85.

25. Sugirtharajah, *The Bible and the Third World*, 186.

26. Lee, "Two Stories of Loyalty," 24–40.

27. *The Injustice Done to Tou Ngo* is a drama set during the Yuan dynasty (1271–1368). In the story, a father and son try to force two widows to marry them. The older

Sugirtharajah's final mode of vernacular reading is performantial parallels. This mode uses indigenous rituals and behavioral practices to help explain biblical concepts. One example he gives of this mode is A. C. Musopole's use of Malawi witchcraft techniques to explain Jesus' teaching in John 6:53–55 that his followers must eat his flesh and drink his blood.[28] Sugirtharajah explains that the use of these witchcraft rituals could be understood metaphorically or literally.[29]

The problem with vernacular hermeneutics, as Sugirtharajah sees it, is that with globalization and the intermixing of many diasporic communities, pure indigenous systems of thought are difficult to find.[30] Moreover, many vernacular interpretations are so particularistic and isolated that they have little to offer the global community.[31] Nonetheless, such hermeneutical methods still have much to offer as a reaction against the forces of globalization in today's world.[32]

Approval of Postcolonial Rereadings

Given some of the weaknesses of vernacular hermeneutics, Sugirtharajah proposes postcolonial interpretation as an alternative. Postcolonial biblical interpretation is in the same stream of interpretation as liberation hermeneutics in that both focus on voicing the concerns of minority groups and confronting dominant ideologies.[33] Sugirtharajah critiques liberation hermeneutics, though, as being too concerned with textual issues and with the homogenization of the poor.[34]

---

widow is amenable, but her daughter-in-law is not. The son then attempts to murder the older widow but accidentally kills his father. He blames the younger widow, Tou Ngo, for the murder, and she is condemned to death. For more information, see Yan, "Theatricality in Classical Chinese Drama," 68.

28. Musopole, "Witchcraft Terminology, the Bible, and African Christian Theology," 352.

29. Sugirtharajah, *The Bible and the Third World*, 189.

30. Sugirtharajah, *The Bible and the Third World*, 198; Sugirtharajah, *Asian Biblical Hermeneutics and Postcolonialism*, 14; Sugirtharajah, *Postcolonial Criticism and Biblical Interpretation*, 190.

31. Sugirtharajah, *Asian Biblical Hermeneutics and Postcolonialism*, 14.

32. Sugirtharajah, *Troublesome Texts*, 127–28.

33. Sugirtharajah, *The Bible and the Third World*, 244.

34. Sugirtharajah, *The Bible and the Third World*, 244.; Sugirtharajah, *Troublesome Texts*, 123.

Postcolonial hermeneutics is a reaction against the dominant interpretational techniques of the colonial period. Sugirtharajah explains, "Postcolonialism is about a set of measures worked out by diasporan Third World intellectuals in order to undo, reconfigure, and redraw contingent boundaries of hegemonic knowledge."[35] This type of interpretation is concerned with giving a voice and a new identity to those once colonized.[36]

The first concern of postcolonial hermeneutics is to scrutinize biblical texts for their colonial entanglements.[37] Sugirtharajah explains that numerous biblical texts were written in colonial contexts. In light of these contexts, "Postcolonial reading practice will reconsider the biblical narratives, not as a series of divinely guided incidents or reports about divine-human encounters, but as emanating from colonial contacts."[38] As an example, Sugirtharajah considers the liberating purposes of the book of Esther to demonstrate how the contents of the book might relate to those in areas formerly colonized.[39]

The second concern of postcolonial hermeneutics is to reread biblical texts in light of postcolonial concerns.[40] To accomplish this task, Sugirtharajah explains that biblical texts will be read "from the perspective of postcolonial concerns such as liberation struggles of the past and present; it will be sensitive to subaltern and feminine elements embedded in the texts; it will interact with and reflect on postcolonial circumstances such as hybridity, fragmentation, deterritorialization, and hyphenated, double or multiple, identities."[41] Such a reading will utilize texts in a way in which they speak to these issues.

As one example of this type of reading, Sugirtharajah considers Elijah's confrontation with the priests of Baal at Mount Carmel. He explains how this reading would affect the interpretation of this passage:

> Postcolonial reading will, for instance, see the confrontation of Elijah and the priests of Mount Carmel, not as a straight theological conflict between two deities, Yahweh and Baal, nor as one religious community and its gods pitched against another and its

---

35. Sugirtharajah, *The Bible and the Third World*, 246.
36. Sugirtharajah, *Asian Biblical Hermeneutics and Postcolonialism*, 16.
37. Sugirtharajah, *The Bible and the Third World*, 251–52.
38. Sugirtharajah, *The Bible and the Third World*, 251.
39. Sugirtharajah, *The Bible and the Third World*, 251.
40. Sugirtharajah, *The Bible and the Third World*, 252–55.
41. Sugirtharajah, *The Bible and the Third World*, 252–55.

gods, but as a complex issue where communities intermingle and the gods are significantly beyond their theological propensities.[42]

A third task of postcolonial hermeneutics is the interrogation of colonial interpretation.[43] The task here, as Sugirtharajah sees it, is to overcome the oppressive interpretations of the colonial period. Such an interpretation will be a reaction against or an interrogation of the dominant Western-influenced interpretations of the colonial era.[44]

Evaluation

Sugirtharajah's hermeneutic proposals are helpful in emphasizing the need to study the cultural concerns of various people groups in both native and diasporic settings. To communicate the gospel effectively with those peoples, one needs to study the people's indigenous perspectives, context, history, and methods of interpretation.

Unfortunately, though, it is at this point that the benefits of Sugirtharajah's approach end. His pluralistic denial of the Bible as the authoritative word of God and of Jesus Christ as the sole mediator of salvation is a rejection of historic Christianity. His argument that understanding Jesus as the authoritative, sole provider of faith for all mankind is oppressive and outdated is an affront to evangelical Christianity. The attempt to "refashion" Jesus in a way that is more receptive to Asian audiences is misguided and is a failure to understand the very nature of the Gospels.

Moreover, his argument that John's Gospel and the other New Testament documents were written to Christians, thus nullifying any sense of mission in verses like John 14:6 or Acts 4:12, is erroneous. Andreas Köstenberger argues cogently against this understanding of John's purpose, showing that John wrote with an evangelistic purpose.[45] This view was the dominant one until the onslaught of historical criticism in the twentieth century.[46] These passages display the fact that the missionary nature of the church is a fundamental aspect of the Christian faith.

---

42. Sugirtharajah, *The Bible and the Third World*, 253.
43. Sugirtharajah, *The Bible and the Third World*, 255–57.
44. Sugirtharajah, *Asian Biblical Hermeneutics and Postcolonialism*, 17.
45. Köstenberger, *The Mission of Jesus and the Disciples According to the Fourth Gospel*, 8.
46. Carson, *The Gospel According to John*, 91.

From a missiological perspective, another weakness is that in reacting against the non-contextualization of the colonial period, Sugirtharajah has moved directly to over-contextualization. One wonders if contextualization is even appropriate to describe his proposals when Sugirtharajah himself explains that he desires to go beyond contextualization altogether in refashioning the very nature of the gospel.

In terms of hermeneutics, Sugirtharajah's proposals are in line with the radical reader-response hermeneutics of Stanley Fish.[47] His desire to read postcolonial and vernacular concerns into the text strips the locus of authority away from the author and places it in the hands of the reader. In his view, readers, in their own cultural settings, are able to utilize texts in any way they see fit. This lack of authorial control over the written word leads quite naturally into syncretism, which is evident in many of the examples Sugirtharajah gives.

His treatment of 1 Kings 18:20–40 and Elijah's defeat of the prophets of Baal is an attempt to eisegetically read his concerns for globalization, diversity, and pluralism into the text. His rejection of this passage as a narrative that displays God's superiority over the false religions of this world fails to deal with the fundamental aspects of the narrative. His pluralistic perspective simply will not allow him to admit that the clear teaching of this passage is that the worship of the God of Israel is true and the worship in all other religious systems is false.

In the end, Sugirtharajah's system is nothing more than repackaged postmodernism for cross-cultural situations. Sugirtharajah speaks positively of postmodernism but concludes that it is too Western a concept to be useful in the Majority World.[48] Nonetheless, his rejection of absolute truth, his pluralistic outlook, and his desire to question and confront historic interpretation are postmodernism. As a result, his hermeneutic system is too subjective for evangelical interpreters.

---

47. For a summary of Fish's perspective, see Brooks, "Critiquing Ethnohermeneutics Theories," 36–41.

48. Sugirtharajah, *Asian Biblical Hermeneutics and Postcolonialism*, 15.

6

Cross-Textual Hermeneutics

In the last chapter we looked at the postcolonial hermeneutic approach, which sought to make sense of the current situation of believers who live in areas that were formerly colonized by Western powers. Part of the challenge in these contexts is the existence of multiple sacred texts or traditions. How do Christians in East Asian contexts navigate the similarities and contradictions in their traditional creation stories and those in the Bible? These are the kinds of questions that the cross-textual approach to hermeneutics considers.

The primary proponent of the cross-textual view is Archie Lee. He is a professor of Old Testament and hermeneutics at the Chinese University of Hong Kong. His writings display an interest in traditional Chinese religious practices, biblical interpretation in multicultural and pluralistic contexts, and cross-textual hermeneutics.

Summary

Lee's hermeneutic proposal is what he terms "cross-textual hermeneutics."[1] It is similar in approach to Sugirtharajah's vernacular hermeneutics in that it seeks to take the traditions, customs, and sacred texts of a people and relate them to the narratives and teachings of the Bible. He explains that in light of the diverse, multiscriptural context of Asia that "Asian Christians should venture to read their own classical texts and the biblical text together and

---

1. Lee, "Cross-Textual Hermeneutics," 60–62; Lee, "Cross-Textual Hermeneutics on Gospel and Culture"; Lee, "Cross-Textual Reading Strategy," 1–27.

let one text shed light on or challenge the other, so that creative dialogue and integration can take place."[2]

Lee criticizes those theologians and missionaries who have denounced Chinese sacred texts and other classical works.[3] He argues that those who hold that the Christian faith is the universal and absolute truth and those who hold to historic interpretation practices do not take the Asian religious and cultural setting seriously. He states that both the Bible and the religious context should be equal contributors, and no one text should hold sway over the others. He writes that at times the cultural context even critiques the biblical text.[4]

Lee argues that historic methods of interpretation are outdated. He explains,

> More recently, however, biblical scholars have acknowledged the limitations of [the historical-critical] approach, especially with regard to the fact that it presupposed an alleged objectivity on the part of the reader with regard to the text, established by means of a supposed scientific method, and thus fails to take into account the vital interaction between the received text, the contemporary reader, and the act of reading in the process of interpretation. As a result, the enormous impact of the social location, cultural background, economic context, and political situation of the reader on the process of interpretation has been completely ignored.[5]

With these concerns in mind, Lee states that if biblical interpretation is to be relevant in the Asian context, interpreters must relate the story of Scripture to the story of indigenous religious culture.[6]

In several articles, Lee displays how his model of cross-textual interpretation should be used. In one article, he examines how Chinese culture views the symbol of the dragon, and he contrasts that perspective with how

---

2. Lee, "Cross-Textual Hermeneutics," 61.
3. Lee, "Cross-Textual Hermeneutics," 61.
4. Lee, "Cross-Textual Hermeneutics," 62.
5. Lee, "Cross-Textual Interpretation and Its Implications for Biblical Studies," 247. It is important to note that when Lee critiques the historical-critical method, his critique applies to the grammatical-historical method as well. He is not critiquing the critical stance of those who have a historical-critical perspective, but he is critiquing the viability of analyzing the historical and grammatical setting of the text. He is also challenging the grammatical-historical approach's objectivity of meaning.
6. Lee, "Cross-Textual Interpretation and Its Implications for Biblical Studies," 248–49.

the dragon is conveyed in Scripture.[7] In Chinese culture, the dragon represented the imperial authority and was thought to convey blessing, but in the Bible, the dragon is a symbol of chaos and evil.[8] After explaining this difference, though, Lee does little to alleviate these divergent understandings of this symbol.

In a second article, Lee examines the Chinese creation myth, which states that the world was created through a female creator, Nu Kua.[9] He then relates the myth to the biblical account of creation. Once again, though, after examining some of the discrepancies between the biblical text and cultural myth, Lee does little to offer a way forward in light of the differences.

In a similar article that relates the Chinese flood narratives to the biblical ones, Lee explains that among the fifty-six ethnic minority groups in China, some 568 versions of a flood narrative exist.[10] He examines some of the common themes of these Chinese myths, one of which is the intermarriage between the divine and the humans that remain after the flood. Lee explains,

> This insight about a divine-human continuum in Chinese religious belief and mythological representation will present a challenge to the Chinese reading of the Bible. Humanity's aspiration for immortality or divinity will help to detect the same human yearnings recorded in the tradition of the Genesis story. When the biblical materials are read cross-textually with Chinese resources, it is hoped that new light can be shed on the different layers of the biblical text, and that often-neglected features will be seen clearly against the contours created by the nonbiblical text being brought into the reading process.[11]

Once again, though, after explaining the differences between the Chinese flood narratives and the biblical ones, Lee never proposes a solution to these discrepancies.

---

7. Lee, "The Dragon, the Deluge, and Creation Theology."

8. Lee, "The Dragon, the Deluge, and Creation Theology," 99–102.

9. Lee, "The Chinese Creation Myth of Nu Kua and the Biblical Narrative in Genesis 1–11," 312–24.

10. Lee, "When the Flood Narrative of Genesis Meets Its Counterpart in China," 87.

11. Lee, "When the Flood Narrative of Genesis Meets Its Counterpart in China," 96–97.

Lee examines, in a fourth article, the abuse of power in the story of David and Bathsheba and then applies it to the contemporary situation in Hong Kong.[12] The article was written in 1985, when people in Hong Kong were anxiously anticipating the return of Hong Kong to Chinese rule in 1996. Lee considers David's abuse of power and Nathan's role of rebuking David's sinful action. Lee then calls the church to fulfill Nathan's role in rebuking the abuses of power from contemporary governmental regimes.

In a final article, Lee considers Isaiah 56–66 in light of the handover of Hong Kong to China.[13] In this article, he reads the situation in Hong Kong back into the biblical text. Picking up on Gadamer's wording, he explains that the study is a fusion of the two horizons.[14] His study of Isaiah displays a commitment to historical critical methods.

Critique

Like Sugirtharajah, Lee's hermeneutic proposals are concerning. His desire to implement a strategy that allows the contemporary culture to critique the biblical text is a departure from evangelical Christianity. Likewise, his proposal that indigenous texts should be integrated with biblical texts and that neither should have a position of authority is an encouragement toward syncretism. Both issues display a rejection of the Bible as the inerrant, infallible, authoritative word of God.

At the same time, though, his handling of some biblical texts in the articles examined displays a commitment to study and apply the details of the text. As a result, his analysis of the various texts, although dependent on historical critical methods, is more in line with the original author's intent than Sugirtharajah's handling of various texts. In several of the other articles, he raises discrepancies between Chinese culture and the biblical text but fails to propose a way forward. In the end, his model fails due to its rejection of historic Christianity, its tendency toward syncretism, and its failure to alleviate the differences between the biblical text and the cultural context.

---

12. Lee, "The David-Bathsheba Story and the Parable of Nathan"; Lee, "Doing Theology in the Chinese Context," 243–57.
13. Lee, "Returning to China," 156–73.
14. Lee, "Returning to China," 161; Gadamer, *Truth and Method*, 306–07.

7

Rhetorical-Interactive Hermeneutics

THE PRIMARY PROPONENT OF this view is K. K. Yeo. Yeo brings a unique perspective to the issue of cross-cultural hermeneutics. He is ethnically Chinese, was reared in the multicultural context of Malaysia, received his theological education in the US, and has taught in both Hong Kong and the US. His outlook on this issue has three characteristics: a historical-critical perspective, a rhetorical-interactive hermeneutic, and a cross-cultural intention.

Historical-Critical Perspective

Yeo utilizes historical-critical tools to analyze the text of Scripture. In addition to his direct statements about the use of historical-critical methods,[1] his use of these methods is displayed in his study of 1 Corinthians 8 and 10. His basic method of exegesis is rhetorical criticism, which he states explores the persuasive nature of discourse as it relates to the original author and his

---

1. Yeo, *Rhetorical Interaction in 1 Corinthians 8 and 10*, 53; Yeo, *What Has Jerusalem to Do with Beijing?*, 65.

audience.² This method, though, utilizes other critical tools such as literary criticism, redaction criticism, and textual criticism in analyzing the text.³

He applies redaction criticism to 1 Corinthians and determines that the text contains a total of six different letters (Letters A through F) that were edited together by a later Pauline school.⁴ While he does believe that Paul wrote the original letters, he agrees with Robert Jewett that the letter in its current form was redacted together by a conservative Pauline school for their purpose of fighting heresy.⁵

In a later work in which he examines the letters of Paul and the writings of the Chairman Mao,⁶ he relates the process of canonization of Paul's writings to that of Mao's:

> As charismatic leaders of social and religious movements, Paul and Mao were not ordinary persons. Both had extraordinary ideas that had worldwide impact. If they had not been great persons,

---

2. Yeo, *Rhetorical Interaction in 1 Corinthians 8 and 10*, 53. Rhetorical criticism is one form of literary criticism that has developed in New Testament scholarship that seeks to ascertain the specific type of rhetorical devices that were utilized in the formation of the letter. Most of these discussions focus on Paul's letters. For a brief introduction and critique of rhetorical criticism from an evangelical perspective, see Carson and Moo, *An Introduction to the New Testament*, 59.

3. Redaction criticism is one aspect of historical criticism that developed out of source, form, and tradition criticism. Source criticism focused on the sources that were utilized in the forming of the Gospels and Epistles. Carson and Moo explain that "each source, real or imagined, was thought to reflect the theology and outlook of different communities, or different writers, or of the same community at a different time" (Carson and Moo, *An Introduction to the New Testament*, 55). This focus gave rise to form criticism, which focused on the form of the documents. Out of form criticism, tradition criticism developed as a response. It focused on the traditions of the communities that stood behind the formation of the various New Testament documents. As a reaction to the weaknesses of tradition criticism, redaction criticism developed. It argues that the communities behind the New Testament documents edited them to produce Gospels and letters that voiced the concerns of the evangelist and fulfilled the purposes of the community. Literary criticism picks up on many of these historical critical tools by analyzing the specific literary devices employed in the New Testament documents. For a brief historical survey of these developments and for a critique of this perspective, see Carson and Moo, *An Introduction to the New Testament*, 54–59.

4. Yeo, *Rhetorical Interaction in 1 Corinthians 8 and 10*, 81–82.

5. Yeo, *Rhetorical Interaction in 1 Corinthians 8 and 10*, 79.

6. Mao Tse-tung, or Chairman Mao, was the leader of China from 1949, when the communist army first came to power, until his death in 1976. Although history has had a positive outlook on his leadership of China, recent research has shown that his leadership was responsible for the deaths of 70 million Chinese, and that during a time of peace. For more information, see Chang and Halliday, *Mao*.

their ideals would not have been canonized. But neither Paul nor Mao thought of writing "scriptures." Both were practical theorists writing out of the necessity of situations and addressing problems in their communities. The canonization process of both Mao's and Paul's thought reached a point of becoming divine (the divine word itself or the agent of divine word) when devotees began to memorize and imitate the rhetoric. Any canonized text contains codes that believers assume to be the lenses through which reality should be viewed. Christians believe that sacred Scripture views reality as God sees it; Maoist followers believe that the Little Red Book views reality as Mao sees it.[7]

He goes on to explain that it was after Paul's death that the Pauline school collected, redacted, and circulated his writings. It was at this point that Paul gained prestige and power, and "his legacy gained its mystified and divinized qualities."[8]

The result of this historical-critical perspective is that at times Yeo views the Pauline letters on equal ground as Chinese sacred texts and other writings.[9] They are not inspired by the Holy Spirit but are elevated to the place of Scripture because of the radical commitment of devotees. In his study he writes of how a reading of Confucian ethics "helps to correct or supplement Paul's theology."[10] He reads the writings side by side and seeks to create a dialogue between the two.

Rhetorical-Interactive Hermeneutic

Yeo describes his hermeneutical approach as one of rhetorical interaction. He explains that this approach is concerned with "the interactive and communicative process of utterance between the rhetor and audience in the rhetorical situation."[11] He continues in stating that this approach "accepts the subjectivity of an interpreter and the role of interpreter in interaction with the text."[12] By using this approach, he seeks "to work out the triangular

---

7. Yeo, *Chairman Mao Meets the Apostle Paul*, 192.
8. Yeo, *Chairman Mao Meets the Apostle Paul*, 193.
9. K. K. Yeo, "Messianic Predestination in Romans 8 and Classical Confucianism," 273; Yeo, *Chairman Mao Meets the Apostle Paul*, 192; Yeo, *Musing with Confucius and Paul*, 430; Yeo, "Paul's Theological Ethic and the Chinese Morality of Ren Ren," 120.
10. Yeo, *Musing with Confucius and Paul*, 430.
11. Yeo, *Rhetorical Interaction in 1 Corinthians 8 and 10*, 16.
12. Yeo, *Rhetorical Interaction in 1 Corinthians 8 and 10*, 17.

interactive relationships among the utterance/text, the rhetor/audience, and the hearer/interpreter."[13]

Yeo picks up on the hermeneutical ideas of Gadamer and Ricoeur.[14] With Gadamer, Yeo agrees that the interpreter's understanding of the text comes through a dialogical process.[15] In other words, meaning and understanding are fused together in interpretation as the interpreter interacts with the text. This process is a communicative dialogue, and meaning is derived partially from the situation of the text and partially from the situation of the interpreter.

As a result of these insights from Gadamer's hermeneutic, Yeo understands reading as both reproductive and productive.[16] He explains:

> The processes of reading and meaning-production are always dialogues between the writers and the readers. The authority of interpretation does not reside in the frozen text or in the first writer but is to be found in the interactive process of the text, involving both the writer and the reader, which I have previously called "rhetorical interaction."[17]

He continues by explaining how this understanding of authority affects the determination of meaning:

> This reproductive and productive process of reading allows and requires text/writer and reader/interpretation to be intersubjective. A text not only carries meaning but allows readers to create meanings. Similarly, readers not only interpret texts, they are being "read" by texts, that is, their stories are made meaningful by the texts. Because understanding and reading processes are reproductive and productive, a writer cannot control the meaning of a text and limit that meaning to *just* his or her own "original" intention.[18]

---

13. Yeo, *Rhetorical Interaction in 1 Corinthians 8 and 10*, 17.

14. For a summary of these views, see Brooks, "Critiquing Ethnohermeneutics Theories," 30–36.

15. Yeo, *Rhetorical Interaction in 1 Corinthians 8 and 10*, 18.

16. Yeo, *Rhetorical Interaction in 1 Corinthians 8 and 10*, 16.

17. Yeo, "Culture and Intersubjectivity as Criteria for Negotiating Meanings in Cross-cultural Interpretations," 86.

18. Yeo, "Culture and Intersubjectivity as Criteria for Negotiating Meanings in Cross-Cultural Interpretations," 87; Yeo, *Musing with Confucius and Paul*, 34; Yeo, "Messianic Predestination in Romans 8 and Classical Confucianism," 260; Yeo, "Introduction," 20. In "Introduction," Yeo states, "Thus, it is not just the scriptural text that determines the

Rhetorical-Interactive Hermeneutics

For Yeo, then, the intersubjective nature of interpretation results in the fact that the meaning of a text is both reproduced and produced. In light of this dynamic, Yeo explains that the original author is not the sole determiner of meaning.

Yeo also adopts some aspects of Ricoeur's hermeneutics. He agrees with Ricoeur that it is not the text of Scripture which is sacred, but it is the one to which Scripture points, namely God, that is sacred. Yeo continues,

> In other words, the biblical text is sacred not in its ontological nature but in its interpretive and communicative process. That hermeneutical process is exercised by the biblical writers who claim that the Holy Rhetor of the texts wills the utterance to speak over time and space. Once the power or effectiveness of that speaking is evident and beneficial, we say that the text has its enduring quality. The enduring quality of the text is manifested not in the "pure" or "objective" or "arbitrary" exegesis of the historical meaning of the text but in the interaction of the text with the exegete and the audience.[19]

While Yeo draws from Ricoeur's hermeneutical system, he also critiques some aspects of it.[20] Even though Yeo argues that meaning does not reside only with the original author, he disagrees with Ricoeur's understanding of texts as "autonomous" or independent from the author's intent. Instead of suspending the original context of the text, Yeo picks up on Gadamer's language of fusing the horizons of the original author/original context and the contemporary interpreter/contemporary context.

Yeo likewise accepts the possibility of multiple interpretations for any given text of Scripture. He argues that "interpreters cannot recover completely the cultural meaning of Paul."[21] Since interpreters cannot know what Paul meant, Yeo states that there is a "plausibility of divergent interpretations."[22] For him, then, more than one interpretation to any given text is reasonable.

---

meaning" (Yeo, "Introduction," 20).
19. Yeo, *Rhetorical Interaction in 1 Corinthians 8 and 10*, 19.
20. Yeo, *Rhetorical Interaction in 1 Corinthians 8 and 10*, 20.
21. Yeo, "Introduction," 19.
22. Yeo, "Introduction," 20.

Cross-Cultural Intention

Yeo describes his cross-cultural hermeneutic as one of intertextual intentions.[23] He points to Julia Kristeva's definition of intertextuality[24] to explain that texts do not exist in isolation, but they interrelate with other texts that preceded them or currently coexist with them. The aim of an intertextual study, then, is to uncover these areas of similarity and difference between two texts that have influence on some specific group of people.

These intertextual studies, Yeo explains, have their foundation in the intersubjective nature of interpretation.[25] Since interpretation is a dialogue between text and reader in which readers both reproduce and produce meaning, Yeo argues that this intertextual type of study creates an environment in which a dialogue between two textual influences takes place. It is a method of analyzing the specific ways in which the biblical text and a cultural text interact with and influence one another.

In his study of Confucius and Paul, Yeo explains the benefits of the intertextual approach to cross-cultural interpretation: "The intertextual perspective will help us see the commonality and commensurability between Confucius and Paul. It is their profound differences that distinguish the cultural-specific context of Confucian China from that of the Protestant West."[26] He goes on to state that the areas of difference can be either obstacles or resources depending on how readers respond to them.

Yeo then explains the importance of dialogue between these two sources that shape the worldview of Chinese Christians:

> Confucius and Paul are very close at certain points while differing radically from each other in terms of the larger frames of reference or their thought. On the one hand, these basic differences of the origin or cause of determinative concepts of Confucius and Paul shape in a complementary way the contours of my identity as a Chinese Christian, just as they make up the principles of my hermeneutical investigation. On the other hand, there are basic differences that are simply irreconcilable, and holding on to them

---

23. Yeo's intertextual study is different from the type of intertextual study that compares motifs from two different biblical authors. For Yeo, intertextual studies compare the stories and teachings of the biblical texts with the texts of other religious traditions.

24. Kristeva, "Word, Dialogue and Novel."

25. Yeo, *Musing with Confucius and Paul*, 33–34; Yeo, "Messianic Predestination in Romans 8 and Classical Confucianism," 260, 273.

26. Yeo, *Musing with Confucius and Paul*, 35.

Rhetorical-Interactive Hermeneutics

in radical tension is an ever-present challenge. The incommensurability between Confucius and Paul does not mean that one is right and the other wrong. Rather it means that on different issues both are incomplete and that one is needed for the fulfillment of the other.[27]

Elsewhere, Yeo fleshes out the results of this dialogue in more practical terms when he explains that through this intertextual study, "Paul's christological lens is colored with the social and moral aspects of ethics and politics, and Confucius's humanistic lens is colored with theological necessity."[28]

Yeo explains that there are three aspects to his conception of the possibility of knowing truth that guide his cross-cultural hermeneutic. These aspects include, "(1) that complete knowledge of the truth cannot be attained, (2) that all truth is God's truth, wherever it is found, and (3) that provisional knowledge of the truth can be known by all peoples (not just Christians)."[29] He then explains that his reservation about the possibility of knowing truth "invites us into a dialogical process between cultures, a dialogue in which we can both accept but also transcend the limits of our specific cultural locations."[30]

Yeo encourages performing these intertextual studies by beginning with an exegetical study of the biblical text.[31] In actuality, though, he states that his study of the biblical texts is guided by the teachings and concerns of certain cultural documents or cultural presuppositions. In one study, immediately after stating that he will begin his study by examining the biblical text, he states that he will be "imposing a certain principle (the yin-yang understanding) on the text."[32] Another study analyzes "Paul's messianic (Christological) predestination language using the lens of the Confucian millennial understanding of *Datong* (Great Togetherness)."[33]

Despite the concerns raised by Yeo's imposing certain principles upon the biblical text, his study of the text focuses on ascertaining the message

---

27. Yeo, *Musing with Confucius and Paul*, 36.
28. Yeo, "Messianic Predestination in Romans 8 and Classical Confucianism," 274.
29. Yeo, "Culture and Intersubjectivity as Criteria for Negotiating Meanings in Cross-Cultural Interpretations," 99.
30. Yeo, "Culture and Intersubjectivity as Criteria for Negotiating Meanings in Cross-Cultural Interpretations," 99.
31. Yeo, *What Has Jerusalem to Do with Beijing?*, 51, 65.
32. Yeo, *What Has Jerusalem to Do with Beijing?*, 51.
33. Yeo, "Messianic Predestination in Romans 8 and Classical Confucianism," 259.

that the original author intended to convey to the original audience. In one study, he examines the uses of "weak" and "strong" in 1 Corinthians 8 and 10. He seeks to identify which heretical groups these terms might apply to, and he considers what Paul hopes to communicate to these groups through the use of these terms.[34] In another example, he considers four interpretations of Romans 7 and then proposes an alternative view.[35] His alternative view arises from concerns like the context of Romans 7 and the usage of specific words. After explaining his view, he proceeds to relate his interpretation to Confucian ethical traditions.

After examining the biblical text and the cultural text, Yeo simply juxtaposes the similarities and differences without providing solutions for the reader. After explaining the eschatological views of Paul and Mao Tse-tung, Yeo states in conclusion,

> In contrast to the secular faith of Mao's view of history, Paul's eschatology is Christ-centered: it has an openness to the future. It acknowledges the limitation of the human and urges one to place one's trust in the Divine, who determines the future. For Mao, death for the people was the highest virtue as well as the ultimate end of the utopian hope. In other words, Mao's utopian vision was a "fully realized eschatology" in the now because of his rejection of the eternal future.[36]

Not making a clear statement about which perspective is correct and which one is not, he avoids making a harsh critique of Chinese culture and is able to simply have the dialogue between two competing influences on the Chinese Christian worldview.

There are a few times in his writings that Yeo does critique certain aspects of Chinese culture. He examines the Confucian ideals of *li* (holy ritual) and *ren ren* (being a loving person) and compares them with Paul's teachings on the cruciform life. He concludes,

> Chinese Christians can learn from Paul that *li*, including its expression in acts of filial piety, does not have the power to break

---

34. Yeo, *Rhetorical Interaction in 1 Corinthians 8 and 10*, 142–55.

35. Yeo, "Culture and Intersubjectivity as Criteria for Negotiating Meanings in Cross-Cultural Interpretations," 94–95. While I do not agree with his interpretation of Romans 7, my point here is simply to show that his interpretation arises from his study of the text. He then relates his conclusions about Paul's concerns in Romans 7 to Confucian cultural considerations.

36. Yeo, *Chairman Mao Meets the Apostle Paul*, 224–25.

sin's grip over humanity. Moral formation through *li* animated by *ren ren* needs something more than the right social context and good intentions. It requires death to self and the world through the cross of Christ.[37]

Since the Confucian ideals of *li* and *ren ren* serve as the foundation for ancestor worship, Yeo then addresses that subject:

> This suggests that Paul's theology calls for Chinese Christians to abandon the assumptions and practice of ancestor veneration or to reshape them in the light of the Pauline gospel so that they express, rather than conflict with, that gospel of the crucified and exalted Christ, who is lord of the powers and who creates a new spiritual family in which old relationships are brought to an end and love reaches out not just to one's biological family and one's friends but to all, even to outsiders and enemies.[38]

Yeo advocates that when examining many of these Confucian teachings, one must distinguish between the religious practices and the ethical ones. After explaining that Confucianism is a dominant cultural force even for Chinese Christians, he states that "this definition of Chineseness should not be taken as a subscription to Confucian forms of worship (e.g., offering food to the dead and burning incense to the ancestors) but to the practice of Confucian ideals (e.g., reverence for elders)."[39] He states that only those aspects of culture that reject the cruciform life need to be changed.

Yeo, though, tends to see Paul's teachings as "fulfilling" Confucian ideals, or he utilizes Confucian ideals to reread Paul's letters.[40] He explains his perspective on these issues when he writes, "In my case, the Christian reading of Confucian texts and the Confucian reappropriation of Christian theologies are my way of being faithful to being Chinese."[41]

Evaluation

There are a number of aspects of Yeo's hermeneutical system that are worth commending. First, his argument that culture needs to be corrected on

---

37. Yeo, "Paul's Theological Ethic and the Chinese Morality of Ren Ren," 140.
38. Yeo, "Paul's Theological Ethic and the Chinese Morality of Ren Ren," 140.
39. Yeo, *Musing with Confucius and Paul*, 425.
40. Yeo, *Musing with Confucius and Paul*, 406, 429.
41. Yeo, *Musing with Confucius and Paul*, 425.

those points where its norms depart from the expectations of the crucified life is a helpful one. Although this point is a minor one in his overall hermeneutic system, and though he rarely critiques Chinese culture in his discussions, his statement does reflect how the authoritative biblical text does confront and reshape cultural standards.

A second helpful area in Yeo's system is the distinction he draws between religious and ethical aspects in Confucian teaching. Again, this position is a minor one in his overall system of interpretation as he tends to see biblical truth fulfilling Confucian ideals, but it does not lessen the usefulness of his statement. One might argue, though, that making such a separation is easier with Confucianism than it would be in other contexts where culture and religion are so closely intermingled. Since Confucianism is an ethical system in which religious rituals were later added to help people fulfill those ethical guidelines, it is often easy to draw the distinction between religion and culture in that tradition.

Third, Yeo's general commitment to study Chinese culture is helpful. He displays a wealth of knowledge concerning Chinese ethical, philosophical, and religious practices in his writings. While the writings focus on Confucian and Taoist teachings, he also recognizes that contemporary Chinese are more likely to be affected by materialism and consumerism.[42] His knowledge of these issues enables him to better understand the complexities involved in developing a Chinese Christian worldview. It also enables him to understand the barriers that keep non-Christians from responding to the gospel.[43]

A fourth strength of Yeo's approach is his commitment to begin each study with an examination of the biblical text. While concerns exist about Yeo's understanding of Scripture, this principle is helpful for those who are committed to Scripture as the authoritative word of God. For such interpreters, hermeneutics should always begin with a study of the biblical text, allowing Scripture to address those areas of culture that contradict its teaching.

While there are some positive aspects to Yeo's approach, several negative ones also exist. First, Yeo's use of historical critical methods is a problem. His critical stance toward Pauline authorship through his statements about the Pauline school is an attack on the traditional understanding of the nature of Scripture. Such a position questions the inspiration and

---

42. Yeo, "Paul's Theological Ethic and the Chinese Morality of Ren Ren," 119.
43. Yeo, *What Has Jerusalem to Do with Beijing?*, 196–97.

inerrancy of the Scriptures, and it challenges the unique place of Scripture as the authoritative word of God.

Moreover, Yeo's understanding of the canonization process of the Scriptures is equally troubling. To argue, as Yeo does, that Paul did not envision his writings as Scripture misrepresents the response of other New Testament authors to Paul's writings (2 Pet 3:15–16). More troubling, in fact, is the view he espouses that the canonization process of Paul's writings was the same as that of Mao Tse-tung's.

Similar to the first concern, a second problem is Yeo's commitment to rhetorical criticism. Numerous scholars have pointed out the weaknesses of rhetorical analysis of the biblical texts.[44] While rhetorical criticism was a popular approach from 1970 to 1990, contemporary New Testament scholars recognize that little has been gained from the overly technical labeling of certain sections of the text.[45] This view fails to recognize that the Greco-Roman system of rhetoric was designed for orators, not letter writers.[46] Moreover, one questions the validity of these insights when even the church fathers, who were still living in the Greco-Roman period, failed to comment on such rhetorical categories.[47]

Third, the subjective nature of Yeo's hermeneutical perspective is a drawback. Although he critiques Ricoeur for completely abandoning the original author, Yeo goes almost as far by allowing the reader to dialogue with the text and create his own meaning. Yeo strips authority away from the original author and places it in the hands of readers by arguing that readers both recreate and create meanings to texts with which they interact.

Moreover, Yeo's explanation of the interpretation process blurs the distinction between meaning and application. Yeo states that the meaning of a text is found partly in the situation of the text and partly in the situation of the reader. This intersubjective approach blends together what the text means and how it applies.

A fourth negative aspect of Yeo's system is his commitment to intertextual readings. Yeo's intertextual, cross-cultural hermeneutic fails in not recognizing the authoritative place of the biblical text. It has already been shown that this attack on the Bible's authority is due to Yeo's historical

---

44. Carson and Moo, *An Introduction to the New Testament*, 59; Plummer, *40 Questions about Interpreting the Bible*, 302, 309.

45. Plummer, *40 Questions about Interpreting the Bible*, 309.

46. Carson and Moo, *An Introduction to the New Testament*, 59.

47. Carson and Moo, *An Introduction to the New Testament*, 59.

critical perspective, but it is necessary to note that the result of such a perspective is that Yeo places the Bible on equal grounds as other sacred texts.

Similarly, his practice of reading Scripture through the lens of Confucian teaching or other cultural principles is eisegetical. While Yeo is correct to note that no interpreter is presupposition-less,[48] wise interpreters seek to overcome the presuppositions they bring to the text by allowing Scripture to confront and critique their own worldview. Reading Scripture to confirm or fulfill one's own concerns is misguided.

As a result, Yeo's system for cross-cultural biblical interpretation is not an appropriate model for evangelical interpreters. The problems with his view include his commitment to historical and rhetorical critical methods, his arguments that the reader creates the meaning of a text, and his eisegetical tendencies.

---

48. Yeo, "Introduction," 3–4.

8

Ethnohermeneutics

The primary proponent of the view known as "ethnohermeneutics" is Larry Caldwell, who studied at Fuller Seminary and then later served as a professor of hermeneutics and missions in the Philippines. He now serves as the Chief Academic Officer and Dean at Sioux Falls Seminary. Caldwell is an Evangelical who believes that "the Bible is God's authoritative, inerrant word, and that it is the final authority for all matters of faith and practice."[1] His interest in ethnohermeneutics grows out of his commitment to missions and his desire to reach all the cultures of the world with the gospel.

Before we delve into the view, let me add a brief word about how much I respect Caldwell. In 2011 I presented some of the material in this chapter at a meeting of the Evangelical Theological Society. A few days before the meeting I found out that Caldwell himself would be attending, so I reached out to him to let him know about my presentation. When the meeting rolled around, there I was critiquing Caldwell with him in the room. After it finished, he came up and said, "This is great! Let's go out to dinner and continue the conversation."

To be clear, he didn't mean that my presentation was so great that I'd persuaded him! But in his humility, he was willing for his writings to be discussed, evaluated, and critiqued by a room full of strangers—because he recognized that all of us think better and more clearly when we have healthy and respectful dialogue about complex issues. Academia could often use a bit more of this type of humility.

---

1. Caldwell, "A Response to the Responses of Tappeiner and Whelchel to Ethnohermeneutics," 136.

To begin our discussion, it's helpful to know that Caldwell defines ethnohermeneutics as "Bible interpretation done in multi-generational, multicultural and cross-cultural contexts that, as far as possible, uses dynamic hermeneutical methods which already reside in the culture. Its primary goal is to interpret and communicate the truths of the Bible in ways that will be best understood by the receptor culture."[2] He argues that faithful Bible interpreters in intercultural situations ought to study and utilize indigenous hermeneutic methods because doing so will ensure greater receptivity to the proclamation of the gospel message.[3]

Cultural Outlook

Caldwell's perspective on culture is a basic premise that predisposes him to accept indigenous hermeneutic systems. Caldwell adopts Charles Kraft's position of God-above-but-through culture. Kraft writes, "This model holds that the Christian God should not be perceived either as against, merely in, or simply above culture. It sees God as outside culture but working in terms of or through culture to accomplish his purposes."[4] Kraft goes on to explain that "though God exists totally outside of culture while humans exist totally within culture, God chooses the cultural milieu in which humans are immersed as the arena of his interaction with people."[5]

Since Caldwell agrees with Kraft that God should not be perceived of as against culture, his overall view of culture is positive. Caldwell explains his perspective on this issue when he writes, "God is at work in each culture drawing individuals from within each culture to himself."[6] His point is that God is at work, using the unique aspects of each culture to help the people in that culture come to a more complete knowledge of who he is. This understanding of God working through culture, he believes, is the foundation for why missionaries utilize culturally sensitive methods to communicate the truths of the gospel.[7]

---

2. Caldwell, "Part 2: Reconsidering Our Biblical Roots," 67.

3. Caldwell, "Towards an Ethnohermeneutical Model for a Lowland Filipino Context," 170; Caldwell, "Towards the New Discipline of Ethnohermeneutics," 31–32; Caldwell, "Third Horizon Ethnohermeneutics," 324.

4. Kraft, *Christianity in Culture*, 88.

5. Kraft, *Christianity in Culture*, 89.

6. Caldwell, "Towards the New Discipline of Ethnohermeneutics," 31.

7. Caldwell, "Receptor-Oriented Hermeneutics," 31.

Caldwell then argues that if missionaries are willing to use culturally sensitive methods to communicate the gospel, they should also be willing to use indigenous hermeneutic methods to help determine the most culturally sensitive way to communicate that gospel. He explains,

> What I am arguing for here is an acknowledgment that God not only works through the culture of each particular society—hence the need to communicate the truths of Scripture in culturally relevant forms that the society will understand—but, correspondingly, that God also works through the hermeneutical processes inherent in each society.[8]

He encourages Bible interpreters to ask two questions: "What are the hermeneutical method, or methods, found within the culture of the people whom I am ministering; and, how can I possibly use this method(s) when I attempt to communicate the truths of the Bible to individuals in or from this culture?"[9]

Caldwell distinguishes between surface-level ethnohermeneutics and deep-level hermeneutics.[10] Surface-level ethnohermeneutics involves using culturally appropriate methods to communicate the truths of the Bible. Interpreters operating at this level will take a specific teaching of Scripture and seek to communicate that truth in a culturally sensitive manner. These interpreters will look for culturally appropriate methods of communication or specific illustrations or analogies that arise from that culture to help better convey the truth of Scripture to people within this culture.

Deep-level ethnohermeneutics, on the other hand, uses culturally appropriate methods of interpretation to discover the truths of Scripture.[11] Instead of simply communicating the truths of Scripture in a culturally appropriate manner, at this level interpreters will use indigenous hermeneutical systems to determine the truths of Scripture for the people in that culture. Doing so will enable the interpreter to communicate the uncovered truths in the most culturally sensitive way possible.

Caldwell is careful to note that while he advocates the use of indigenous hermeneutical methods, he does not support using the content of

---

8. Caldwell, "Receptor-Oriented Hermeneutics," 279.
9. Caldwell, "Towards the New Discipline of Ethnohermeneutics," 31–32.
10. Caldwell, "Towards an Ethnohermeneutical Model for a Lowland Filipino Context," 170–71.
11. Caldwell, "Towards an Ethnohermeneutical Model for a Lowland Filipino Context," 170–71.

those indigenous religious systems.¹² He recognizes that some may question how this approach avoids incorporating the theological content associated with those methods of interpretation. He responds,

> However, an answer is not very difficult when we understand that we are not necessarily taking the *content* in which the hermeneutical methodology of the society is used—for example, in a Hindu society some of the *Upanishads*—but rather developing a *dynamically equivalent hermeneutical methodology* that incorporates as many acceptable elements as possible of the hermeneutical methodology that a particular Hindu society uses when it interprets the *Upanishads*. The theologically unacceptable content of the *Upanishads* will be disregarded in the same way that the New Testament writers disregarded the spurious elements of the hermeneutical methodology of *midrash* of their day—those elements that were both disallowed by God's Word as well as not receptor-oriented, like the interpretations that were popular at Qumran—nevertheless using many of the same elements of the common midrashic methodology, now in dynamic ways.¹³

Caldwell encourages using the methods of interpretation but not the theological content associated with those methods.

Jewish Hermeneutic Foundation

One of the primary aspects of Caldwell's argument for the use of ethnohermeneutics is his understanding of the New Testament authors' use of the Old Testament. He explains that the New Testament writers utilized Jewish cultural methods of interpretation when they interpreted the Old Testament. He states that these methods, which were culturally appropriate to Jewish audiences, are quite different from the grammatical-historical methods utilized by contemporary interpreters. Since the authors of Scripture used culturally appropriate methods of interpretation that were different

---

12. It is important to note that Caldwell's position here is what differentiates him from some of the other authors already considered. It has already been shown that Sugirtharajah, Lee, and Yeo support using the theological content of indigenous systems to interpret and sometimes even critique the biblical content.

13. Caldwell, "Receptor-Oriented Hermeneutics," 282–83. As is evident from this quotation, Caldwell's understanding of how the New Testament authors interpreted the Old Testament is vital to his argument for the use of ethnohermeneutics. His position on this issue will be explained under the next subheading.

from the grammatical-historical method, he argues that contemporary interpreters in other cultures ought to have the freedom to use their indigenous hermeneutical methods when they interpret Scripture.

Caldwell explains the significance of this argument,

> The New Testament writers, through the guidance of the Holy Spirit, used their own culturally relevant hermeneutical methods in communicating Old Testament truths to their particular audiences. As a result, the discipline of ethnohermeneutics places a renewed emphasis upon the New Testament's use of the Old Testament for the purpose of discovering some of the hermeneutical methods employed during the first century AD. By discovering these methods it can be shown that the hermeneutical milieu of that time period directly influenced the hermeneutical methods of the New Testament writers as they interpreted the Old Testament text for their various audiences. This implies that what the New Testament writers wrote is inspired, but not their specific hermeneutical methods. And this fact is terribly significant for all Bible interpreters today. Why? Because it means that no one hermeneutical method is inspired; each and every method simply emerges from its own unique hermeneutical milieu.[14]

Since the New Testament authors used hermeneutical methods that were influenced by their cultural situation, Caldwell argues interpreters today can use the indigenous methods that are appropriate to their context.

Caldwell also explains that the New Testament interpreters utilized three types of Jewish hermeneutical practices.[15] The first method they utilized was rabbinical *midrash*. *Midrash* is a set of exegetical principles developed by Jewish rabbis that sought to contemporize or adapt the text to the current situation.[16] Caldwell gives examples in his dissertation of *midrash* in the Old Testament, the intertestamental literature, and the New Testament. The New Testament examples include Jesus' teaching, Matthew's writing, Paul's preaching in Acts, Paul's writing in Romans, and John's writing in John 12.

---

14. Caldwell, "Towards the New Discipline of Ethnohermeneutics," 32.
15. Caldwell, "Third Horizon Ethnohermeneutics," 322–23.
16. Caldwell, "Receptor-Oriented Hermeneutics," 115–18; Caldwell, "Third Horizon Ethnohermeneutics," 322. Caldwell references New Testament scholar Richard Longenecker to define *midrash*, whose comments can be found in Longenecker, *Biblical Exegesis in the Apostolic Period*, 37.

One example that Caldwell gives of *midrash* in the New Testament is Romans 10:6–8. He states that throughout church history, interpreters like John Calvin have been confused by the way Paul references Deuteronomy 30:12–14 in this passage. Caldwell explains that what Paul is doing is utilizing Jewish hermeneutical techniques to apply the passage to his readers' contemporary context. He writes,

> Thus exegetes, like Calvin, need fret no longer concerning the supposed irregularities of Paul's use of the Deuteronomy passage here. The point in all this discussion of Romans 10:6–8 is not so much to accurately define the specific hermeneutical technique used by Paul in this instance—*pesher* vs. targum—but rather to show that in either case Paul is using the hermeneutical methodology of his day. Paul simply quotes the "that" of Deuteronomy (based upon both his and his audience's understanding of the common targumic interpretation of the "that") and interprets it in light of the "this" of Jesus Christ. The quotation of the Deuteronomy passage, in other words, is actualized and reinterpreted in light of the new context of Paul and those to whom he is writing the epistle. The present situation of his audience compels Paul to adapt this Old Testament quote for purposes of New Testament faith.[17]

Caldwell argues that Paul, in Romans 10:6–8, is referencing a targumic explanation of Deuteronomy 30:12–14 and then using midrashic methods to apply the text to the contemporary hearers.

Caldwell summarizes the ways Jesus and the New Testament authors used the Old Testament:

> Consequently, in their "actualization" of the Old Testament Scripture, Jesus and the writers of the New Testament had little interest in attempting to discover the original context of the particular Old Testament text that they quoted. They, likewise, cared little if their interpretation of a particular Old Testament text varied from the use of that same text by another New Testament writer, or even with their own previous usage of that same text (as we saw in the case of Luke). Instead, the New Testament writers were more concerned with *the application of these texts to their present audiences* in light of the person and work of Jesus Christ. In other words, the needs of their audiences were the primary concern of the New

---

17. Caldwell, "Receptor-Oriented Hermeneutics," 225; Caldwell, "Third Horizon Ethnohermeneutics," 322–23.

Testament writers, and the hermeneutical methodology of *midrash* allowed them to communicate their message accordingly.[18]

For Caldwell, then, it is not a problem that Jesus and the New Testament authors take Old Testament verses out of context because they are simply using Jewish interpretive techniques to better communicate with their audiences. In fact, Caldwell argues that the primary interpretive technique of Jesus and the New Testament authors is that meaning is shaped by the interpreter's context.[19]

To support his view of the New Testament use of the Old, Caldwell quotes New Testament scholar Richard Longenecker, who explains,

> It is hardly surprising to find that the exegesis of the NT is heavily dependent upon Jewish procedural precedents, for, theoretically, one would expect a divine redemption that is worked out in the categories of a particular history—which is exactly what the Christian gospel claims to be—to express itself in all its various manifestations in terms of the concepts and models of that particular people and day.[20]

The problem with Longenecker's position, as Caldwell sees it, is that although Longenecker argues that the New Testament authors used Jewish hermeneutical practices, he also argues that those methods should not be duplicated by contemporary interpreters.[21]

Caldwell disagrees with Longenecker and argues, "Just as God used the cultural forms of the first century AD to communicate the message of the NT to a new generation of believers in Jesus Christ, so today we also need to recognize that God can use culturally relevant hermeneutical models to carry the gospel message within cultures and across cultures."[22] Since the New Testament authors used culturally relevant hermeneutical methods when they interpreted the Old Testament, Caldwell explains,

---

18. Caldwell, "Receptor-Oriented Hermeneutics," 249. Caldwell only references *midrash* as the technique that Jesus and the NT authors used to be receptor-oriented because in his dissertation he focused primarily on how they used *midrash* techniques. His later writings explain that the *pesher* and allegorical techniques also helped Jesus and the NT authors helped them to focus on their audiences.

19. Caldwell, "Third Horizon Ethnohermeneutics," 32.

20. Longenecker, *Biblical Exegesis in the Apostolic Period*, 207; quoted in Caldwell, "Third Horizon Ethnohermeneutics," 323.

21. Longenecker, *Biblical Exegesis in the Apostolic Period*, 218–20; quoted in Caldwell, "Third Horizon Ethnohermeneutics," 324.

22. Caldwell, "Third Horizon Ethnohermeneutics," 324.

contemporary interpreters should also use indigenous hermeneutical methods to communicate better with their audiences.

Receptor Orientation

The goal of Caldwell's system is a more receptor-oriented message. He explains the missiological thrust of ethnohermeneutics:

> We must always keep in mind that the primary motivation behind ethnohermeneutics is missiological: to help a new generation of missionaries, pastors, and church planters make the gospel message as relevant as possible to other audiences so that more unreached people groups will be reached and more individuals will acknowledge Jesus Christ as Savior and Lord.[23]

He argues that the use of ethnohermeneutics results in a more receptor-oriented presentation of the gospel. His hope is that as the gospel is presented in understandable ways, more and more people will put their faith in Jesus Christ as Lord.

To this end, Caldwell adapts anthropological theories of communication to biblical interpretation. He explains what it means to be receptor-oriented: "To be receptor-oriented means to deliver a message that is *understandable within the frame of reference of the target audience*; it does not guarantee that the message will be *accepted* by that audience."[24] Caldwell's receptor-oriented hermeneutics, then, seeks to use the target audience's hermeneutic methods to determine and present a more understandable gospel message.

Returning to Jesus and the New Testament authors, Caldwell states there is no doubt that their communication style was receptor-oriented.[25] He explains,

> Since *midrash* was a part of the hermeneutical milieu of Jesus and the New Testament writers, it is not surprising that their receptor-oriented communication often employed this culturally appropriate hermeneutical methodology. This methodology helped their

---

23. Caldwell, "A Response to the Responses," 139–40.
24. Caldwell, "Receptor-Oriented Hermeneutics," 252.
25. Caldwell, "Receptor-Oriented Hermeneutics," 249.

messages to be better understood, and accepted, by their first-century-AD audiences.²⁶

The New Testament authors, as Caldwell understands them, practiced deep-level contextualization or deep-level ethnohermeneutics, using Jewish hermeneutical practices to better communicate with Jewish audiences.

With the goal of being receptor-oriented, Caldwell critiques the usefulness of the traditional two-step method, which he refers to as the historical-critical method,²⁷ in cross-cultural contexts. After explaining that historical criticism is one of many helpful models for interpretation, he writes,

> At the same time, however, this two-step method based on historical criticism has often times proven itself woefully inadequate for interpreting Scripture in cross-cultural situations. While the two-step method of interpretation may indeed be a good model for interpreting Scripture in the Western world, it must be seen that this particular model has arisen out of Western philosophy after the Reformation and such has little relevance in cultures which do not have a similar Western philosophical background.²⁸

Caldwell goes on to state that Western missionaries have exported their hermeneutical models along with the gospel. He explains,

> However, with the dominance of the Western church in worldwide missionary endeavors over the past two centuries came the dominance of this western hermeneutical method. So it was that Bible schools established by western missionaries had curriculums that resembled curriculums in the West, complete with an emphasis on Greek and Hebrew, etc., in a nutshell, historical criticism. It was

---

26. Caldwell, "Receptor-Oriented Hermeneutics," 252.

27. See Caldwell, "Third Horizon Ethnohermeneutics," 315n2. Caldwell incorrectly equates the historical-critical method with the grammatical-historical method. Whelchel critiques Caldwell at this point and notes, "A significant difference can be found, however, between the attitude of enlightenment rationalism which assumes the *cogito* is the judge of all, and that of evangelical grammatical historical hermeneutics which actively seeks the illumination of the Holy Spirit as the ultimate determiner of scriptural meaning. Historically Evangelicals have been skeptical (and rightly so) of the rationalistic attitude of the enlightenment which elevated human reason above the authority of the scripture as interpreted to us through the mediation of the Holy Spirit" (Whelchel, "Ethnohermeneutics," 127). The major difference between the historical-critical method and the grammatical historical approach is the former's skepticism over the supernatural events recorded in Scripture.

28. Caldwell, "Third Horizon Ethnohermeneutics," 315.

just *assumed* that it was the proper approach. And the nationals who were trained by westerners, or who were trained in the West, simply learned this same Western system. It was seldom, if ever, questioned.[29]

Forcing believers in other cultures to learn hermeneutic models influenced by Western philosophy, he argues, is another form of Western paternalism.[30] In Caldwell's view, if missionaries desire to adequately contextualize the gospel and present an understandable message, they should loosely hold to their own Western hermeneutical assumptions and look for possible indigenous hermeneutical methods.

Caldwell laments how seldom this deep-level contextualization is done:

> Unfortunately, most contextualizers have not taken the time and effort necessary to really understand the prevalent hermeneutical methods at use in their target cultures, despite the fact that many of these cultures contain vast oral or written scriptures. Instead, for whatever reasons, most contextualizers have been content with using the hermeneutical methods (predominantly Western historical criticism) that they were already familiar with when interpreting the Bible and making it relevant for their various cultures. Consequently, this surface-level contextualization has been an incomplete contextualization.[31]

Good contextualizers, he argues, are receptor-oriented, and being receptor-oriented means being aware of and utilizing the target group's traditional methods of interpretation.

Doing such contextualization, Caldwell explains, requires revising the two-horizon view of interpretation to include a third horizon.[32] Following David Hesselgrave, Caldwell proposes adding a third horizon, the receptor culture, to this process. He explains,

> In a cross-cultural situation, the attempt to fuse the various horizons is extremely complicated. For communication to happen,

---

29. Caldwell, "A Response to the Responses," 139–40.
30. Caldwell, "Receptor-Oriented Hermeneutics," 345.
31. Caldwell, "A Response to the Responses," 138.
32. Caldwell, "Receptor-Oriented Hermeneutics," 271; Caldwell, "Cross-Cultural Bible Interpretation," 21–24. Caldwell's proposal here builds off the insights of Nida, *Message and Mission*, 33–58; Conn, *Eternal Word and Changing Worlds*, 188–90; Carson, "Church and Mission: Reflections on Contextualization and the Third Horizon," 17–20.

there should be the fusion of *three* horizons, a *tri-fusion* as it were. Once again, the burden for this tri-fusion rests upon the interpreter. Aside from fusing with the Original Bible Culture, the interpreter must also try to fuse with the *Receptor's Culture*.[33]

Interpretation, Caldwell states, involves familiarity with the culture of the biblical text, one's own culture, and the culture of the recipients. He argues that good interpreters will fuse these three horizons to ensure effective communication from the interpreter to the receptors.

That said, while Caldwell criticizes traditional Western approaches to interpretation, he does argue that the focus of interpretation in any context should be a study of the text. In his book *Doing Bible Interpretation*, he lays out a seven-step process for engaging the text and communicating its truth to others that incorporates a genre-specific approach.[34] Because of his missional perspective, he seeks to provide a process for interpreting the Bible using only the Bible—that is, without so many aids that are emphasized in the West but unavailable in the Majority World.

Much of the process Caldwell lays out in this book are similar to the principles we will consider in chapter 10. Thus, it's best to see his overall perspective as a hybrid approach that combines many insights from Western approaches to engaging the text and considering the unique features of different genres while remaining open to the insights of other hermeneutical approaches that arise from different cultural contexts.

Along the same lines, while Caldwell encourages the use of indigenous hermeneutic approaches, he would not encourage a full-on reader-centered approach of interpretation. Even when using indigenous approaches to interpretation, the resultant explanation of the text must fall within the bounds of healthy theology. The reason for emphasizing ethnohermeneutics is that sometimes these approaches to the text "might better help us understand what God, the original author, was attempting to communicate both then and now."[35]

---

33. Caldwell, "Cross-Cultural Bible Interpretation," 21–22.
34. Caldwell, *Doing Bible Interpretation!*
35. Caldwell, personal communication.

Evaluation

There are several positive aspects of Caldwell's proposal. First, his commitment to Scripture as the authoritative word of God is a clear positive. The fact that he sees Scripture as authoritative and the final word on faith and practice of the church is helpful, and those with an evangelical perspective will agree with Caldwell on this issue. In fact, Caldwell's stance on this issue sets him apart from some of the other authors considered in this study who have placed Scripture on common ground with other sacred texts.

A second positive of Caldwell's proposal is his commitment to missions. Again, unlike some of the other authors already considered, Caldwell's aim is missiological—he desires more of the world's people groups to come to know Jesus Christ as Lord and Savior. His proposal is not solely an academic exercise but is born out of the efforts to reach people with the gospel. His missiological aim comes through in his desire to respect the cultures of people in other contexts and especially in his desire to develop a system where interpreters don't need to rely on a myriad of tools and resources since many of these are not available in the Majority World.

Third, his commitment to being culturally sensitive is another positive. Caldwell displays a strong desire to study the target culture of the people he is trying to reach and to use his knowledge of the culture to communicate the gospel message in more understandable ways. His desire to study the thought processes and the worldview of a people strengthens the contextualization process.[36]

Caldwell's commitment to learn the indigenous hermeneutic systems of a specific culture is equally positive. His critique that Western missionaries often fail to consider the hermeneutical assumptions of their target group is accurate. He is correct that when missionaries "do their homework"[37] and learn a culture's indigenous hermeneutical methods, it aids the communication process.

Finally, Caldwell's critique of the two-horizon model of interpretation is well stated. Caldwell is correct to note that in cross-cultural and intercultural situations interpreters must handle three cultures, including the culture of the target group. His discussion on this issue is helpful to those who seek to communicate God's word with people of a different culture.

---

36. Caldwell, "A Response to the Responses," 139; Caldwell, "Towards an Ethnohermeneutical Model for a Lowland Filipino Context," 178–80.

37. Caldwell, "A Response to the Responses," 139.

Ethnohermeneutics

While there are many positive aspects of Caldwell's proposal, there are also some troubling aspects. First, his perspective on culture is too positive. His God-above-but-through culture position leaves out the critical God-against-culture perspective. Every culture has some qualities that are sinful and contradict the clear commands of God's word. Missionaries and pastors need to recognize that while God can use some aspects of culture, he is against those aspects that are sinful and in violation of his word. Cultural relativity may be applied in amoral areas of culture, but in those areas that Scripture addresses, biblical authority must take precedence over culture.

Caldwell's positive view of culture leads him to propose that God works through the hermeneutical processes of a culture. In a response to one of Caldwell's articles, Daniel Tappeiner comments, "If by 'works through' Caldwell means only that contextualizing is useful in the missiological task, he is on solid ground. If he means to say that God uses ethnohermeneutics to discover 'what it meant,' he has established hermeneutical pluralism."[38] Since Tappeiner's critique, Caldwell has clarified that he is arguing the second, that proper contextualization requires the utilization of indigenous hermeneutical methods. Such an approach allows the standards of a culture to determine the teaching of Scripture, elevating cultural relativity above biblical authority.

Caldwell is quick to respond that he is not open to hermeneutical relativity and does not believe that every hermeneutical method or every interpretation is valid.[39] He does believe that there is more than one valid way of interpreting Scripture and more than one meaning for any given text of Scripture. Each proposed meaning, he argues, must be evaluated based on the overall thrust of Scripture.[40] Nonetheless, Tappeiner's critique remains a valid one. Allowing each culture to determine its own rules of biblical interpretation at least opens the door to hermeneutical relativity.

A second concern relates to Caldwell's emphasis on *midrash*. While some scholars agree that the NT authors utilized *midrash* and other Jewish approaches when interpreting the OT, many others disagree.[41] In fact,

---

38. Tappeiner, "A Response to Caldwell's Trumpet Call to Ethnohermeneutics," 227.

39. Caldwell, "A Response to the Responses," 144.

40. Caldwell, "A Response to the Responses," 144.

41. One of the primary opponents of such a view is Kaiser. For his arguments against this view, see Kaiser, *The Uses of the Old Testament in the New*; Kaiser, "The Single Intent of Scripture," 123–41. Other scholars who have critiqued such a view include Beale, "Positive Answer to the Question," 89–96; Dodd, "The Old Testament in the New," 167–81; Marshall, "An Assessment of Recent Developments," 1–21.

in the *Commentary on the New Testament Use of the Old Testament*, the authors go to great lengths to show how each NT citation and allusion falls within the range of meaning intended by the OT author. Thus, a careful analysis of each Old Testament citation will reveal that Jesus and the New Testament authors respected the Old Testament contexts.

In one work, Caldwell references a Darrell Bock article in which Bock lists four schools of understanding the New Testament use of the Old Testament.[42] Responding to Caldwell at an EMS discussion, Henry Holloman noted that three of these four schools argue that the New Testament authors used the Old Testament in accordance with its original context.[43] His point is that the evidence favors this view, and Evangelicals have correctly recognized that evidence. To support his statement that this view is the standard among Evangelicals, Holloman references Article XVIII from *The Chicago Statement of Biblical Hermeneutics*: "We affirm that the Bible's own interpretation of itself is always correct, never deviating from, but rather elucidating, the single meaning of the inspired text."[44]

In recent scholarship, Abner Chou has made a similar argument in *The Hermeneutics of the Biblical Writers*.[45] He provides an exhaustive examination of the OT use of the OT and the NT use of the OT in an attempt to understand the type of hermeneutic approach the biblical authors used. As a result, he argues, "Their faithful hermeneutic provides us the certainty that the way we were traditionally taught to interpret the Bible is the method the Bible upholds. Literal-grammatical-historical hermeneutics is not a modern formulation but how the biblical writers read the Scriptures."[46]

Finally, Caldwell does not encourage a subjective approach to interpretation where interpreters in any context can do whatever they want with the text. It is concerning, though, that with Caldwell's approach, interpreters in different contexts utilizing their own indigenous approaches may end up with different explanations of the same text. Such an approach moves away from the traditional one meaning / many applications approach of interpretation to a many meanings approach, where meaning includes the contemporary application. Some Evangelicals have adopted this approach,

---

42. Caldwell, "Third Horizon Ethnohermeneutics," 321–22.
43. Holloman, "Response," 2.
44. "The Chicago Statement on Biblical Hermeneutics," 881.
45. Chou, *Hermeneutics of the Biblical Writers*.
46. Chou, *Hermeneutics of the Biblical Authors*, 23.

and like Caldwell they see the boundary of possible meanings as determined by theology or by the rest of Scripture.[47]

The problem with this view is that it takes right interpretation to arrive at right theology, and a multiplicity of meanings leads to a multiplicity of theologies.[48] Meaning is not determined by right theology or by the contemporary context but by the original author. The contemporary context determines what significance the author's meaning has in the interpreter's life and cultural setting, but it does not determine meaning itself.

We will return to this issue in chapter 10 as one of the principles explores the interaction between theology and interpretation—that is, does good theology guide interpretation? Or does faithful interpretation lead to good theology? In reality, the truth is somewhere in the middle, but even with good theology, we must always return to the text and ask the question, "What did the original author mean?" It is for this reason that Evangelicals have long held, and should continue to hold, to the one meaning / many applications theory of interpretation.

---

47. The approach known as "theological interpretation of Scripture" encourages this view of interpretation. For a proponent of this view, see Treier, *Introducing Theological Interpretation of Scripture*. For a brief description and critique of this position, see Plummer, *40 Questions about Interpreting the Bible*, 313–20; or Allison, "Theological Interpretation of Scripture," 28–37.

48. Several others have stated this same critique of Caldwell's proposal. For their critiques, see Tappeiner, "A Response to Caldwell's Trumpet Call to Ethnohermeneutics," 226; Espiritu, "Ethnohermeneutics or Oikohermeneutics?," 278; Whelchel, "Ethnohermeneutics," 131–32; Holloman, "Response," 1.

9

OTHER MODELS

SEVERAL OTHER AUTHORS HAVE written concerning issues related to cross-cultural hermeneutics. For the purpose of better understanding the various issues involved in interpreting Scripture in multicultural contexts, we will examine the processes of these authors and then provide some summary statements.

Elizabeth Mburu

Elizabeth Mburu is an associate professor of New Testament and Greek at several schools in Nairobi, Kenya. Her book *African Hermeneutics* presents an argument for a contextualized approach to hermeneutics.[1] While her book focuses specifically on the African context, she presents many principles of interpretation that are helpful in thinking through how to interpret the Bible in any specific cultural context.

In her approach, Mburu advocates starting from what is known and then moving to what is unknown.[2] With this statement she builds on the similarities between the biblical worldview and the African one and explains that her approach starts with what is familiar in the African worldview and uses that as a bridge to better understand the unfamiliar world of the biblical culture. In that sense, her approach is a contextualized hermeneutic.

---

1. Mburu, *African Hermeneutics*.
2. Mburu, *African Hermeneutics*, 7.

Other Models

To guide this process, she provides four considerations that help guide this process. She writes:

- Africans tend to have an inherently religious or spiritual worldview that is not lost when they become Christians.
- The philosophy and method used in an African hermeneutic must address issues that are relevant to African Christians.
- An African hermeneutic must ground abstract thinking in concrete realities.
- An African hermeneutic must be comprehensible to all Christians and not just a select group of intellectuals. The goal is for millions of believers who live in Africa to truly understand the biblical text and apply it in their lives.[3]

While making these statements about the African worldview that guide the interpretative process, Mburu adds that this approach does not advocate a reader-response hermeneutic or one that exalts the local context above that of Scripture. She explains that in any context the goal of interpretation is not to read meaning into the text because doing so misses the intention of the original author.[4]

Mburu then goes on to explain a process for interpreting the Bible in an African context. She uses the illustration of a four-legged stool and explains that the four legs of the stool relate to: 1) parallels to the African context; 2) theological context; 3) literary context; and 4) historical and cultural context. Finally, the seat of the stool serves as the model for the application of the text.[5] She adds that while we begin with leg 1 because it is the most familiar, actually "the legs are not independent of each other, and we will find that we will be moving back and forth between them as we try to find the right balance."[6]

Another important feature of this approach is the use of insights from African oral literature. Similarities exist between traditional African storytelling and the ways that narratives are told throughout Scripture. Since many of the stories in Scripture were originally told in oral format, an understanding of oral storytelling tradition provides us with new insights into

---

3. Mburu, *African Hermeneutics*, 7.
4. Mburu, *African Hermeneutics*, 8.
5. Mburu, *African Hermeneutics*, 65.
6. Mburu, *African Hermeneutics*, 66.

the text. For example, in studying the book of Ruth, Mburu notes, "Some Bible stories are linear and clearly express the intended message, but many others, like the book of Ruth, are similar to African stories in that they have a non-direct approach."[7] Again, the similarities between the two cultural traditions provides new insight into the text.

One of the benefits of Mburu's approach is the emphasis on simultaneous study of the various legs of the stool. Oftentimes approaches to hermeneutics emphasize a process where it seems one step in the process happens independently of all the others. Mburu rightfully recognizes that sometimes an insight in the area of literary context will lead to greater insights in the area of theological context and vice versa. Not only is such a perspective correct, but this recognition relates well to many of those in the Majority World. Especially in Asia and Africa, people don't think in terms of logical step-by-step progressions, but they think in more circular ways. Thus, those textbooks and processes that emphasize a Western, highly logical progression for how to interpret the Bible are often difficult to apply in Majority World contexts.

That said, Mburu doesn't see her approach as a contradiction or replacement to Western methods of interpretation. Rather, it is complementary. Her goal is to pursue the author's meaning, but African storytelling and traditional aspects of African culture provide many new inroads and insights into the text. Thus, her approach builds on and modifies traditional Western approaches to interpretation in a way that leads to both greater insight while studying the text and to more faithful application of the text to the local context.

Another strength of Mburu's work is that she recognizes that no one reads the Bible as a blank slate. Every person approaches the Bible with a certain worldview and cultural perspective that influences how they read Scripture and what details in the text they pay attention to. Such a statement should not lead to eisegetically reading one's own culture into the text, but it should lead to a recognition that every person has certain biases as they interpret.[8] Good interpreters recognize these biases and the way they influence their reading of Scripture.

---

7. Mburu, *African Hermeneutics*, 128.

8. Friedrich Schleiermacher referred to this concept as "preunderstanding." He explained that one's understanding of a given text is always conditioned by the understanding he has before coming to the text: "The understanding of a given statement is always based on something prior, of two sorts—a preliminary knowledge of human beings, a preliminary knowledge of the subject matter" (Schleiermacher, *Hermeneutics*, 59).

At this point we might ask why Mburu's approach of starting with culture is a legitimate approach to interpreting Scripture when the goal of interpretation is to understand the original author's intention. Doesn't this approach just lead to reading one's own cultural perspective into the text? The reason it doesn't is because she seeks to leverage preunderstanding for better recognition of the text's meaning, which is a unique aspect of Mburu's approach. Since she is developing a contextualized hermeneutic for Africa, she recognizes that the cultural context of Africa shares many aspects of the original cultural context of Scripture. Differences certainly exist, but there are many more similarities. This allows interpreters of Scripture to utilize aspects of their own context to better understand the text of Scripture.

She gives a couple of examples of how leveraging one's cultural perspective can aid in better understanding of the text. With the woman caught in adultery (John 7:53—8:11), Africans can relate to the harsh punishment for adultery and can also relate to the honor/shame dynamic at play in this narrative.[9] Another example she gives comes from the story of Hannah (1 Sam 1–2) and the aspect of that text where barrenness is considered shameful.[10] It is important to note that these examples are simply entry points into the text. They create understanding and common group for deeper study of the theology and grammar of the text. Since the goal is understanding, Mburu notes that this approach also applies not just when there are similarities between the two cultures but also when there are differences as well.[11]

Enoch Wan

Enoch Wan is a professor of intercultural studies at Western Seminary. He is ethnically Chinese and has written several articles on issues related to ethnohermeneutics and contextualization.

Wan defines ethnohermeneutics as

> the principles and procedures by which the interpreter determines the meaning of the Holy Scripture, inspired by the Primary Author (triune God within theoculture) and inscripturated through the secondary authors (human agents of varied

---

9. Mburu, *African Hermeneutics*, 68–69.
10. Mburu, *African Hermeneutics*, 69.
11. Mburu, *African Hermeneutics*, 69.

historio-culturo-linguistic contexts of homoculture) for the recipients (of various historio-culturo-linguistic contexts).[12]

Important to Wan is the understanding of God communicating to humans through the words of the human authors of Scripture. Since the world contains a variety of human cultures, ethnohermeneutics involves interpreters of Scripture wrestling with how to understand the message of Scripture within these various cultural contexts.

Wan explains that this ethnohermeneutic process is a difficult one. He writes, "There remains the distance and difference between the Author, writers and interpreters/recipients of the Scriptures due to the different multiple-contexts involved; there is the inevitable difficulty of ethnohermeneutics for all Christians of all times."[13] Since the process of interpretation involves individuals from multiple cultural contexts, it is a process that is best done in community with others.

Wan states that in general Evangelicals agree that the historical-critical method is the best model for interpretation.[14] He then explains that this method is not without its weaknesses. As Wan sees it, the weaknesses of the historical-critical method arise from the unchecked presuppositions of interpreters that use this approach. One of these presuppositions that Wan critiques is the understanding of a plain meaning or only one meaning to any given text. Wan describes such a perspective as "questionable."[15]

The benefit of ethnohermeneutics, Wan writes, is that interpretation done in the context of multiple cultures prevents individualistic heresy.[16] The presence of interpreters from multiple cultural contexts forces each interpreter to look beyond his own cultural biases. Wan explains that such an approach produces an interpretation of Scripture that is biblically based and scripturally sound.[17]

---

12. Wan, "Ethnohermeneutics," 1.
13. Wan, "Ethnohermeneutics," 1.
14. Wan, "Ethnohermeneutics," 8–9. Like Caldwell, Wan groups the historical-critical method together with the grammatical historical method.
15. Wan, "Ethnohermeneutics," 9.
16. Wan, "Ethnohermeneutics," 10.
17. Wan, "Ethnohermeneutics," 10.

Other Models

Paul Hiebert

Chapter 4 examined Hiebert's explanation of the history of contextualization. Here we look at his views on the role of hermeneutics in the contextualization process. Hiebert critiques the views of Kraft and Caldwell and calls their proposals "uncritical contextualization."[18] He writes that

> in applying ethnoscience to missions there is the danger of letting the context determine the meaning of biblical texts. The meanings of scriptural passages become what people believe them to be, not a communication from the outside. Ultimately this leads us to an uncritical contextualization that is willing to bend the gospel to fit each culture and to neglect the prophetic call for all cultures, societies, and peoples to be transformed by the power of God.[19]

While ethnoscience has made many positive contributions to the missionary task, the uncritical contextualization that is characteristic of its approach is ultimately problematic.

In light of these weaknesses, Hiebert proposes a critical contextualization process.[20] This process begins with exegesis of the culture. Local leaders and the missionary uncritically gather information about traditional beliefs and customs. Hiebert explains that the goal of this part of the process is simply to understand the former beliefs and practices.

The second step in Hiebert's process is the exegesis of Scripture and the hermeneutical bridge.[21] During this step, the pastor or missionary leads the people in a study of certain passages of Scripture that relate to the cultural practices in question. This step is also a chance for the pastor or missionary to train the people in the correct ways to read and interpret Scripture. Hiebert explains,

---

18. Hiebert, *The Gospel in Human Contexts*, 97–98. What Hiebert refers to as "uncritical contextualization," I have called "over-contextualization."

19. Hiebert, *The Gospel in Human Contexts*, 98.

20. Hiebert, "Critical Contextualization," 109; See also Hiebert, *Anthropological Reflections on Missiological Issues*, 88. Less than being a hermeneutical process for the interpretation of any and every passage of Scripture, Hiebert's process is more focused on contextualization and the redemption of specific cultural practices in light of the community's recent commitment to Christ. It is for this reason that his proposal begins with a study of culture—one must first study the culture in order to find out those areas of the culture that are inconsistent with the Christian gospel.

21. Hiebert, "Critical Contextualization," 109–10.

> New believers have little knowledge of the Scriptures and often cannot read. They are dependent upon the missionary for an understanding of what the Scriptures mean, and for guidance in dealing with the questions they face. It is the responsibility of the missionary not only to teach the people the Scriptures, but also how to study the Scriptures for themselves, and to apply them to their own lives. As they mature, he or she must make it clear that they must be obedient to the voice of God as it comes to them through the Word of God, not as it comes to the missionary nor even to the church that sent the missionary.[22]

While Hiebert does not advocate a specific method of interpretation, he does emphasize the church as the hermeneutical community.[23] He explains that this community guards against errant hermeneutical practices:

> Exegesis and hermeneutics are not the rights of individuals but of the church as an exegetical and hermeneutical community. And that community includes not only the saints within our cultural context, and even the saints outside our culture, but also the saints down through history. To become a Christian is to become a part of a new history, and that history must be learned.[24]

Hiebert stresses the role of each group of believers in joining the larger church community. He also emphasizes the role of the Holy Spirit in guiding each community's interpretations. He writes, "We must never forget that the same Holy Spirit who helps us to understand the Scriptures is also interpreting it to believers in other cultures."[25]

The final two steps in Hiebert's critical contextualization process involve the critical response of the believers and the adoption of the new contextualized practice.[26] As the believers examine their cultural practices in light of the teaching of Scripture, they may change, reject, or modify those practices. He states, "Here cultures are viewed as both good and evil, not simply as neutral vehicles for understanding the world."[27] Many aspects of

---

22. Hiebert, *Anthropological Insights for Missionaries*, 215.

23. Hiebert, *The Gospel in Human Contexts*, 183; Hiebert, "Critical Contextualization," 110.

24. Hiebert, "Critical Contextualization," 108.

25. Hiebert, "An Introduction to Mission Anthropology," 59–60.

26. Hiebert, "Critical Contextualization," 110.

27. Hiebert, *The Gospel in Human Contexts*, 29.

culture, Hiebert explains, must be changed by the objective truth of God's word.[28]

Daniel Tappeiner

Daniel Tappeiner was a Pentecostal theologian who served as a missionary in the Philippines. His article on cross-cultural hermeneutics was written in response to an article by Larry Caldwell.[29]

Tappeiner rejects the possibility of multiple hermeneutical methods.[30] He explains that interpreters can distinguish between the meaning and application of a text by determining "what it meant" and "what it means."[31] He writes, "There really is only one valid way in which 'what it meant' can be discovered. The grammatical historical method is simply the developmental result of a process of discovering explicitly the laws which govern the proper and valid recovery of 'what it meant.'"[32] The grammatical historical method, Tappeiner argues, is the only proper way, in any culture, for determining the meaning of any text.

Tappeiner states that when applying the meaning of a text to a specific context, a number of different approaches may be utilized.[33] He argues that even local indigenous hermeneutic or communication methods can be used to convey the contemporary application of that historical meaning. He writes that "there is only one theology (one supra-cultural truth), but many ways, culturally sensitive, in which to expound and communicate that one theology."[34] Contextualization, he explains, is the application of the timeless truth of Scripture to the contemporary context.

---

28. Hiebert, "The Missionary as Mediator of Global Theologizing," 306.
29. Tappeiner, "A Response to Caldwell's Trumpet Call," 223–32.
30. Tappeiner, "A Response to Caldwell's Trumpet Call," 226.
31. Tappeiner, "A Response to Caldwell's Trumpet Call," 226.
32. Tappeiner, "A Response to Caldwell's Trumpet Call," 229–30.
33. Tappeiner, "A Response to Caldwell's Trumpet Call," 226, 229.
34. Tappeiner, "A Response to Caldwell's Trumpet Call," 226–27.

Daniel Espiritu

Daniel Espiritu is a Filipino Pentecostal minister who teaches Philosophy in the Philippines. Like Tappeiner, Espiritu wrote his article on cross-cultural hermeneutics in response to Caldwell.[35]

Espiritu's proposal is for what he terms "oikohermeneutics." He explains that the work of missions will require the entire household of God praying, talking, and working together to reach the world.[36] His proposal is similar to Hiebert's as he sees hermeneutics not as the role of an isolated believer or community but as belonging to the church. Likewise, he argues that the theology of the local church needs to be worked out in communion with the universal church.

Espiritu argues that Caldwell's proposals and many of the hermeneutic methods of believers in Asia are characterized by postmodernism and cultural relativism.[37] He laments the current situation in the Philippines, where preachers use sermons full of allegories and folk illustrations, and he wonders if Caldwell's call for the use of indigenous hermeneutic systems might actually delay the work of missions in Asia.[38]

Espiritu states that given the basic evangelical worldview, interpreters with this perspective must use caution in how they handle the text. He writes that "we cannot engage in an 'endless play' with the biblical texts."[39] He also states that the grammatical historical approach is not so much a Western approach as it is an outgrowth of the evangelical worldview:

> The evangelical insistence on doing rigorous exegesis to get at the probably intended meaning of biblical texts, replacing allegorizing, spiritualizing, and moralizing, is not so much the outgrowth of western worldview as it is the inevitable offshoot of evangelical presuppositions and worldview.[40]

For Espiritu, then, grammatical historical is the natural method of interpretation given the evangelical understanding of truth.

---

35. Espiritu, "Ethnohermeneutics or Oikohermeneutics?"
36. Espiritu, "Ethnohermeneutics or Oikohermeneutics?," 281.
37. Espiritu, "Ethnohermeneutics or Oikohermeneutics?," 272.
38. Espiritu, "Ethnohermeneutics or Oikohermeneutics?," 270, 279.
39. Espiritu, "Ethnohermeneutics or Oikohermeneutics?," 278.
40. Espiritu, "Ethnohermeneutics or Oikohermeneutics?," 278.

Conclusion

This chapter summarized the views of Mburu, Wan, Hiebert, Tappeiner, and Espiritu. Together they provide many helpful insights into the work of cross-cultural biblical interpretation. In the next section we turn our attention to the task of synthesizing the helpful aspects of these views into principles that will enable us to interpret Scripture in intercultural contexts.

SECTION 3

Section 3

A FEW WEEKS AGO, I played rugby for the first time. As an American, the game looks similar to American football, but the rules are very different. As the game started, my instinct was to run a certain way or to throw the ball in a certain direction, only to be told by my friends that those actions were considered illegal. I felt a bit lost, not knowing what I was supposed to do.

At times we may feel the same way when interpreting Scripture. Just the other day my son was looking at a difficult passage in one of the Gospels, and he told me, "I have no idea what this means." Sometimes we read a passage that's hard to understand, and our response is the same. We don't even know where to start. For some of us, the same may be true when we interpret alongside those whose cultural perspective is different than ours. It may be confusing why their explanation is different or why the details they pay attention to are different from the ones we think are important.

What helped me when I was playing rugby was having a few friends who knew the rules and had more experience playing the game than me. Every minute or two they would pull me aside and say, "In this situation, you need to be in this position," or "If they line up there, you need to drop back five yards." These directions (or "principles") gave me some kind of framework for understanding both how the game was played and how I was to navigate it. Even then, though, I still didn't really understand what I was doing—I needed more practice.

This section of the book attempts to do the same thing. In chapter 10 I provide some principles that enable us to interpret Scripture in any cultural context. These principles work through the exegetical process while focusing on the unique challenges of interpreting Scripture in intercultural or multicultural situations. But just like I needed (and still do need!) practice in rugby, chapter 11 will attempt to flesh out what those principles look like when we apply them to specific texts. We'll also examine one cultural practice to see how we might interpret and apply the truths Scripture to that practice in a way that leads to a biblically faithful, contextualized approach.

Then, in chapter 12, we will apply the principles of chapter 10 to the issue of orality. In a sense, in that chapter we are considering the question of how the principles would work if people can't read or if they choose not to read. This situation is an increasing reality for the church given the influence of technology and the availability of vast information in non-literate forms. Like an American learning to play rugby, this is a difficult question to answer, but we'll give some guidelines to help those ministering in this type of intercultural context.

10

Principles for a Cross-Cultural Author-Oriented Approach[1]

On July 14, 2021, the group known as WhatCulture posted a video to YouTube titled "10 Movie Scenes Everyone Gets Wrong."[2] In the video they provide a list of famous movie scenes that moviegoers have misunderstood because of ambiguity in the scene. Not only do fans sometimes misunderstand the intent of these scenes, but sometimes it even affects their perception of the entire movie. And how do these YouTubers know that fans have misunderstood the scenes? Because they neglected key details in the scenes, fans did not rightly discern the author or director's intention.

In this book I argue that an author-oriented approach is the one best suited to evangelical biblical interpretation. That is, the goal of interpreting the Bible is to understand what the original author meant by his use of words and grammar in his specific cultural and historical setting. As we saw in the first few chapters, though, some challenges exist in pursuing the author's meaning, especially when it is done in an intercultural context. For one, in contrast to understanding the intention of movie directors, the authors of Scripture are no longer living, so we can't ask them if we've misunderstood what they've written. In addition, in chapter 1 we saw that our own cultural perspective can sometimes hinder us from understanding the original author's meaning.

---

1. Some overlap exists with the material in this chapter and in my article titled "Grammatical-Historical Exegesis and World Mission," 239–267. However, I have attempted to reword the material to be less of a "process" and more of a set of principles.

2. WhatCulture, "10 Movie Scenes Everyone Gets Wrong."

In this chapter, then, my goal is to attempt to provide some principles that 1) address the challenges raised in previous chapters and 2) combine the helpful aspects of other views examined. Many helpful books exist that address the issue of how to interpret and apply the Bible, and my goal is not to reproduce what those books offer. Instead, my hope is to think about how culture affects these various aspects of interpretation. Thus, in this discussion, I will focus more on how interpreters can pursue the original author's meaning while simultaneously navigating their own cultural influences and those of their target audience.

Similarly, a secondary goal is for the discussion to be practical. My aim is to equip church leaders, especially those serving cross-culturally, to be better interpreters and communicators of God's word. With that in mind, I won't delve too deep into the philosophical questions related to hermeneutics and the question "What is meaning?" As we saw in chapter 1, with more and more of our world being characterized by interaction with those of different cultural backgrounds, it is more urgent than ever to consider how we interpret the Bible alongside brothers and sisters whose cultural perspective differs from ours. In other words, the question driving this chapter is how can we "rightly handle the Word" (2 Tim 2:15) in intercultural and multicultural contexts?

Overview

We start with a simple review of some of the challenges we considered in section 1 and how they affect this process. In doing so, we can consider diagram 5, which gives us a visual reminder of some of these challenges.

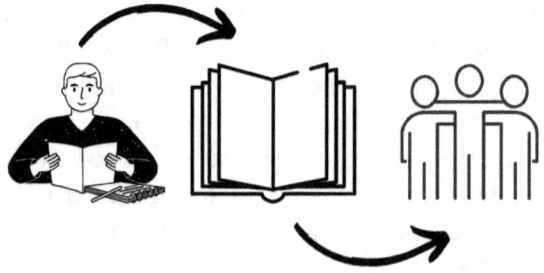

Diagram 5: The Interpretive Process

Principles for a Cross-Cultural Author-Oriented Approach

The left side of the diagram reminds us of chapter 1, where we examined how our own worldview and cultural perspective (the ideas, feelings, and values) serve as a preunderstanding. At times where one's cultural perspective is similar to that of the biblical text, this preunderstanding may help the interpreter to "enter" the text and more easily understand the content. At other times, the differences between the worldview of the interpreter and the worldview of the text not only create a challenge to overcome but also create the potential of misunderstanding.

In the middle of the diagram, we see the text itself. This image reminds us of chapter 2, where we saw that in spite of the challenges our cultural perspective creates our goal in interpretation is to understand the meaning of the original author. Such a statement does not mean we hope to climb back into the mind of the author but that we hope to understand the message the author intended to communicate through the text he wrote.

On the far side of the diagram, we see the "hearers" of the text, which is symbolic of the application of the truth of the text to the contemporary context. Such an image should remind us of chapter 4, where we considered contextualization and the challenge of implanting the word in the local context. In that chapter, we looked at the historical progression of that discussion, which pointed us of the centrality of the word in that process. We must know the text and original author's intention in order to adequately communicate it or live it out in culturally appropriate ways.

Finally, on the right side of the diagram, we see multiple people. This graphic illustrates the need to implant the truth of the word in the cultural context—that is, to communicate truth in a way that addresses the *shared* ideas, beliefs, and values of a group of people. In the same way, it also speaks to the topic of chapter 3 and the need for indigenous interpreters. In other words, modeling faithful interaction with the text and doing so in community with others raises up future leaders in that context that can continue to interpret the word faithfully.

With this general summary of the process of cross-cultural interpretation in mind, we now want to consider ten principles that will aid us in this process. Some principles are more directed to the "front end" and the need to examine our own worldview, while some are more directed towards engaging the text or applying the text to the local context.

Principle 1: Consider Our Own Cultural Influences

We have already considered this principle in the first chapter, where we examined the ways our cultural perspectives affect what we pay attention to in the text. The father of modern hermeneutics, Friedrich Schleiermacher, referred to this concept as preunderstanding when he wrote, "The understanding of a given statement is always based on something prior, of two sorts—a preliminary knowledge of human beings, a preliminary knowledge of the subject matter."[3] In simple terms, no one reads Scripture as a blank slate.

In his book *Reading While Black*, Esau McCaulley makes a similar point when he states that "the social location of enslaved persons caused them to read the Bible differently."[4] But it wasn't just slaves who read the Bible through the lens of their situation. Slave masters did something similar, emphasizing the slave texts in Paul's letters because they reinforced their preexisting worldview.[5] But where slave masters read the text for the sake of justifying their worldview, slaves read Scripture to make sense of their situation. Thus, while all Christians approach Scripture through the perspective of their own context, seeking understanding and asking questions that are prompted by their situatedness, the more faithful process of interpretation allows the text to speak.

Such recognition is especially important in intercultural and multicultural contexts. Consider a possible scenario: a missionary has only read a text from in his home culture. Most likely, he has only ever read explanations of that text by those from his own cultural context. It is possible that his understanding of that text is limited, or that it is influenced or affected by his own cultural perceptions.

When that missionary attempts to teach or study that text alongside believers from a different cultural context, what will the result be? This believer will be unaware of the ways in which his own cultural perspective has affected his understanding of the text. He may be confused by the fact that believers in this context pay attention to details in the text he never noticed. Or it is possible that those believers may be confused as to why this brother

---

3. Schleiermacher, *Hermeneutics*, 59; Larkin, *Cultural and Biblical Hermeneutics*, 37; Thiselton, *Hermeneutics*, 155.

4. McCaulley, *Reading While Black*, 25.

5. McCaulley, *Reading While Black*, 26–28. To be clear, McCaulley argues rightly that the biblical interpretation of slaves was more faithful to the biblical story because it was both canonical and theological in the ways they read texts in light of God's character.

Principles for a Cross-Cultural Author-Oriented Approach

explains the text in the way he does. The worst situation is that because he is unaware of the way his culture is affecting his reading of the text, he may unwittingly force the new believers to add something to the text that isn't necessarily there.

A danger here is when cultural manifestations of Christianity become known as the biblical forms of those truths. One example is the teaching that is often described as "biblical manhood." One book on the topic has the subtitle *How to Mold Men through Baseball*. It has a picture of duct tape on one of the first few pages, and later lists things like how to handle a gun, iron a shirt, and to tip as things dads should teach boys.[6] While these may all be helpful topics in a specific location, they are not "biblical." In fact, many of these ideas are more influenced by the culture than they are the Scriptures.

Our point here is that for those teaching in intercultural and multicultural contexts, they need to be aware of their own cultural perspective. They need to realize the ways their perspectives on some issues are influenced more by their culture and worldview than they are by Scripture, and this may influence the way they interpret Scripture or teach cultural norms as "biblical" truth. Again, since I have proposed an author-oriented approach to interpretation, it is critical that we identify the ways our own cultural perspective and preunderstanding keep us from identifying the original author's meaning.

Principle 2: Study the Target Culture

The first principle leads naturally into the second one. Those in intercultural and multicultural contexts must adopt the approach of a learner. Not only do they need to think critically about the ways their own cultural perspective influences their reading of the text, they must also be students of the target culture, always studying and considering key issues in the new context that may help or hinder understanding.

This principle is often discussed by missionaries in terms of learning the worldview of the people and being able to communicate effectively. It is less frequently discussed, though, in terms of its potential impact on interpreting the Bible. Chapter 1 already showed some of the ways that the specific norms, values, beliefs, etc. may influence how interpreters in that culture may approach the text of Scripture. Intercultural interpreters, then,

---

6. Stinson and Dumas, *A Guide to Biblical Manhood*, 2, 88–89.

must commit to learning the worldview of the people in the hopes of helping indigenous believers navigate these issues. As we have also discussed, sometimes the unique perspective of a culture may help them to make connections that those in other cultures overlook. At other times, their perspective may be a hindrance to understanding. Either way, the missionary must study the culture to be able to identify these issues.

Not long after I moved to Taiwan I was teaching a group of believers there. We were studying 1 Peter 1:14–16 and discussing how holiness should affect every area of our lives. The discussion then turned to what areas and in what ways believers should pursue holiness. After considering a number of issues, these believers mentioned finances in the life of a believer and then mentioned playing the lottery. Without much hesitation, I gave the traditional American, evangelical response about the dangers of playing the lottery. These believers stopped me and explained that the lottery system functioned differently in Taiwan.[7] Though this example is more of an issue of application or implication of the biblical text, still, I had not studied the target culture well enough to explain how the text related to their situation. Thankfully, these believers helped me.

Principle 3: Learn the Biblical Culture and Historical Context

Numerous authors have mentioned the three horizons of biblical interpretation in intercultural contexts, which include the missionary's culture, the target culture, and the biblical culture.[8] Intercultural interpreters need to be well versed in all three horizons. And while the first two principles have touched on the missionary's culture and the target culture, understanding the biblical culture is clearly critical to being able to rightly interpret Scripture in any context.

Other hermeneutics texts are certainly able to cover this topic in more depth than I do here, but to just consider one example, let us look at Colossians. We see the high Christology throughout the letter, where we read

---

7. In the US, one purchases a lottery ticket; thus there is an economic investment by the individual to participate. In Taiwan, one is given a number on a receipt of *any* purchase. So, while there may be an incentive so buy more products to get more numbers, there is no economic investment to specifically participate in the lottery.

8. Nida, *Message and Mission*, 33–58; Hesselgrave, *Communicating Christ Cross-Culturally*, 108; Caldwell, "Receptor-Oriented Hermeneutics," 271; Caldwell, "Cross-Cultural Bible Interpretation," 21–24.

of Christ that "all things were created through him and for him" (1:16), and that in him are "hidden all the treasures of wisdom and knowledge" (2:3). These are more than just theological descriptions, though; the animism of the first century puts these statements in a new light. Knowing that people in this context were concerned about the spirit world and thought it had power over all the affairs of men, we can see how Paul's teaching addresses the issues of this context and reorients their worldview to be more Christ-centered.

Every part of Scripture is situational in that it was written for a specific people at a specific time. Such a statement doesn't contradict the timeless nature of Scripture, but it does recognize that modern-day interpreters need to do the hard work of attempting to understand how the cultural and historical context at the time of writing affected the authors and what they wrote. Understanding the biblical culture enables believers to rightly discern the original meaning of texts. But more than that, it also equips them to make connections with their own situations.

To return to our example of Colossians, the background of animism in the New Testament (cf. Acts 19:11–20) correlates to the worldview of many in the Majority World. In many African and Asian contexts, people still consult a shaman to determine spiritual forces that need appeasement; they see deceased ancestors as part of the spiritual world who still have some power over the material world; and even in the Muslim world, people use talismans to protect themselves from spiritual powers. Thus, recognizing this similarity between the historical context of the letter and the current context, makes it easier for many believers to understand and apply the truths of this letter.

Principle 4: Study the Grammar and Syntax of the Text

When it comes to an author-oriented approach to interpretation, obviously the text itself plays a paramount role in determining the author's meaning. It is only through the study of the words, grammar, and syntax used by the original author that readers can determine the meaning he desired to communicate. For this reason, the grammatical-historical method of interpretation is the one that is best suited to an author-oriented approach to interpretation.

Of course, the grammatical-historical method of interpretation is easily misunderstood. It is not the same as the historical critical method, which adopts a critical stance toward the reliability or trustworthiness of the text. Some might also contrast this approach with a more biblical-theological or redemptive-historical approach, but the differences are often exaggerated. To speak of grammar and history is not at the expense of the theological or in neglect of the redemptive story, but, as Gaffin states, "Redemption is historical."[9]

Others have argued that a grammatical-historical approach to interpretation is a Western method, and to seek to employ it as cross-cultural hermeneutic that enables interpreters in any context to determine the author's meaning is arrogant and paternalistic. I have tried to respond to this critique more fully elsewhere,[10] but here I'll just state that the study of words in their contexts as the original author intended is not a uniquely Western approach. Because as we have already seen, in any cultural context the primary means we have for understanding the author's intention is through the study of what he wrote.

My purpose here is not to defend this approach but to explain how one might utilize a grammatical-historical approach when doing intercultural interpretation. For example, we can consider a familiar text like Psalm 23, which starts with the words, "The Lord is my shepherd." In some cultural contexts, there may be no such concept as a shepherd, and thus the missionary may need to provide some explanation.

In actuality, though, the grammar helps us here. Even though the author assumes some common knowledge about what a shepherd does based on Israel's history, from the following verses we can still learn about some of the things a shepherd does as the Psalmist describes the ways that the Lord is like a shepherd. The shepherd provides what the sheep need, thus "I shall not want" (23:1). The shepherd leads the sheep, thus "He makes me lie down in green pastures" (23:2). And the shepherd protects the sheep, thus "I will fear no evil for you are with me" (23:4). The grammar and the author's own explanation provide understanding.

In other cases, the biblical author's usage of specific terms or phrases may be different than the common use in that context. A clear example is the NT use of "hope." In every day life, the word "hope "is often used to convey something one wants to happen but is uncertain if it will. For example, many sports fans become optimistic "hoping" their favorite team will win a championship, though only one team actually does. The NT

---

9. Gaffin, "The Redemptive-Historical View," 91.
10. Brooks, "Grammatical-Historical Exegesis and World Mission," 242–47.

Principles for a Cross-Cultural Author-Oriented Approach

usage, though, is different. An example of the difference comes from 1 Peter 1:3 where Peter qualifies the term hope with the adjectival participle translated "living." Peter also adds the phrase "through the resurrection of Jesus Christ from the dead" to further clarify the fact that a believer's hope is certain because it is based on the resurrection of Christ, and it increases in strength throughout time. Thus, even in instances where the local cultural understanding of certain phrases is different or even opposite from the biblical meaning, the grammar of the text enables interpreters to discern the original author's meaning.

Principle 5: Consider the Literary Structure of the Text

Another principle we need to consider in terms of developing a cross-cultural approach to interpretation is literary analysis. This principle overlaps with the previous one since considering many aspects of literary analysis is part of the grammatical-historical approach. In that sense, many other authors have recognized the value of considering specific principles for different literary genres, and my approach builds on their insights.[11] With this aspect of interpretation we would also need to consider the overall literary context and the way one specific text relates to the overall purpose of the book.

For example, with the verses we looked at in the last section, we might consider how the message of hope in 1 Peter 1:3 relates to hope in 1:3–9 or even how hope within 1:3–9 relates to the overall message of 1 Peter. In the same way, with Psalm 23 we can consider how lying down in green pastures relates to the overall message of the Psalm or even how Psalm 23 relates to the messianic trilogy of Psalm 22–24 or even the broader structure of Royal Torah in the Psalms.

At other times, though, certain types of literary analysis like narrative analysis can simply be an academic tool to investigate and identify certain unique features of the text. Several of the examples we considered in chapters 6–7 would fall in this category as they looked for narrative, structural, or rhetorical insights from a text and then contrasted those features with similar aspects in some specific cultural context. And yet, identifying key aspects of an overall narrative can aid an interpreter in determining the

---

11. Among the many books that take this approach, see Stein, *A Basic Guide to Interpreting the Bible*; Osborne, *Hermeneutical Spiral*; Brown, *Scripture as Communication*; Mburu, *African Hermeneutics*; Caldwell, *Doing Bible Interpretation!*

original author's intention. In other words, the author has designed the story in a way that things like the flow of the story, key developments in the story, interrelationship of characters, and climax of the story all relate to the author's meaning.

For example, Miki Lo argues that if we look at the Jesus childhood narrative in Luke 2:41–52 and interpret it only as an example of obedience to parents, we miss Luke's point.[12] To interpret this story correctly, we need to see the way Luke incorporates suspense in his echoes of the story of the childhood of Samuel and in the way he puts the question of "Is this really the Messiah?" in the reader's mind. This question keeps the reader searching as he/she reads the rest of the narrative. Thus, narrative analysis, combined with grammatical-history interpretation, provides a way for interpreters to analyze the storytelling methods of the author and more accurately determine his meaning.

When we consider this aspect of interpretation in terms of developing a cross-cultural approach to interpretation, we can make a couple points. First, different cultures may tell stories in a variety of ways. Some cultures have unique ways of indicating suspense, tension, or any aspect of storytelling. For example, when he was living among the Sawi people in Papua New Guinea, Don Richardson told the gospel story and people celebrated Judas as the hero.[13] Why? They told stories differently and defined the actions of heroes differently in their context. Thus, the people misunderstood the meaning intended by the Gospel writers (told in oral form by the missionaries).

Another point we can make in terms of a cross-cultural hermeneutic is the fact that different cultures may emphasize or be drawn to different genres. Many Westerners are drawn to the Epistles because of the logical progression of thought and argumentation. In Asia and Africa, though, many believers gravitate toward wisdom literature like Proverbs both because of its practical nature and because of similarities with cultural forms of communication.[14] For example, Chinese language contains thousands of proverbs which can be deep and practical at the same time.

---

12. Lo, "Using Narrative Analysis to Find the Author's Meaning."

13. Tucker, *From Jerusalem to Irian Jaya*, chapter 18. As Tucker explains, for a number of reasons in this context, they saw deception as an ideal, and the heroes of their stories were those who betrayed or deceived others.

14. For a discussion of the importance of proverbs in African cultures, see Mburu, *African Hermeneutics*, chapter 7.

The point here, though, is that they even though they have cultural ways of forming stories and they may be drawn to specific genres of Scripture, that doesn't mean interpreters in these contexts can do whatever they want with the text. They also can't simply focus on one genre that best fits their communication style. Interpreters in any context need a full-on understanding of Scripture. They need the emotion of the Psalms, the logic of the Epistles, and the tension and character development of the narrative sections of Scripture. Each different genre provides a unique aspect of the overall story of Scripture, and each genre provides a different lens through which God's people learn to understand and live out God's truth.

Principle 6: Examine the Literary Genre of the Text

Another critical aspect of interpreting any specific text is the analysis of the theological emphases of that text. Whenever we interpret a specific text of Scripture, we need to recognize that it has something to say theologically. Sometimes scholars reflect on this question in relation to the Gospels by asking what genre the Gospels are. Are they primarily history or theology?[15] The reality, we realize, is somewhere in the middle, because the Gospels are historical, verifiable events told through the lens of theology in an attempt to show how the events of Christ's life, death, and resurrection fulfilled God's historical salvation plan.

We can make similar statements for other genres of Scripture as well. Wisdom literature is practical advice based on God's ordering of the universe and on what it means to live a righteous life based on God's truth. Poetry and especially many Psalms reflect of what it means both to trust and to praise God in the midst of every circumstance of life. OT narrative is a demonstration of God's faithfulness, oftentimes in spite of the faithlessness of his people. In the Epistles we see the gospel explained in a way that addresses key issues of a specific context. Moreover, we see the "already / not yet" dynamic of the NT in that believers experience in light of the cross and resurrection but also with a future-oriented faith that awaits Christ's return.

When we study a specific text, regardless of its genre, it should stir us to reflect on God's attributes and character—his holiness, goodness, faithfulness, mercy, and grace. As we seek to develop a cross-cultural approach to interpretation, though, we should recognize that there are really two types of theology that result from our study of Scripture. One is

15. Pennington, *Reading the Gospels Wisely*, esp. chapters 1–2.

more top-down; that is, we reflect on and consider the categories that God himself gives to us in Scripture. This type of theology is what we do in systematic theology as we examine what Scripture says about God, man, the church, etc. The second type of theology is bottom-up; that is, we come to Scripture with questions that grow out of our context. Oftentimes, this type of theology is harder, since Scripture wasn't written to address these more specific, contextual issues.

For the health of the local church, both types of theology are important. In terms of a cross-cultural approach to interpretation, though, the first type of theology is more supracultural in that there should be more similarity in how people in different cultural contexts articulate their viewpoints on these issues. However, as we saw in chapter 1, interpreters in different cultural contexts will still notice certain details and aspects of a text that others have overlooked or not paid as much attention to. Thus, while we can say this aspect of theology is *more* supracultural, that is not to say that the theologies that flow out of Scripture will necessarily be the same in every context. We will return to this point in principle 8.

While top-down theology is more cross-cultural and similar in any cultural context, bottom-up theology will vary a great deal. The reason for this variety is because different issues and questions will arise in different cultural contexts. It is also a more complicated theological process, since Scripture doesn't directly address many of these issues. Interpreters, then, need to have the ability to synthesize insights from multiple texts, likely multiple genres. Doing so requires a higher degree of interpretive ability as opposed to simply recognizing the theological implications of one single text of Scripture.

While both types of theology are important and essential, the questions they answer arise from very different places. Moreover, they require slightly different levels of interpretive ability. But both are critical to the overall health of a church. To return to the challenge examined in chapter 3, indigenous interpreters in every context need to have the ability to interpret Scripture in a way that leads to healthy theology—both top-down and bottom-up types of theology.

Principle 7: Evaluate the Theology of the Text

Scripture is the fountain of theology. Good interpreters don't let theology influence how they interpret a specific text; rather, theology flows naturally

Principles for a Cross-Cultural Author-Oriented Approach

out of the text itself. Thus, as the church interprets Scripture, Scripture is always critiquing and refining the theology of the church. Such a statement is especially important in the Majority World, where church leaders have access to fewer theological resources. Their theology, as it should for all believers, must be text-dependent, or else they may be swept away by false teaching.[16]

At the same time, though, given our discussions in other chapters on preunderstanding and the ways that culture influences how we approach the text, all interpreters need to recognize that their preexisting theological convictions can and do influence their understanding of any given text. For example, in chapter 1 we considered how an individualistic versus collectivistic mindset might affect how we interpret the conversion of the Philippian jailer in Acts 16. Apart from the cultural considerations, if we hold that conversions can only be individual, this theological conviction may also influence how we interpret that text.

This principle relates to the broader discussion on the theological interpretation of Scripture (TIS). TIS is "reading the Bible with a concern for the enduring truth of its witness to the nature of God and humanity, with a view to enabling transformation of humanity into the likeness of God."[17] This definition attempts to relate the value of reading Scripture through the lens of theology. That is, it considers how the church's theological positions ("enduring truth of its witness") guide and inform the range of appropriate interpretations of any given text.[18]

While a variety of views and opinions exist related to TIS, on a fundamental level we need to recognize that the theology of the interpreter does impact interpretation. Ideally, interpreters of Scripture would simply be able to read the text and not be influenced by their own presuppositions, but no one can read any text of Scripture in a vacuum. Every interpreter is influenced by his or her own cultural context and preexisting theological convictions. Obviously, these preexisting theological convictions can help or hurt one's ability to discern the meaning of the text. For example, if we consider Hebrews 6:1–8, our theological perspective on issues like Calvinism or Arminianism may influence us to read the passage in a certain way.

One important aspect of this discussion is biblical theology, which some scholars see as synonymous with theological interpretation and as

---

16. Hanna Tawadrous, personal communication.
17. Moberly, "What Is Theological Interpretation of Scripture?," 163.
18. Plummer, *40 Questions about Interpreting the Bible*, 313–20.

a key link between exegesis and systematic theology.[19] In addition to the two types of theology described above, biblical theology can be considered a third, as it attempts to trace the biblical storyline and analyze the major themes that arise out of the grand narrative of Scripture. Wendel Sun describes the biblical story in this way: "God, the creator King, is reestablishing his kingdom in the world through keeping his covenant promises to Abraham, Israel, and David in the life, death, and resurrection of his Son Jesus Christ, who will reign forever in the new creation with his new-covenant people."[20] As Sun goes on to explain, such a statement not only explains the story, but it also provides the major theological aspects of the story as well.

Having a solid grasp of the biblical storyline will aid interpreters in being able to place the text under study within an overall framework of God's redemptive plan. For example, when interpreting the Gospels, we can see the importance of Jesus as the faithful covenant keeper who fulfills the OT story. Thus, in Sun's formulation, we see Jesus' role in "reestablishing the kingdom" in the ways he fulfills God's covenant promises. Or, in the case of the Epistles, they are written post-resurrection but pre-reign. Thus, this "already / not yet" dynamic affects the way the authors simultaneously point readers back to the cross and forward to his return.

In terms of developing a cross-cultural model for interpretation in any context, we can make a couple points. First, though we recognize that theology should flow out of Scripture, and any text we study should correct and adjust our theological convictions, no one can escape the reality that their theology affects how they read and interpret Scripture. For better or worse, theology is part of the preunderstanding we bring to the text. Thus, reflecting on chapter 3, the need in every context is for indigenous interpreters who not only have a strong understanding of how to handle the text but who also have strong theology. Such theology certainly includes top-down theology as well as a thorough understanding of the biblical story. A good grasp of these issues will guide them in doing the more difficult bottom-up theology.

At the same time, in any context as interpreters engage the text, they need to let the word speak for itself. So, while theology can guide us, Scripture must constantly correct and adjust our theological convictions. The responsible interpreter is aware of the influence of his/her own theology

---

19. Treier, *Introducing Theological Interpretation of Scripture*, chapter 4, section 3.
20. Sun, "Biblical Theology and World Mission," 69.

Principles for a Cross-Cultural Author-Oriented Approach

and of differing interpretations of the text, especially the more well-known controversial texts. This should position him/her well to approach the Scripture humbly and discern its meaning.

Principle 8: Display Openness to Other Cultural Perspectives

In chapter 1 we saw a few examples of how one's cultural perspective can affect the details and theological themes an interpreter pays attention to in the text. Like the last point on theology, this type of preunderstanding can aid or hinder interpreters depending on their cultural background and the text being studied. In my own personal experience, I had never paid much attention to the corporate nature of many commands in the NT until I lived among a people who have a collectivistic mindset. Living among people with this perspective opened my eyes to new ways of thinking, and only then did I begin to notice this theme in Scripture as well.

This is not to say that interpreters are unable to notice concepts or themes in Scripture until they experience them in other cultures. Western interpreters are certainly able to study, analyze, and grasp ideas like idolatry, collectivism, honor/shame, or emphasis on the spirit world that are much more prevalent in Majority World locations.[21] Living among a people, though, whose culture shares those values with the first-century world brings them to life in new ways and enables interpreters to read Scripture with fresh eyes.

While some contemporary cultures may have more in common with the first-century worldview than others, *all* cultures are disadvantaged to some extent. Every cultural perspective is limited because, as we saw in chapter 1, each culture prioritizes certain values over against other ones. Thus, when interpreters approach Scripture, their unique cultural perspective enables them to clearly recognize those concepts their culture values while unintentionally minimizing the themes their culture does not value.

One coworker of mine shared with me that when he first graduated seminary in the US, he felt confident on issues related to the eternal security of the believer.[22] After graduating, though, he moved to a former Warsaw

---

21. By "idolatry" here I'm not referring to the term in a spiritual sense, but in a literal one, as many Asian contexts are still filled with temples housing literal idols to which people bow down.

22. Preston Pearce, personal communication.

Pact nation in Eastern Europe where they were many people who committed apostasy during the time of communism. As he met with believers, they would discuss these issues. He would point to texts that seemed to support eternal security, and the local believers would point to texts that seemed to support the possibility of falling away. Studying Scripture with believers who had experienced different things historically forced him to reevaluate how he understood key texts related to this topic. As a result, he "came to see security, perseverance (expected and promised), and assurance are closely related topics."[23]

On a personal level, I experienced this principle when I married someone from a different cultural background. Until I married my wife, I didn't realize how family-centered Chinese culture is in its nature. This is true so much that in that culture people organize their lives around the needs of the family. After we got married, my wife's (extended) family would sometimes ask for help with certain things, and as an individualistic American, I assumed we could tell them we didn't have the time or ability to help. But my wife would say, "You don't say no to family." Being a part of a family that was collectivistic and that emphasized the responsibility we have to one another gave me a new perspective on the depth of dishonor displayed in the parable of prodigal son (Luke 15:11–32) when he abandons his family and pursues his own desires.

Additionally, a few years ago I had the chance to visit India and interact with church leaders from areas where there had formerly been no churches.[24] These leaders were from multiple cities and multiple ethnicities, but they gathered to study the Scriptures *together*. In their context, it makes sense to study key issues as a group rather than just as isolated leaders. They come together with pressing issues of their context, study those issues through the lens of Scripture in small groups, and then critique each other as a large group. As they do so, they are forced to express the different key aspects of the text and how they understand them through their own unique cultural perspectives. The result is a doctrinal statement that expresses the view of the whole group on how Scripture addresses the issue. This culturally appropriate process of interpreting Scripture as a

---

23. Preston Pearce, personal communication.

24. Though I experienced one of these trainings in person, I learned more about the background and structure from a leader who oversees this work. See also Lawless, "Urgency and Healthy Church Planting."

group, with participants from multiple cultural backgrounds, leads them to greater theological fidelity.

Interacting and interpreting Scripture with those of different cultural backgrounds makes us better interpreters. People with different cultural perspectives often pay attention to aspects of the biblical text that we have overlooked. Studying Scripture with others also forces us to reevaluate our own presuppositions and conclusions we make about specific texts. This process helps us to be better interpreters, and this principle helps us to see why we need global theology. The global church needs to hear a diverse set of voices to see the complete picture of God's revelation. Such a statement does not mean that we need diversity in theology necessarily, but only that interpreters from one context may see or better understand certain theological themes because of their unique cultural perspective.

In reflecting on chapter 3, then, and considering the missionary task of taking the gospel and planting it in new cultural contexts, the great need for these newly planted churches—and for the good of the global church as a whole—is indigenous interpreters. Thus, as I have argued elsewhere,[25] when it comes to theological education and leadership development in these contexts, the goal is not simply for the missionary to teach them his/her theological beliefs. It is not enough to "give them our notes" and just teach them how to pass on those notes to others. Missionaries must equip local leaders with the biblical and exegetical skills to interpret Scripture and to do theology *on their own*.

Principle 9: Apply the Truth of the Word to the Local Context

Perhaps the most challenging part of the interpretive process is determining how the unchanging truth of God's word intersects with the changing world we live in. Though challenging, it is still significant and a critical part of interpretation. Here's how Osborne describes the importance of this principle:

> The study of Scripture can never be complete until one has moved from text to context. The static study of the original meaning of a text dare never be an end in itself but must at all times have as its goal the dynamic application of the text to one's current needs and the sharing of that text with others via expository teaching

25. Brooks, "Theological Education as an Integral Component of World Mission."

and preaching. Scripture should not merely be learned; it must be believed and then proclaimed. This dynamic aspect of the Word is the task of contextualization and homiletical analysis.[26]

To some readers it may seem obvious to speak of the need for application of the text, but recall chapters 5–7 and the postcolonial, cross-textual, and rhetorical interactive approaches: each of these approaches engage the text as simply an academic study, and in terms of their engagement with the local context, these scholars simply compare the biblical text with the local context in order to identify similarities or differences. These approaches display little intent to apply the message of the text to the situation of the local context. For evangelical interpreters with a commitment to the inerrancy and sufficiency of Scripture, an attempt must be made to not only understand the meaning of the original author but also to apply that meaning to the contemporary context.

Given its importance, then, how should interpreters go about applying or contextualizing God's word? This is a critical question related to cross-cultural interpretation for a few reasons. One is simply because application of the text can be a difficult and complicated process for many interpreters. When it comes to intercultural interpretation, though, the process becomes even more complicated because of the existence of multiple cultural perspectives. In chapter 1 we saw that in missionary contexts, missionaries must consider three separate cultural influences: their own culture, the biblical culture, and the target culture. Navigating these distinct cultures means recognizing the ways they influence how we see the text (preunderstanding) in addition to their influence on how we apply the text.

To faithfully interpret Scripture in this kind of intercultural setting, then, missionaries must diligently study the target culture. They must also be aware of the ways their own cultural perspective can influence the way they read and apply the text. As I shared earlier in the chapter, in one case I was quick to make applications of a text to the lottery system in Taiwan without realizing how the lottery system actually worked in that context. In that case, I made assumptions about the local culture without really studying it; thus, my application of the biblical text to that practice was inaccurate.

In chapter 9 we examined Paul Hiebert's critical contextualization approach. This is a helpful process for evaluating cultural practices in light of biblical teaching. These new believers work with the missionary to identify

---

26. Osborne, *Hermeneutical Spiral*, 410.

Principles for a Cross-Cultural Author-Oriented Approach

certain practices which may or may not be contrary to Scripture. They study the practices and specific biblical texts that speak to the various cultural and worldview issues involved in the practice. The group then decides together a biblical way forward, which often means some biblically appropriate substitute for the aspects of the practice that contradict Scripture.

For example, in animistic contexts, people fear the spirit world, and many practices are adopted as a result of that fear. It drives them to avoid certain phrases or wear certain amulets as means of protection. When people from this context become believers, they need to evaluate these practices. While Scripture does teach about a spirit world, it also teaches that believers should not fear evil spirits because Christ reigns over the entire created order (Col 1:15–20, 2:8–15). Knowing Christ and living in Christ provides believers with the power they need to live a fruitful, God-honoring life (Eph 6:10–20; Col 2:2–3). Thus, studying Scripture together does not lead them to completely abandon everything in their worldview, but it enables these believers to adjust their practices in a way that aligns better with the truths of Scripture.

In fact, this type of contextualization is not a one-time event. Situations may exist when a special concerted effort is needed to evaluate certain cultural practices. In a healthy church, though, the body of believers is constantly evaluating their lifestyle and practices to ensure they align with Scripture more faithfully. This process happens as the church gathers and studies Scripture together and is why the church is sometimes referred to as the "hermeneutical community."[27]

The first type of process (seen in Diagram 6) is what Hiebert envisions in critical contextualization. This is where the community gathers to investigate a specific cultural practice and evaluate its various components in relation to the truths of Scripture. They may keep some aspects of the practice while modifying other aspects.

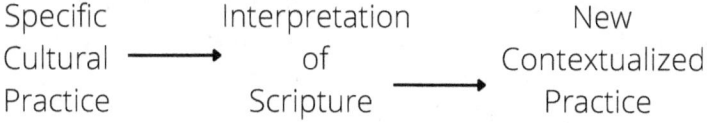

Diagram 6: Starting with the Local Culture

---

27. Hiebert, *The Gospel in Human Contexts*, 183; Hiebert, "Critical Contextualization," 110.

In the second type of process (seen in Diagram 7), the starting point is not a cultural practice but is a specific text of Scripture. This type of process is similar to traditional interpretive approaches or traditional preaching and teaching models, where the pastor starts with the text and only moves to consider how the truth of the passage addresses specific aspects of the culture. What is similar is that in both cases the worldview of the people and the cultural practices are evaluated in light of the teaching of Scripture.

Diagram 7: Starting with a Specific Biblical Text

An important insight from the second model is that this type of contextualization is ongoing throughout the life of the newly planted church. In contrast to those who see contextualization solely in terms of how to frame the gospel in an initial evangelistic conversation, this view sees contextualization as a process whereby the people are constantly evaluating and refining their cultural practices to align with biblical teaching. Such a process enables them to flesh out the gospel in culturally appropriate and biblically faithful ways.

We will look at more examples in chapter 11, but for now we can consider a simple one that illustrates both what it looks like when interpreters start from a biblical text and also how application will be more subjective and depends on the local context. Consider a command like "love one another earnestly from a pure heart" (1 Pet 1:22). Much could be said about the context and purpose of the letter and how it influences why Peter felt the need to issue such a command. To fully understand the command, we would need to do some work to understand that context. Nonetheless, it is a simple command, and a command that strikes at the very heart of the nature of community in the local church.

Exactly *how* that love is communicated, though, will vary in different cultural settings. In the US people demonstrated their love and care for others with acts of service, but they also literally used the word. I can personally remember some church members who after our service would say, "We love you, pastor." Where I currently live in Asia, though, people would almost never use the word in direct communication with others. They communicate their love and concern for others in different ways: by asking about family, by giving food or other gifts, etc. Oftentimes they give advice, even about topics some people consider to be personal or individual matters, which often makes foreigners uncomfortable. But these are simply culturally appropriate ways of showing care, concern, and love.

The point here is that applying Scripture to the local context needs time, care, and a commitment to studying the worldview and cultural norms of the people. The specific ways in which the truths of Scripture are lived out in a specific context are going to be different in different cultural settings. Especially in missionary contexts, when those teaching are not native to that cultural context, they need to give extra care to thinking through how the text under consideration addresses cultural practices in that context. But even when cultural insiders are teaching, they also need to reflect on questions like: What are the culturally appropriate ways to obey this truth of this text? Or: What are the common ways people in this context disobey or don't live out this command? Asking these kinds of questions will enable them to lead believers through the process of taking the truth of one specific biblical text and fleshing it out in that context.

Principle 10: Communicate the Text in Culturally Appropriate Ways

A final principle to consider is the process of communication. While we may not include such a principle in a normal process of biblical interpretation, it is important to consider this topic in the discussion of cross-cultural hermeneutics because different cultures have unique processes for communication. If missionaries desire to communicate biblical truth in a way that people from a different cultural background understand, they must take into account the communication patterns and styles of those people.

One recent experience of mine exemplifies these different communication styles. One seminary where I teach requires all graduating students to preach a sermon before graduation. This sermon is not only preached before the entire student body, but also the faculty and president. What is interesting is that these students come from a variety of backgrounds and often communicate in different ways. One day we had two preachers from two different home countries, and the churches in these two countries tend to have very different preaching styles. One is more forceful and authoritative, and the other is much more relaxed and conversational. Sure enough, when these brothers preached, they personified the two different styles that tend to be used in their home countries.

We also have a time of feedback after the preaching, and it was interesting to hear people who are used to the relaxed conversational approach to preaching describe the authoritative preacher as "running over people" or "forcing people into submission." At the same, those who were used to his style described his sermon as "encouraging." Some of these stylistic differences were certainly due to the personalities of the preachers, but it was also clear how much they were influenced by the ways people normally communicate in their home countries. In the same way, people responded not just to the *content* of the sermon, but their evaluation was largely dependent upon the *communication methods* used to convey that content.

Even in intercultural settings, though, many people communicate in the way the two preachers above did—without considering their audience and only speaking in ways that people from their cultural context tend to communicate. Missionaries may be more inclined to consider the worldview and communication patters of those they interact with. But this lesson is not just for missionaries. As we've seen in multiple chapters in this book, we live in a multicultural world where people we interact with may have been influenced by any number of different competing worldviews. Thus, every communicator of God's word needs to take into account the cultural background and worldview of the people they interact with.

While many people simply say, "I just want to communicate truth," in reality *how* the truth is communicated also matters. In fact, we see this fact modeled in Scripture as well, where the Bible presents several models for using illustrations to communicate in culturally relevant terms. The Old Testament prophets often acted out their messages (Isa 20:3-4, Ezek 4:1-4; Zech 11:4-17). Jesus used parables to illustrate the truths he was teaching and utilized culturally appropriate metaphors his listeners could relate to. Likewise, Paul used cultural statements and beliefs to connect with his audiences (Acts 17:23; Titus 1:12). Thus, we recognize the importance of intercultural interpreters considering the worldview and communication patters of those they teach.

Conclusion

Rather than considering a specific process or methodology for interpreting Scripture, this chapter has focused on principles that guide cross-cultural interpretation. At the same time, since many books have fleshed out specifics of interpretation in helpful ways, we have put less emphasis on those issues and have given more attention to how culture affects these various principles.

Our goal has been to consider how, in any context, one must interpret Scripture in a way that both respects the intention of the original author while recognizing that we all interpret Scripture in a specific context. The contexts where we live and the cultural perspectives we have influence the way all of us read and interpret Scripture and must be taken into account. Moreover, given that we often interpret Scripture in and for the local church, we must give attention not only to the ways our culture affects the ways we read and interpret as individuals, but we must also give attention to the cultural perspectives of others. Doing so ensures that all people can hear, understand, and live out the truths of God's word.

11

Applying the Model in Various Contexts

I FREQUENTLY GIVE ThM- or doctoral-level students an opportunity to teach. This teaching practice is part of their academic journey as they learn to communicate good content but do it in a way where it educates and equips others to be able to do the same. On one occasion one of my students was teaching and, in part because of miscommunication on my end, the student focused the lecture on some complicated theoretical ideas that the students had not been exposed to before. Without any real-life illustrations to which they could relate, the students found it hard to follow the lecture. After listening patiently for a long while one animated student finally spoke up and said, "We need examples if we're going to understand these concepts!"

This chapter is my attempt to answer that student's question. In chapter 10, I tried to give examples and illustrations while also explaining each of the principles. At the same time, though, I recognize that some readers need more concrete examples to see how the principles function and interact in relation to some specific texts. Thus, in this chapter, my goal is to illustrate the principles by examining four specific texts. And, similar to the previous chapter, the goal is not to provide an exhaustive exegetical explanation, but rather it is to show how the principles can help us in any cultural context and to show the complexity of doing exegesis when people from multiple cultural backgrounds are present.[1]

---

1. Admittedly, most of my intercultural experience has been in working with those in the East Asian context. So my applications and reflections here will reflect that.

Applying the Model in Various Contexts

In the last chapter, when examining principle 9, we saw that in addition to starting from specific biblical texts, some situations exist where it is necessary to start with a specific cultural practice in mind. Thus, in this chapter, we will also look at the issue of ancestor veneration, both looking at the cultural background of this practice and attempting to examine and apply a few biblical texts that could help Christians navigate this issue. We'll start, though, with a review of all the principles we examined in the last chapter:

1. Consider our own cultural influences.
2. Study the target culture.
3. Learn the biblical culture and historical context.
4. Study the grammar and syntax of the text.
5. Consider the literary structure of the text.
6. Examine the literary genre of the text.
7. Evaluate the theology of the text.
8. Display openness to other cultural perspectives.
9. Apply the truth of the word to the local context.
10. Communicate the text in culturally appropriate ways.

Text 1: OT Narrative (Judges 3)

One of the interesting aspects of doing biblical interpretation is the fact that multiple genres exist in Scripture. These different genres complicate the interpretive process, because the original authors wrote with different styles and with different orienting principles in mind. Robert Stein referred to this dynamic as "the rules of the game."[2] In chapter 10, we touched on this issue in principles 5–6 and saw that understanding narrative in Scripture can be difficult because in different cultural contexts stories are told and interacted with in unique ways.

In this section, then, we want to look at one specific narrative text and consider some of the challenges of interpreting it in different cultural contexts. Judges 3:12–30 is particularly challenging for a few reasons. On a literary level, it is complicated because, like much biblical narrative, the

---

2. Stein, *A Basic Guide to Interpreting the Bible*.

main point is communicated primarily through the subtleties of the text. These subtleties can often be missed by the casual interpreter.

Complicating matters even further is the fact that while we are used to telling and hearing stories, our cultural patterns for interpreting stories may be different from the way the biblical authors tell stories. For example, in traditional East Asian narrative style, the storyteller typically does not emphasize the faults or failures of the main characters.[3] Perhaps because of the honor/shame aspect of their culture, they only emphasize the strengths and victories. Contrast this type of storytelling with, for example, that of the Gospel writers who at times emphasize the weakness and humanity of Christ, or by contrast the consistent failures of his closest followers, and we can see where misinterpretation may happen.

From another perspective we might say that the cultural values or the way certain cultures describe heroes often varies from culture to culture. This text from Judges 3 is a good example of how such contrasting paradigms can create confusion. From a Western perspective, we might consider the plethora of movies in which the hero is wronged in some way in the beginning of the movie but then single-handedly achieves vengeance on his enemies. Movies like *Die Hard*, *Braveheart*, or *John Wick* tell this kind of story and set something of a cultural paradigm. Thus, when Westerners who are familiar with such movies read the narrative of Ehud, they would tend to read him in the same vein. For that matter, those familiar with East Asian storytelling might do the same, since they are familiar with stories emphasizing the strengths and valiant deeds of heroic warriors.

In this text, though, several details exist that show that the author is emphasizing the opposite. That is, the author is communicating more than just an amazing feat of deliverance for God's people. He is actually emphasizing that *the methods* of deliverance also matter. Moreover, we see the deterioration of integrity and holiness in exchange for an increase in sinfulness, arrogance, and self-sufficiency. Daniel Block makes this argument from the broader narrative of Judges 3:7—16:31 when he calls it the "Canaanization of Israel."[4] He notes that the stories of deliverers all follow a general structure or cycle, but what is fascinating is that statements that mark the various components of the cycle slowly become less and less clear. Whereas the stories of Othniel and Ehud contain all six elements, the final story of Samson contains only two. Thus, "the breakdown of the structures

---

3. Insight from Miki Lo, personal communication.
4. Block, *Judges, Ruth*, 143–49.

of the accounts is a rhetorical device paralleling the general moral and spiritual disintegration of the nation."[5]

More specifically in the Ehud narrative, the author provides details that display the same deterioration in holiness and character. For example, whereas in 3:7 the author only states once that the people of Israel did evil in the sight of the Lord, in 3:12 he states it twice. Then in 3:15 we see Ehud described as left-handed, which serves as another subtle indication of his deception, since he is of the tribe of Benjamin, literally "son of the right." As Kuruvilla explains, "The anomaly of a member of a right-handed tribe being a left-handed man seems to be hinting at the theological oddity of a deliverer raised up by Yahweh (3:15) resorting to underhanded tactics."[6]

Far more significantly, Ehud is duplicitous in his actions. Twice he tells the king that he has a "message" for him (3:19, 20), and yet what he actually has is a sword. Kuruvilla makes the point that the sword is doubly concealed, "physically under Ehud's cloak (3:16), and verbally, by referring to it as a 'message/thing' (3:20)."[7] Similarly, he is self-sufficient in his actions; that is, he is not depending on Yahweh. Whereas in 3:10 (in the previous story) Othniel is said to be empowered by Spirit of the Lord, no similar statement is made about Ehud. In contrast, he fashions the sword "for himself" (3:15) and commands the people, "Follow after me" (3:28).[8]

Much more could be said about the narrative and the author's subtle use of key details that help us see the so-called Canaanization of Israel and its leadership during this period. For our purposes, though, the above explanation of the text is enough for us to reflect on a few of the principles from chapter 10. Noting the different cultural paradigms in storytelling should remind of us principles 1 and 2. Principle 1 helps us to see that the cultural norms that shape our thinking may be different from those that shaped the biblical author. In this case, Western interpreters need to exercise caution that their culture's tendency to celebrate a self-sufficient warrior hero who accomplishes deliverance by the strength of his might doesn't lead them to miss the actual intention of the biblical author.

This point overlaps with principle 2 where we likewise need to consider the target culture's traditional ways of reading and interpreting narrative.

---

5. Block, *Judges, Ruth*, 147.

6. Kuruvilla, *Judges*, 73.

7. Kuruvilla, *Judges*, 75.

8. See Kuruvilla's explanation on self-sufficiency in *Judges*, 73, and of the lack of Yahweh in 69–71.

How these two principles interact will depend upon the worldview of the interpreter and the worldview of the people in that place where he/she is interpreting. In my case, as a Westerner living in Asia, principle 2 helps me to see that those in my context would not be familiar with a narrative that emphasizes the weakness, failures, and arrogance of a leader.

Along the same lines, they would not be familiar with the ways this individual story is part of a larger narrative framework. We mentioned that the author emphasizes the deterioration of holiness in the way that the clear organization and structure of each cycle becomes less and less clear as he progresses through the stories of these seven judges. Since indigenous narratives don't emphasize this type of broad structure, interpreters in the context would likely miss such an emphasis.

The same could be said in relation to principles 6 and 7, as they emphasize the importance of understanding this single text in relation to the broader biblical story. The biblical story helps us to see the contrast here between the faithful, covenant-keeping God and a stubborn, disobedient people. The failures, weaknesses, and self-centeredness of Ehud point to the need for God's people to have deliverance accomplished on their behalf by one who is perfect, sinless, and willing to lay down his life for others. The biblical story helps us to see how this single narrative points us forward to the coming of Christ.

Text 2: Poetry (Psalm 24)

We first looked at a narrative passage, and now we want to consider a poetic text. As I said above, principles 4–6 remind us of the importance of recognizing different literary styles and emphases in different genres of Scripture. Perhaps this contrast is never clearer than when we compare the subtleties of narrative with the emotional and often exaggerated language of poetry. In fact, we already considered the symbolic language of Psalm 23 a few times in chapter 10, and now we will consider one of its partners in the messianic trilogy, Psalm 24.

Psalm 24 contains three sections, each with a fairly distinct topic. Verses 1–2 focus on God's work in creating the world. Verses 3–6 list the characteristics of one who is pleasing to God, namely the one who might "ascend the hill of the Lord." And finally, in verses 7–10 we see a song celebrating the entrance of the conquering "king of glory." Craigie and Tate note the difficulty of finding a central unifying theme of the Psalm, but ultimately describe it as a "celebration of the Lord's kingship."[9] They explain that the first section points to creation as the foundation of God's kingship, the second section as the conditions for those who wish to worship the king of creation, and the third section "celebrates the kingship of God in military language."[10]

Again, our purpose here is less to explain the text and more to focus on the challenges of interpretation in various contexts and to see how the principles help us. In approaching the text, principles 4 and 5 remind us that we need to consider the ways that the target culture tends to interpret this specific genre. For example, examining the various historical interpretations of the 诗经 (Shijing) or *Book of Songs* in the East Asian context, Chen explains how the lack of focus on the author led to existential readings of the poem:

> In reviewing the history of the *Shijing* hermeneutics from the Spring and Autumn period to the present, one is struck by its utilitarian nature, whether political, moralistic, or educational . . . With a few exceptions, one finds little discussion on authorship throughout this history. By ignoring the question of authorship, there is more room to interpret the poems and to draw conclusions as one sees fit. Thus, instead of using the poem to express the author's emotion or aspiration, the poems can be used freely by the readers as a sophisticated vehicle to utter their inner feelings.[11]

As we saw in chapter 2, though, interpreters should consider authorial intent, and the reflections on specific applications in their context should be related to the meaning of the original author. Thus, such an approach could be dangerous if indigenous interpreters simply utilize their indigenous hermeneutics approaches instead of considering the original author's intention. Thus, interpreters in a context where the church is newly planted should be taught to consider and apply the original author's intention.

Reflecting again on chapter 10, principles 1 and 2 help us to reflect on our own preunderstanding and on specific issues in other cultural contexts which might help or hinder a correct understanding of the author's meaning. As we saw in chapter 6, many contexts already have some sort of creation story as part of their worldview. In animistic contexts like in Africa, though, that story is followed by the creator no longer associating

---

9. Craigie and Tate, *Psalms 1–50*, 332.
10. Craigie and Tate, *Psalms 1–50*, 349.
11. Chen, "The Book of Odes," 58.

with creation, leaving them to be ruled by various spirits and powers. Thus, though people in these contexts possess some knowledge of a creator, this preunderstanding is not complete in terms of understanding Psalm 24:1–2.

Nonetheless, some preunderstanding does give them an entryway into understanding the text. We would need to build upon that knowledge with principles 3, 4, 5, and 6. For example, principle 3 points to the study of the culture and history that informed the text. One aspect of this would be previous revelation, where the history of God's covenant relationship with Israel informs the theology in the text (which of course overlaps with principle 6). In that sense, the idea in these verses of a powerful, sovereign Creator is informed by previous revelation that describes the Creator as good, loving, and one who cares for and is at work in the lives of people to accomplish salvation. Such an understanding of the Creator would be a sharp contrast to African traditional religions' understanding of a creator who is distant and not involved in daily life.

We can say the same thing about the second section of the text, which lists out the characteristics of those who worship the Creator King. Since this psalm is messianic, we recognize that these characteristics are only completely fulfilled and personified in the person of Christ. Even still, they do provide a picture of the blessed life that has been transformed through a relationship with the Creator King. Since African biblical hermeneutics tends to be existential,[12] the question in verse 3, "Who shall ascend the hill of the Lord?" provides a practical entryway into the text.

In terms of principle 9 and the application of the text to this context, Weanzana provides two salient points for the African context. First, verses 5–6 explain that "blessings come through our obedience to the Word of God in our daily life, in our family, workplace, and school."[13] Second, these blessings come from God alone, and not from some self-appointed distributor of blessings. Both points are necessary amidst the neo-Pentecostal prosperity gospel that is rampant in the African context.[14]

Moving on to the third section of the Psalm, and for the purpose of considering a different principle let us reflect on principle 8, which reminds us of the need to consider possible insights from a different cultural perspective. This section of the Psalm speaks of the city welcoming home the

---

12. Adamo, "The Task and Distinctiveness of African Biblical Hermeneutics," 31–52.
13. Weanzana et al., "Psalms."
14. For more on this topic, see Arnett, *Pentecostalization*; Barnes et al., *The Abandoned Gospel*.

victorious King of Glory. On one hand, those contexts which have a historical monarch may have more insight into the idea of a people celebrating the accomplishments and reign of their sovereign ruler. These practical insights from their culture may make it easier for them to relate to the celebratory attitude the Psalmist describes, which clearly points to the victorious Messiah's rightful reign over all the created order.

We can recognize the same dynamic with the idea of glory. Certain cultures tend to emphasize the ideas of honor and shame over against other paradigms. Georges and Baker explain that these are "collectivistic societies where the community tends to shame and exclude people who fail to meet group expectations and reward loyal members with honor."[15] They categorize this type of culture over against cultures that tend to emphasize guilt/innocence (Western) or power/fear (animistic) perspectives and argue that 80 percent of the world's population has an honor/shame worldview.[16] They then go on to state that the most common biblical term for this cultural paradigm of honor is the word "glory."[17] Thus, cultures that emphasize this paradigm may have an easier time recognizing and interpreting this theme as they read Scripture, including Psalm 24:7–10.

In fact, several scholars have made a similar point. Jerry Hwang argued that in lament poetry the poet often links the honor and shame of God's people with God's as a means of strengthening their covenantal relationship.[18] Jackson Wu makes the same point about Romans, arguing that Western interpreters have often "overlooked or underemphasized" these key terms even though they often appear in the Epistle.[19] The remedy to this problem comes in the title of his book, *Reading Romans with Eastern Eyes*; that is, when we read Scripture from a different cultural perspective, we notice themes that formerly went unnoticed. Throughout this book I have argued that the same dynamic happens when we interpret Scripture alongside believers who have a different cultural perspective.

The point here that I'm trying to make is not that we use certain cultural ideas and read them into the text or that we look for textual justification to support cultural ideas or norms. No, our goal is to understand the original author. But my point is that interpreting Scripture interculturally,

---

15. Georges and Baker, *Ministering in Honor-Shame Cultures*, 18.
16. Georges and Baker, *Ministering in Honor-Shame Cultures*, 19.
17. Georges and Baker, *Ministering in Honor-Shame Cultures*, 47.
18. Hwang, "'How Long Will My Glory Be Reproach?,'" esp. 686.
19. Wu, *Reading Romans with Eastern Eyes*, 2.

that is, with those who have a different perspective than us, can help us more accurately understand the original author's intent. In this case, since the OT authors often had a collectivistic honor/shame mentality, those whose contemporary worldview also emphasizes such ideas may see details that other overlook.

Text 3: Parable (Luke 15:11–32)

For our third example we look at a parable. Considering that each text we have examined is from a different genre, it is worth noting the difficulty of interpreting parables. On that point, Plummer writes that parables are "notorious for their frequent misinterpretation."[20] Because parables use an earthly situation to explain a spiritual reality, it is common for interpreters to allegorize and over-interpret the various details.

When we consider the idea of a cross-cultural hermeneutic approach that could be utilized in any cultural context, we need to take this challenge seriously, since interpreters in some cultural contexts may be especially prone to allegory. Elsewhere I have shown the tendency of East Asian Christian interpreters to spiritualize or allegorize the text of Scripture much in the same way that East Asian Confucian, Daoist, or Buddhist interpreters have interacted with their sacred texts.[21] Such an approach is dangerous, since it lays aside the original author in pursuit of a higher, more pure, spiritual meaning, and also because it disconnects the Spirit's guidance of the human author, separating the words of Scripture into one meaning for the human author and a distinct meaning intended by the Spirit.

Another interesting aspect of interpreting parables is the fact that many details are included because of their cultural significance to the original listeners. These culturally significant details create a challenge for modern interpreters whose cultural background and perspective is distinct from the original audience. For example, in our current text, the younger son asks for his share of the inheritance and leaves his father to pursue his own interests (Luke 15:11–13). Those with a Western, individualistic, task-oriented cultural perspective might not find such a request unusual. Though the negativity of the younger brother's actions are eventually displayed by his "reckless living" in 13b–16, initially his desire to leave the family and find his own path embody many Western cultural values.

20. Plummer, *40 Questions about Interpreting the Bible*, 265.
21. Brooks, "Critiquing Ethnohermeneutics Theories," 207–17.

Applying the Model in Various Contexts

In contrast, Kenneth Bailey explains, "but it is and most certainly was unthinkable for any son to request his portion of the family wealth while his father was alive. Every Middle Eastern peasant understands this instinctively."[22] For this reason, many Western commentaries begin their discussion of these verses by explaining the cultural reasons why his request would have been shocking.[23] For example, Garland starts by explaining the perspective of the Jewish audience, that is, the one listening to Jesus' initial telling of the parable, and then lists the way Roman culture, that is Luke's original readers, would have understood the request.[24] In both cultural contexts, the son's request would have been offensive.

In contrast to the need for additional explanation in Western contexts, East Asian interpreters have an easier entryway into the parable given that their cultural perspective is similar to many aspects of the first-century world. Shaped by Confucian ideals, which sought to provide stable and harmonious relationships in society, the family is the central, most important relationship in the East Asian worldview. As Poceski explains, "While early Confucianism was concerned with the whole spectrum of social relationships, the basic pattern of interpersonal interaction was formulated in terms of the parent-child relationship, which became the principal relationship in Chinese society."[25]

This family-centeredness is still evident in the East Asian worldview today, where it is common (and even expected) for adult children, even those already married, to continue living at home. In contrast to this perspective, Westerners have traditionally encouraged their children to move out and live independently after college. In fact, one researcher called the results of a 2019 survey "shocking" when it revealed that student debt was causing many students in the US to move back home after graduating from college.[26] In East Asian contexts, young adults often lay aside their personal ambitions for the greater good of serving their family or maintaining the family business. Family always comes first.

---

22. Bailey, *The Cross & the Prodigal*, 46.

23. Garland, *Luke*; Edwards, *The Gospel According to Luke*; Bock, *Luke*; Green, *The Gospel of Luke*.

24. Garland, *Luke*, 624.

25. Poceski, *Introducing Chinese Religions*, 43.

26. Friedman, "50% of Millennials Are Moving Back Home with Their Parents After College."

An important saying of Confucius that likewise displays commitment to family is 父母在不远游, or, "As long as your parents are alive, don't travel far." Much more could be said about concepts like filial piety, communal living, or the various aspects of East Asian festivals which all show the family-centered nature of the worldview, but these points are sufficient to show that, like Jesus' original audience, an East Asian reading this parable for the first time would have been shocked at the younger son's question. This perspective gives them an easy entry point into the parable as they would respond in the same way as Jesus' listeners who "would have thought that the younger son's place was to stay at home, to labor, and to obey his father as the older son did."[27]

In fact, numerous details exist in the text which people of different cultures may notice or be drawn to. For example, Mark Allen Powell asked students from different contexts to recount this parable.[28] Only six out of one hundred seminary students from the US mentioned the detail from verse 14 about the famine. In contrast, forty-two out of fifty students from Russia mentioned that detail. Similarly, students from Tanzania noticed the detail of verse 16, related to no one giving him food. In each case, the cultural perspective of the students made a difference to what details they paid attention to and remembered.

Reflecting on chapter 10, we might see these examples as the convergence of several principles. For example, a Western interpreter reading the text alongside an East Asian would benefit from considering the East Asian's cultural perspective (principles 2, 8). The honor/shame and family-centered dynamics would give him new insight into the tension created in the first part of the parable. At the same time, though, the similarity in cultural perspective to the original audience can also create challenges. In that sense, the East Asian brother needs to be careful that he does not interpret the parable solely according to his cultural values (principle 1), but that he takes careful notice of the nuance of the text (principles 4, 5, 6).

A personal example on this point might help to illustrate this later idea. When studying this passage with my students, I was shocked to find out that many of them had heard this parable explained that the father was wrong to forgive the son. Multiple students from different denominations and different locations had heard the text explained this way. Why? Interpreters (pastors) in their contexts had read the text according to

---

27. Garland, *Luke*, 624.
28. Powell, *What Do They Hear?*, chapter 2, section 1, para. 8–10; section 4, para. 1–3.

their cultural paradigm—in their worldview such blatant disrespect of a son to a father should never be forgiven. In fact, one author notes that from a Taiwanese perspective, the father's response is not only unfair but unbelievable.[29]

Thus, even though these interpreters' worldview shared many aspects of the original audience, they missed the point of the parable. Yes, the father's forgiveness of the son *is* shocking, and it *is* countercultural. That's entirely the point. God's ceaseless willingness to welcome even the vilest, most shameful of sinners into his kingdom is breathtaking. Unfortunately, if these interpreters read the parable according to their own cultural paradigms, they end up in the same place as the older brother—appalled that the father doesn't hold the son accountable for the ways he has shamed the family.

In this case, grammar, context, and some general rules concerning interpreting parables (principles 4, 5, 6) provide balance. The context of the parable helps given that it is the third in a series of parables concerning the joy at finding lost things, where all three parables are aimed at responding to the grumbling of Pharisees in 15:1–2. Thus, the final parable contrasts the father's joy at a repentant son, which characterizes God, with that of the older son's anger and resentment, which characterizes the Pharisees. Plummer has a helpful section on principles for interpreting parables, and he uses the example of this parable throughout that discussion. One of his principles is to consider what happens at the end. He explains:

> As Jesus often stresses his most important point at the end of a parable, the fact that the parable of the prodigal son ends with a rebuke of the older brother (Luke 15:31–32) further supports that Jesus is focusing on correcting a wicked attitude toward God's gracious treatment of sinners.[30]

Thus, while certain cultural perspectives provide us an entryway into understanding the text, context and genre-specific principles will enable interpreters to overcome potential over-emphasis on one's own cultural perspective.

We can also make a couple points concerning principles 9 and 10 related to application and communication of the parable's meaning. First, notice that our desire to apply starts with first understanding the parable and

---

29. 曾昌发。《耶稣的比喻——从亚洲诠释学的角度研究路加福音中耶稣的比喻》。台北: 永望文化事业有限公司.
30. Plummer, *40 Questions about Interpreting the Bible*, 272–73.

the original author's intention. Only once we have a grasp on that meaning do we begin to consider how it might inform certain cultural paradigms. Of course, as we have seen, the worldview of the interpreter comes into play at a number of points throughout the interpretive process, but these aspects of the culture are leveraged for the purpose of *understanding* the original author.

With that point in mind, we can also say that given the importance of family and of harmonious relationships in the East Asian worldview, this parable provides a beautiful picture of the gospel to those with this worldview. Although the son's words and actions have broken the relationship and brought shame on his family, the father welcomes him home, thus restoring harmony. Believers in this context need to be careful that they don't respond to those outside the family of God as the older brother has, that is, according to their previous cultural paradigms. Instead, they must allow the understanding of God's nature as gracious and loving toward his creation to transform their own hearts.

Text 4: Epistle (2 Corinthians 12:7–10)

In the broader passage here, Paul recounts a vision that God gave him and which had the potential to make him arrogant. In spite of this, Paul writes, "on my own behalf I will not boast, except of my own weaknesses" (12:5). Then he goes on in verses 7–10 to explain why this vision did not lead him to arrogance and what he learned from this situation about boasting in weakness. We'll examine these verses and then make some statements about how one's cultural perspective might create some challenges in interpretation.

Paul describes here "a messenger of Satan" that was sent to harass him (12:7). He uses the words "thorn in the flesh" to describe this messenger (12:7). The Greek word here signifies something sharp and pointed, and it denotes "something which frustrates and causes trouble in the lives of those afflicted."[31] While it is impossible to know exactly what the thorn was, Paul's language makes it clear that it caused him a great deal of pain. Schreiner notes that presumably Satan intended the thorn to "inflict misery on [Paul]

---

31. Kruse, *The Second Epistle of Paul to the Corinthians*, 205; Harris, *The Second Epistle to the Corinthians*, 855.

and cause him to doubt God's goodness."[32] It is likely that Satan also sought to use the pain to hinder Paul and limit his ability to preach the gospel.[33]

This painful attack, however, was not the result of any sinful behavior on Paul's part.[34] Paul explains that the attack served to keep him from becoming prideful (12:7). Before his prayer, Paul was not even aware of the reason for the attack (12:7–8). The reality is that sometimes God allows Satan to attack believers for reasons that are unknown to them. Amazingly, this passage also teaches that God is sovereign over these attacks, and he uses them for the growth of the believer and the advancement of the gospel (12:9–10).

While Satan used the thorn to attack Paul, humiliating him through severe weakness, God used the attack for good (12:9).[35] Paul writes that God used the thorn to keep him from becoming too conceited (12:7), and through the weakness he experienced he learned to depend more on God's power than his own (12:9b). In the end, the suffering that Paul experienced actually served to spread the gospel.[36]

Paul explains in verse 9 that after pleading with the Lord to remove the thorn, the Lord said, "My grace is sufficient for you, for my power is made perfect in weakness." The lesson Paul learned was that he was to be content with weakness. He was to rely more on God's grace than on his own ability or his privileged position as an apostle. The main point, then, is that God's grace is sufficient to meet all the needs of believers, even when the circumstances of their lives are difficult or painful.

For this specific passage, Paul's teaching on resting in God's grace and not in one's circumstances contradicts the pragmatic perspective of the East Asian context. This pragmatic perspective, if applied to the Christian faith, could result in a prosperity gospel type of theology where faith in Christ is understood as a means for procuring blessing. The tendency in this context to ask "Does it work?" could lead to a mentality where belief in God is evaluated based on whether or not it leads to an easier or more prosperous life.

This danger is also a reality when it comes to communicating the truth of the gospel to non-believers. Non-believers tend to evaluate the benefits

---

32. Schreiner, *Paul, Apostle of God's Glory in Christ*, 301.
33. Best, *Second Corinthians*, 119.
34. Arnold, *3 Crucial Questions about Spiritual Warfare*, 125.
35. Harris, *The Second Epistle to the Corinthians*, 856–57; Page, *Powers of Evil*, 197.
36. Schreiner, *Paul, Apostle of God's Glory in Christ*, 102.

of conversion to Christianity with a "Does it work?" mentality. Much like the opponents that created havoc in the church in Corinth, they examine the life of Paul with questions related to why someone called by God would face so much suffering in his life. In the end, they might conclude that faith in Christ is not worthwhile since it is not guaranteed that following Christ will result in earthly blessing.

While the East Asian worldview's pragmatic perspective creates challenges when communicating the truth of this passage, its focus on relationship aids in communication. For East Asians, the central priority in life is harmonious relationships. This prioritization of relationships helps them to understand this passage because what Paul is saying is that his relationship with Christ is of greater value than any temporary comfort he could experience in this life. The benefit of Paul's faith in Christ is that through that faith his relationship with God has been reconciled. It is of no consequence if persecution or difficulties befall him as a result of his faith since he is at peace in his relationship with God.

This emphasis on relationships makes sense in the context of the East Asian worldview. Since East Asian are willing to give up their rights and face difficulty to maintain peaceful relations with others, they can understand Paul's perspective when he is content with weakness and hardship as long as he remains in a right relationship with God. In fact, Paul explains, the weaknesses he experiences actually serve to strengthen his relationship with Christ by teaching him to rely more on the power of Christ and less on his own strength. He places the priority in his life on his relationship with Christ and that makes sense to those in the East Asian context.

In chapter 10 we saw that principle 1 emphasized the need to examine the influence of one's own cultural perspective on their understanding of the text. In this situation, a Westerner interpreting this text alongside an East Asian must evaluate how his/her own cultural perspective influences the understanding and communication of the text. Since the central priority in many Western worldviews is belief, a Western interpreter might explain that a Christian's belief in God helps him to understand and overcome difficulties. While this explanation is true, it is not as helpful in an East Asian context, since relationship is more of a central and core part of the East Asian worldview.

Since pragmatism contradicts the truth of this passage, it is best to reinterpret that value in light of what the passage teaches. Instead of asking "Does it work?" about their experiences, believers in this context instead should learn to ask, "How does this situation strengthen my relationship with God?" When East Asian believers ask this question, they adopt the Pauline perspective of focusing on God's grace and boasting in their weaknesses, because when they are weak, they experience more of God's powerful presence.

Cultural Norm: Ancestor Veneration

In chapter 10 we considered the issue of application and saw that some, like Paul Hiebert, propose a process for evaluating certain cultural norms through the lens of Scripture. Up until this point in this chapter we have started with Scripture, first seeking to understand the meaning of the original author and considering the benefits and challenges of doing so in different cultural contexts. Even when we start with Scripture, the goal is to end up considering how the truth of the passage transforms the thoughts, beliefs, or values in the local culture. In this example, we flip that process by first considering a cultural practice and then evaluating that practice according to Scripture.

This process of starting with a specific cultural practice is a bit more like the theological process used when we do systematic theology. After examining and understanding the cultural practice, we need to identify key biblical texts that address certain aspects of the cultural practice. Interpreting each text, we synthesize the insights from each text into a thorough biblical response to the cultural practice. The result of the study is a new cultural practice that may retain some aspects of the former practice and may adjust other aspects in light of biblical truth.

In this example, we want to consider the practice of ancestor veneration. In the history of the church in East Asia, this practice has been notoriously difficult to evaluate. While many missionaries and Christians have rejected the practice, the earliest missionaries to China, the Nestorians, looked favorably on the practice.[37] Later, the Jesuits agreed with the Nestorian perspective, but the Franciscans and Dominicans disagreed, taking the matter to the Pope, who forbade ancestor worship for all Catholics in 1704.[38]

This issue is still contentious today. While most East Asian Christians abstain from ancestor veneration-related practices, some scholars advocate

---

37. Lim, "Contextualizing Ancestor Veneration," 110.
38. Lim, "Contextualizing Ancestor Veneration," 111.

for continued participation in it. For example, Simon Chan gives an argument for it in his book *Grassroots Asian Theology*.[39] Or, from a different perspective, David Lim writes positively of Christians continuing the practice.[40] While Lim argues more from a missiological or theology of culture perspective, Chan evaluates the issue through the lens of the doctrine of the communion of saints. While their insights into the issue are helpful, both consider the issue more theologically instead of looking at specific biblical texts.

With the aim of considering the practice through the lens of specific biblical texts, let us first seek to understand the practice. Hwa Yung explains part of the reason believers have struggled to respond to this issue, since it contains both religious and social components: "To participate in it in its original form does involve a religious act which, as it appears to me, would conflict with the demands of the gospel. But to neglect it altogether would rightfully incur cultural condemnation of being disrespectful to parents."[41] Yung helps us to see that there are both religious and cultural components, which are often intertwined.

From a religious perspective, many ancestor veneration practices have their aim at either gaining some blessing from deceased ancestors or providing some benefit needed by the ancestors. An example of the latter is the offering of food or the burning of certain items that the ancestors will receive in the afterlife.[42] While a blessing is desired from the ancestors, many of these ritualistic actions are driven by fear.[43] These actions lean more toward the reason for defining the process as ancestor *worship* because, like other animistic belief systems, the ancestors have spiritual power that they wield over the natural order.[44]

At the same time, though, these practices play an important cultural role. Chua explains that ancestor veneration provides "solidarity within the organized family system,"[45] and Wong adds that within the Confucian worldview, "ancestor worship is filial piety unto the living and the dead."[46]

39. Chan, *Grassroots Asian Theology*, 188–197.
40. Lim, "Contextualizing Ancestor Veneration," 183–93.
41. Yung, *Mangoes or Bananas?*, 229
42. 黄柏和等, 《基督徒与祭祖》, 54–55.
43. Wong. *Exposing Chinese Ancestor Worship*, 1–2; Chua, *Feeding on Ashes*, 8.
44. Wong. *Exposing Chinese Ancestor Worship*, 1–2.
45. Chua, *Feeding on Ashes*, 8.
46. Wong, *Exposing Chinese Ancestor Worship*, 21.

Applying the Model in Various Contexts

In addition to ancestor veneration's integration with daily life, it plays an important role in many East Asian festivals as well.[47]

In fact, while ancestor veneration is a significant part of East Asian culture, it is not uniquely East Asian. People in many cultural contexts wrestle with issue of deceased loved ones and the afterlife. Even in Eastern Europe, food offerings are left near the graves and in honor of deceased loved ones. Partially seen as a gift for the poor, many people also understand that the offerings will help the deceased in the afterlife. Religiously, such a practice may make sense in light of the Catholic doctrine of purgatory, but these practices even exist in Orthodox countries, thus displaying the cultural aspect of the practice.

As a result of this complicated intermingling of both religious and social components, many Christians have forbidden ancestor veneration altogether. A better approach would be to evaluate each aspect biblically, with the aim of providing a cultural substitute where Christians can continue to participate in the aspects of veneration that are not in contradiction with some clear biblical teaching. Thus, believers can continue to participate in the culturally oriented aspects of the practices while modifying the aspects that contain a religious component that is antithetical to the gospel.

Perhaps the most difficult part of this process comes after we have conducted some evaluation of the cultural norm and how it functions within this worldview. Finding the appropriate biblical passages that can speak to the practice without proof texting or eisegetically importing our preconceived ideas into the text is a challenge. For example, we may make a knee-jerk reaction to ancestor veneration by citing Exodus 20:3, "You shall have no other gods before me," and claiming that in an animistic worldview the ancestors have a god-like status, since they have power to bless or curse.

Such a statement is true, but it also misses the veneration aspect that grows out of Confucianism, whereby these actions are a means of continuing filial piety. Thus, as we mentioned in the introduction, we must balance Exodus 20:3 with 20:12 and the need to honor one's father and mother. And in an East Asian worldview, a need exists to apply this command not just to living parents but also in a way that honors the memory of parents, grandparents, and others who have already departed this life.

Steven Wong cites 1 Timothy 5:8 and Ephesians 6:2–3 to argue that the honoring and caring for parents is only expected while they are alive. Certainly, in terms of provision for their needs (in contrast to the burning

---

47. Zhang, "A Brief Account of Traditional Chinese Festival Customs," 21.

items or sacrifice food for ancestors), he is correct. But in the Old Testament we also see an emphasis on remembering, thus we see in many places the repeated term "your fathers, Abraham, Isaac, and Jacob" (for example, Gen 50:24; Exod 2:24; Deut 1:8). In Deuteronomy, Moses himself instructs the people of Israel by reminding them of their history. In fact, at times he instructs them by saying, "Do not put the Lord your God to the test, as you did at Massah" (6:14), when in fact it was not they who tested God but their parents. Thus, there is a connection between this generation and the previous one and a need to reflect, remember, and honor the legacy of those whose lives have already ended.

To reflect, then, on the principles from chapter 10, we first see principle 2 in the need to study the target culture so that we can accurately apply the truths of Scripture to the context without knee-jerk prooftexting or falsely assuming and reinforcing our preconceived conclusions. In the same way, the example in the last paragraph again reinforces principles 4–5 and the need for rigorous study of the text in its original context lest we miss Exodus 20:12 because we only focus on 20:3.

At the same time, while we see a biblical emphasis on remembering and honoring the memory of ancestors, Scripture also confronts the religiously oriented aspects of ancestor veneration. In this sense, principles 6 and 7 on the issue of theology can help us here. We can consider the theological implications of an OT story like Saul and the witch of Endor in 1 Samuel 28. That narrative starts with a statement that Saul put all mediums out of the land (28:3), but he then contradicts those actions by seeking one (28:7). And while there is no direct condemnation of Saul's actions by the author, Samuel's message to Saul is one of criticism. In fact, Samuel's initial question in 28:15, "Why have you disturbed me by bringing me up?" contradicts the idea that any living person should seek to influence the realm of the deceased.

From another theological perspective, we may consider texts that use the term "Sheol" in the OT. While the use of the term is extensive, a number of texts make clear that humans cannot interfere or interact with those who are in that realm. We may consider Job 7:9, that "he who goes down to Sheol does not come up." Or we can consider those texts that use the term in the sense of despair, as in those who go there have no hope left. An example of this usage would be would be Genesis 42:38, where Jacob says, "You would bring down my gray hairs with sorrow to Sheol," or when Korah and others opposed Moses in Numbers 16, the earth swallowed them

Applying the Model in Various Contexts

and "all that belonged to them went down alive into Sheol, and the earth closed over them, and they perished from the midst of the assembly" (Num 16:33). There was no hope for them.

In reflecting on principle 3 from chapter 10, we can also consider the similarities of the animism in the Greco-Roman world with the animism in contemporary East Asia. While many differences no doubt exist, it is within an animistic worldview that deceased ancestors are seen as being part of the spirit world and are also seen as having power which they wield over the material world. With that in mind, we may consider texts like Acts 19:11–20 which, while not dealing specifically with deceased ancestors, does clearly condemn animistic practices while trying to harness spiritual power from the spirit world. The same could be said for some sections of Ephesians and Colossians, for example Colossians 1:15–23 or 2:3–6, where Christ is seen as sovereign over the spirit world and believers are commanded to walk in him instead of being concerned about those issues.

Much more can and should be said about the issue of ancestor veneration. For example, as we reflect on principle 9 and the issue of application, the specific ways that believers navigate these issues may look different in various East Asian contexts.[48] What is clear from this textual study, though, is that believers in these contexts should be encouraged to find ways to respect and honor the memory of ancestors, while at the same time they should not participate in the religiously oriented practices such as offering food or burning items that the ancestors receive in the afterlife.

Earlier we saw that while some aspects of ancestor veneration are driven by filial piety, much of it is actually driven by fear. Building on the brief look at Colossians 1 above, believers no longer have reason to fear. The NT confronts the fear of spiritual powers, noting that through Christ "all things were created, in heaven and on earth, visible and invisible, whether thrones or dominions or rulers or authorities—all things were created through him and for him" (Col 1:15). In discussions of ancestor veneration, this is an often neglected point, that for Christians the gospel reshapes and reorients their worldview from one of fear and shame to one of hope and victory.

We should also note that this process of starting with a cultural practice in mind is much more complicated than the previous examples where we started with a specific text. In this case, we start with the evaluation of the cultural practice, then must identify multiple texts that speak to the various

---

48. For example, in 黄柏和等,《基督徒与祭祖》, the authors give some practical guidelines for their contexts.

aspects of the practice, interpret each one, and then finally systematize the findings in a way that leads to a contextualized and biblically faithful practice. Doing so requires a high level of interpretive ability and theological acumen while simultaneously being sensitive to the cultural context.

It also requires interpreters to be self-aware, recognizing how their background and cultural perspective may influence their initial perception of the cultural practices being examined. Their initial perspective may also influence which biblical texts they choose to examine, which is also a danger. In the practice we examined, even the term we use, whether ancestor "veneration" or ancestor "worship," will influence our initial response to the practices. As interpreters, we must exert caution so that we allow the biblical text to speak to and adjust (if necessary) the practice under consideration.

Conclusion

After focusing on principles in chapter 10, this chapter has sought to approach cross-cultural interpretation from a practical perspective. We examined several texts and one cultural practice in the hopes of seeing how, as interpreters in a multicultural world, we might be more faithful in studying Scripture with others who have a different cultural perspective than we do. We saw that to do so we must become experts in our own culture, in the target culture, and in the biblical culture. Interpreting Scripture in intercultural contexts means often evaluating the ways our own cultural perspective influences us while also considering insights that those with a different cultural perspective might have that would make the text more understandable.

Of course, in reflecting on this process, we must state again the importance of authorial intent. Hopefully these examples have shown that our goal is not to simply find similarities between the biblical and contemporary cultures. Our goal is to understand the original author's meaning and then apply that meaning to our contemporary situation. We long for God to speak to us and allow us to view our world and the contexts we live in through his eyes. And we long for him to speak as he has throughout church history—through his word.

Throughout the last two chapters, though, we have primarily focused on the literate study of Scripture. What I mean is that with the principles in chapter 10 and the examples in chapter 11 our aim to help those who

Applying the Model in Various Contexts

have the ability to read and engage the written word. Given that so many people in the world today are oral learners, meaning they either can't read, prefer to not gain information through reading, or attach true or important information to stories, we may wonder how these principles apply to them. We may wonder how these oral learners can learn to interpret Scripture. Is the approach I've laid out here too literate and not useful in those kinds of contexts? It is to this question we turn our attention in chapter 12.

12

Applying the Model Among Oral Learners

In 2018 I was in a rural area training pastors. These pastors fascinated me because their native language had no written alphabet, so they learned a second language because that language had a Bible. They learned a second language and learned to read in it just so they could have access to the Scriptures! Then they learned a third language because they felt called to lead their church and leadership training was only available in that third language. Missiologically, we might reflect on the need to translate the Scriptures or provide training in more languages, but what gripped me was their hunger for God's word.

We spent that week together studying how to interpret narrative passages, and specifically we studied the narrative sections of Acts. We considered issues like the context of the story, the key characters in the story, the discourse that took place, repetition of key words, and other issues. After studying several stories together, I asked them, "How would you teach this approach to others in the churches you lead?" And there was silence. Then they told me that since the people in their church were oral learners, they really didn't know how to teach the principles to others.

As I've mentioned a few times in this book, interpreting the Bible is not just an activity for scholars writing commentaries or even just for pastors preparing sermons, but it is a discipleship issue in the local church. The church not only needs leaders who can interpret, but the church needs to model healthy interpretation and teach all believers how to interpret as well. With these brothers, then, we wrestled with the issue of interpretation

Applying the Model Among Oral Learners

among oral learners—specifically those in their churches. How do they themselves interpret Scripture in a literate way while also modeling healthy engagement of Scripture for oral learners? And do the two approaches need to be significantly different?

Much of what I want to say in this chapter is built off reflections on the time I spent with those pastors. Though this chapter is only a brief attempt at addressing this question of oral hermeneutics, my goal is to first review some basic concepts related to orality for readers who may be unfamiliar with the concepts and then to propose a mediating position that argues: 1) all interpreters and communicators of God's word must wrestle with issues of orality; 2) even in places with primarily oral learners, it is good if some people can read and engage the text of Scripture; and 3) oral learners can learn principles for faithful interpretation not only for narrative but also for other genres of Scripture.

Understanding Orality

In the last two chapters, we explored principles for interpreting Scripture in intercultural contexts, that is, situations where interpreters with different worldviews or cultural perspectives are interpreting Scripture together. We examined how these different cultural perspectives may affect their engagement of the text and what issues they need to consider as they seek to understand the original author's meaning. Then we looked at specific biblical texts and one cultural practice in an attempt to see how the principles work together to aid in interpretation.

These discussions, though, were very literate in nature, meaning we focused primarily on how to engage the *text* of Scripture, paying attention to specific words and nuances of grammar or even the literary structure of the text. Even in examining a narrative text in chapter 11, we focused more on literate analysis of the story to help us ascertain the original author's intention, and in principle 5 in chapter 10 we mentioned that literary analysis combined with grammatical-historical exegesis is helping in interpreting narrative.

At the same time, though, we need to recognize at least two thirds of the world's peoples either cannot read or choose not to read.[1] The father of the modern-day orality movement, Walter Ong, differentiates between two types of orality: primary and secondary. He explains:

1. International Orality Network, *Making Disciples of Oral Learners*, 3.

> I style the orality of a culture totally untouched by any knowledge of writing or print "primary orality." It is 'primary' by contrast with the "secondary orality" of present-day high-technology culture, in which a new orality is sustained by telephone, radio, television, and other electronic devices that depend for their existence and functioning on writing and print.[2]

He continues, "Today primary oral culture in the strict sense hardly exists, since every culture knows of writing and has some experience of its effects. Still, to varying degrees, many cultures and subcultures, even in a high-technology ambiance, preserve much of the mindset of primary orality."[3]

Since Ong wrote these words about "high technology" in 1982, they need to be qualified a bit. In today's world the dependence on technology for receiving information has increased exponentially, and by correlation so has the amount of secondary orality. In 2004, the International Orality Network (ION) pointed to research that showed a significant decline in reading that had been caused by an increase in the availability of electronic media. Since 2004, the decline has continued, with recent research showing that the time spent on reading each day for personal interest dropped from 0.36 hours in 2003 to 0.29 hours in 2016.[4] And even since 2016, with more and more people turning to sites like YouTube for instructional videos, finding information through social media, or tuning in to streaming media, this decline is likely to continue for some time.

Thus, while missionaries in some parts of the world have had to wrestle with orality for some time, it is becoming increasingly clear that church leaders in *every location* need to consider communicating using oral methods. Even churches with many young, educated, college graduate types need to wrestle with orality. Just because people can read doesn't mean that they prefer to or even enjoy receiving information through reading. Such a reality has massive implications for not only how the church shares the gospel with the lost, but also how it conducts worship and disciples believers.

This idea, then, of secondary orality or tech-driven orality means that even literates may prefer to learn through stories, songs, pictures, or other

---

2. Ong, *Orality and Literacy*, 11. In fact, some people break these two categories down even further. For example, James Slack gives five categories: illiterates, functional illiterates, semi-literates, literate, and highly literate. Deaf would also be included in this list, since they tend to communicate in non-print methods. For more info on that topic see Sauter, "Theological Education for the Deaf."

3. Ong, *Orality and Literacy*, 11.

4. Crain, "Why We Don't Read, Revisited."

media. Christians have long approached discipleship in the church with a literate "read this" type of approach. Contemporary Christians, though, may not be inclined to learn and grow in the knowledge of God through such means. Teaching all believers to interpret the word can be a significant challenge. We must be creative in the ways we teach believers how to understand the original author's intention.

At the same time, Ong's definition should cause us to reflect a bit on the idea of primary orality. Primary oral learners are those people who don't read or who can't read because no written form of their language exists. The challenge with these groups is not just that they cannot understand or interact with literate resources, but it is also that they think, communicate, and organize information differently. As Ong explains, when information is not stored in written form, "You know what you can recall."[5]

Oral Approach to Hermeneutics

For our purposes, the goal is not necessarily to go deep down the rabbit hole of understanding how oral learners organize information but simply to think through how we might teach people in these contexts to faithfully interpret Scripture. Two fundamental questions arise from the discussion above: 1) How do we train primary oral learners to interpret the forms of Scripture they have? And 2) How do we utilize similar principles to help secondary oral learners who can read but prefer not to? We'll consider them in turn.

When we consider orality and biblical hermeneutics, one significant obstacle is that the Bible has been passed down to us in written form. Such a statement needs to be nuanced in a couple ways. An oral tradition lays behind much of Scripture where, for example, the Gospels were first transmitted orally for many years before being written down. The same can be said for large parts of the OT as well. So, this history of oral tradition informs how we might understand and interpret Scripture as a community of faith.[6] In fact, much of the discussion surrounding discipling oral learners focuses on narrative and the stories of Scripture.

At the same time, we also need to recognize that the Gospels *were* written down. The Gospel writers recognized that a fundamental need

---

5. Ong, *Literacy and Orality*, 33.

6. Steffen and Bjoraker consistently make this case in their book *The Return of Oral Hermeneutics*. See esp. chapter 3.

existed to preserve for future generations an accurate and reliable version of all that Jesus did and said. We also recognize, as was discussed in the last chapter, that this written tradition exists in more than just narrative form. Thus, we need to develop some sort of strategy where those in primary oral contexts can engage, interpret, and understand the truths of Scripture contained in more than just narrative.

One potential help in this discussion is the idea of an oral Bible.[7] An oral Bible is different than a set of stories. Where learning a story set may draw together the overall biblical storyline and help believers see the grand narrative of Scripture, it is a collection of stories that skips over some sections of Scripture. An oral Bible, on the other hand, includes all of Scripture and can be listened to. Still, the question remains: when primary oral learners listen to an oral Bible, how can they learn to faithfully interpret what they are hearing?

When it comes to narrative, a simple solution to this problem comes from genre-specific approaches to interpretation. In the last twenty years, many books on hermeneutics have taken this approach where the authors consider a specific genre and then give principles for interpreting that genre.[8] For narrative, Rob Plummer gives some principles, like: evaluate the context; examine the editorial statements from the author; consider thematic statements; look for repetition of words and phrase; and pay attention to trustworthy characters.[9]

By way of comparison, Jackson Atkins explains the process of storytelling.[10] He explains:

> This process begins with the storyteller asking two questions about the whole story. First, the storyteller asks if anything happened before the Bible story that might make it more understandable. This question places a Bible story in its proper context . . . Next, the storyteller asks about the situation or circumstance of the whole story. This question aims to help the storyteller not miss the main point of the story and to create an emotional connection with the characters . . . After the storyteller has asked these two questions of the whole story he or she continues preparing by going through

---

7. International Orality Network, *Making Disciples of Oral Learners*, 3.

8. For example: Kaiser, *Introduction to Biblical Hermeneutics*; Plummer, *40 Questions about Interpreting the Bible*; Stein, *A Basic Guide to Interpreting the Bible*; Brown, *Scripture as Communication*.

9. Plummer, *40 Questions About Interpreting the Bible*, 193–95.

10. Atkins, "Multiplying Disciples in an Oral Context," 77–84.

the story slowly, section by section, asking the same series of questions in each part.[11]

As they work through the sections of the story, the storyteller poses a series of questions to help listeners understand the main idea(s) of the story. The questions include things like, "What can I learn spiritually about the characters from what they are saying or doing?" and "Did any of the characters make a choice, and if they did, what other choices could they have made?"[12] This process of storytelling, with its evaluative questions and set within the biblical context, is similar to the questions Plummer encourages literates to use in their engagement of the text.

Thus, when it comes to narrative, oral learners can learn many of the same interpretive principles utilized by highly literates. They can learn to consider the context of the story, they can pay attention to the main characters (who often serve as both positive and negative models of behavior), they can notice repetition of key ideas, etc. In this way they are able to evaluate the story and understand the intention of the original author, even though they are not able to read the written version of the story.

In fact, some aspects of this process may actually be easier for oral learners. If a chronological set of stories serves the foundation for their understanding of the overall storyline of Scripture, it will be easier for them to connect the specific story under consideration with the broader story. For example, if they consider an OT narrative from 2 Samuel, their understanding of the grand narrative of Scripture enables them to put that story in both its immediate context of 2 Samuel and also its overall context—looking back to Genesis and forward to its fulfillment in the NT. In the Asian context where I live, this aspect of interpretation is the most difficult for literates. They are often unable to look past the immediate literary context.

Jackson Wu makes this point in his article where he explains how biblical theology informs the process of storytelling among oral learners.[13] He shows that the telling of the Bible's story, or the creation of the story set, is often influenced by the storyteller's own preconceived theological perspective of what is and isn't important. Instead, the set of stories should follow the Bible's own structure and metanarrative. He explains that "the Bible's natural organization simplifies the task of interpretation. One is not forced to speculate how to harmonize doctrines that emerge when philosophical

---

11. Atkins, "Multiplying Disciples in an Oral Context," 80.
12. Atkins, "Multiplying Disciples in an Oral Context," 80.
13. Wu, "Biblical Theology for Oral Cultures," 269–90.

suppositions are forced onto the text. The inherent structure and content of the Bible—which includes Israel's story—help people internalize and understand its message."[14]

At this point we begin to see how primary oral learners can interpret the Bible. Understanding the Bible's own grand narrative through a robust biblical theology (which can also be learned orally) provides believers in these contexts with a framework for interpretation. As they hear and evaluate other stories, they are able to relate them to this broader context, thus increasing understanding of the key themes of the text and how they relate to other portions of Scripture. Such understanding leads to a healthy theological framework that both grows out of the text and informs the study of subsequent texts. This point is similar to what we saw in chapter 10 in principles 6 and 7.

Additionally, while biblical theology informs the broader context and provides these believers with this interpretative framework, principles for interpreting narrative also aid this process. In the same way that believers evaluate the context of the story and reflect on previous stories before this current story is told, after the telling of the story believers can also reflect on and discuss questions that enable them to evaluate the key aspects of the narrative. These questions need not just be focused on application (e.g., What does this story mean to you?), but they can be evaluative and engaging of the story content in a way that leads to understanding the original author's intention.

Hopefully we can also see the benefit of having some in the church community who are able to read and engage the text of Scripture. These with literate ability are able to ensure that the story set follows the Bible's own storyline and that the eventual oral Bible faithfully adheres to the actual words of Scripture. In some situations, the oral learners in the community can only interact with the story when the community gathers to listen to it, but literates can frequently engage the text. They can go deeper in the study of the actual wording and nuance of the language, thus increasing their ability to lead others in the study of the text. Such a dynamic leads to a healthier church.

Trip Whalen has worked extensively with storying among oral learners.[15] In his work, a group often spends a week-long intensive period learning a large group of stories. At the same time, though, when the group

---

14. Wu, "Biblical Theology for Oral Cultures in World Mission," 283–84.
15. Trip Whalen, personal communication.

learns a new story, questions often arise about certain details that are part of the story but not necessarily explained in the story. For example, many stories in the Gospels convey information about the historical and cultural setting, including specific groups of people like Pharisees or Sadducees. Primary oral learners are limited in their ability to consult resources outside the story for information on these critical background details. Thus, it is helpful to have some in the group who can read and consult extrabiblical resources.

Seeing how primary oral learners can learn to interpret Scripture, we can turn to the question of oral preference. In fact, this question is much easier to answer. Since they can read, we can use a hybrid approach to teach them to understand and interpret Scripture. Again, biblical theology and following the Bible's own grand narrative gives them a framework and overall context from which they can understand other portions of Scripture, seeing how the individual text fits together as part of the whole. While orality principles inform how they see the grand narrative, they also have the ability to focus in on the text if necessary for deeper understanding.

In 2014 my wife and I implemented this approach with a group of unbelieving university students in Taiwan. Recognizing the influence of technology on them, we utilized a modified storying approach. We met weekly and focused on a different story each week, starting with creation, and moving chronologically through Scripture. After the story, we used discussion questions to help them evaluate the story and identify the original author's meaning. This process led to further questions, which led us to the text. The back-and-forth between hearing the story and examining the text produced a greater depth of understanding.

Reflecting on principle 10 from chapter 10, that of communication, we may utilize a similar approach in a more traditional preaching context. That is, recognizing the influence of oral communication on many hearers due to the pervasive use of technology, preachers can implement more of a storytelling approach when preaching from narrative texts. They need not always use a deductive point-by-point approach that is emphasized in many preaching textbooks. Instead, they walk listeners through the story, stopping at points to help them evaluate the narrative and apply the theological truths to their lives. In his book, Ajibade recommends using more of an inductive approach, but he adds, "The inductive sermon does not rule out a structure, one that at least guides the preacher but not necessarily one for the listeners to memorize. Such structure serves as a roadmap that guides the preacher-storyteller in telling the story, declares the principles and applies it to the situation of the people."[16]

In chapter 11 we considered the story of Ehud in Judges 3. A more inductive approach to preaching that has oral preference in mind might start with a brief review of Israel's history, i.e., What happened for Israel to end up in this situation? Briefly telling this story provides the broader context and connects the story with the rest of salvation history. Instead of developing a logical, highly structured sermon, the preacher simply tells the story. The preacher might pause after verses 12–14 and the telling of Israel's oppression at the hands of its enemies to reflect with the listeners on what lessons we can learn from Israel's situation or how their situation is similar to our current one. Using this type of approach communicates in ways that are easier for those with oral preference to follow while also modeling and indirectly teaching how to interpret narrative.

Orality and Interpreting Non-Narrative

Since oral learners tend to communicate in and rely on stories as the foundational component of their worldview, it is easier to see how biblical narrative can be utilized in communicating biblical truth and also how oral learners can learn principles for interpreting narrative. But narrative is not the only genre in Scripture. In fact, Scripture contains a diverse collection of genres, including poetry, wisdom, prophecy, apocalyptic, epistle, parable, and others. How can those with oral preference learn to interpret texts from these genres?

Interpreting Poetry and Wisdom Literature

Some non-narrative genres are easier than others. Oral learners already use songs, proverbs, and drama to communicate information and recount previous events. These culturally appropriate communication styles can be used to learn Psalms, Proverbs, or other portions of wisdom literature. Of course, hearing or memorizing these portions of Scripture is not the same as understanding or interpreting. Once again, then, we would return to some principles for interpreting these genres and implement them to help

---

16. Ajibade, *Expository Preaching in Africa*, 154.

listeners reflect on and evaluate the theological aspects of these Scripture portions.

In the last chapter we looked at Psalm 24. Putting the words to song with music will make it memorable and easy to remember. When evaluating the content, listeners can reflect on previous stories and how they inform aspects of the text. The creation story certain serves as the foundation for verses 1–2. For verses 3–6, they may reflect on Exodus 19 and the story of Moses receiving the Ten Commandments. The lack of holiness made the people afraid, a truth that will help the listeners both reflect on the characteristics of verse 4 and begin to look forward to Christ.

In her presentation on Bible translation, Katie Frost considered the topic of "internalization."[17] She points to several internalization techniques that can help listeners understand and apply the content of non-narrative passages. For example, teachers can use visual demonstrations, physical demonstrations like drama, or even pre-selected objects that bring the ideas to life. She has listeners internalize the phrase "rejoice in hope" (Rom 12:12) by relating it to a room in their house. The practice brings back memories and relates the phrase the individual's own experience, thus increasing understanding.

While Frost's approach focuses more on internalization for the purpose of Scripture translation, Ben Rainey explains how this process can also be implemented for interpretation. He also notes how it is similar to the hybrid approach proposed above for narrative:

> In this methodology the teacher is literate and employs discourse analysis, literary analysis and has to bring in historical and cultural commentary. These serve as tools mediated by the teacher for the students to employ as participants to better exegete the passage. The teacher also creatively implements these pedagogical techniques. The teacher does not preach the passage but rather guides the students in utilizing the tools so they can learn to interpret the passage together. The students do not need to access commentaries, historical books, and hermeneutical terms they can't read or understand. And with time and practice they advance in their knowledge and skills.[18]

While Frost's Romans 12:12 example is a single phrase, she also notes that discourse cues like the structure of the passage can also aid in

---

17. Frost, "Non-Narrative Internalization."
18. Ben Rainey, personal communication.

internalization.[19] This point is especially true if it can be diagramed or shown in picture-like form. Thus, with Psalm 24, having a diagram that shows the movement from the creation theme in verses 1–3 to the holiness in pursuit of the Creator theme in 4–6, with a climax on the conquering king of glory, might enable listeners to both understand and evaluate the meaning of the Psalm.

Along the same lines, in her book, Adrian Hinkle shows that the authors of wisdom literature often employ a variety of techniques that aid in understanding and retention of the material. In examining Job, she writes:

> The didactic nature of the book of Job includes literary techniques such as repetition and rhetorical questions to captivate the audience's attention and advance the theological premise of the book. However, in addition to this, Job includes the use of specific pedagogical aids to assist the audience in retaining the religious education contained as well as offer a demonstration of the means by which they too can remember the theological presuppositions recounted in this book. The writers of Job use nature, history, and the Pentateuch to further define the religious ethos of the community and record the pedagogy through which this can be repeated for later faith adherents.[20]

These pedagogical techniques that are built into the structure of wisdom literature provide listeners (and not just readers) an entry point into understanding and interpretation. The fact that Job uses the Pentateuch enables oral learners to reflect on narratives they are already familiar with, and the use of nature enables them to relate some of the content to their own context.

Interpreting Epistles

The Epistles may seem like more of a challenge for oral learners given their didactic nature and logical structure. Especially in the Pauline Epistles, Paul often uses a highly integrated and logical approach to respond to specific issues in these churches. How then can oral learners—who don't use inductive reasoning—learn to interpret these portions of Scripture?

In his article, Grant Lovejoy shows that most of the Epistles already have a narrative context that lays behind and informs the content of the

---

19. Frost, "Non-Narrative Internalization."
20. Hinkle, *Pedagogical Theory of Wisdom Literature*, chapter 4, section 1, para. 12.

letter.[21] He explains how he might connect some of the content from Philippians together with the story of Acts:

> So from its beginning the church in Philippi had a diverse membership. It included a cloth-seller named Lydia and a slave girl from whom Paul had cast out a spirit. It included the Philippian jailer and his household, plus others. The church was strong in its faith and generous toward Paul. Several times they sent him money to support his ministry. He visited them whenever he could and they always enjoyed seeing him again.
>
> But after several years a conflict arose in the church at Philippi. Some church members had a disagreement and it threatened to ruin the congregation's unity and testimony. Someone sent word to Paul to tell him what was happening in the church. When he heard this, he was very concerned and decided to send a letter to the church. He himself could not go because he was under arrest for his Christian faith.[22]

Using this narrative framework puts the Epistles within their canonical context and allows a somewhat seamless connection with the rest of the New Testament. Admittedly, it requires a bit of mirror-reading, but it nonetheless sets up the reason, context, and much of the teaching content of the letter.[23]

For some individual texts this "narrative" explanation of a Pauline Epistle is possible because Paul himself provides some historical context for his teaching. In the example of 2 Corinthians 12:1–10 we considered in chapter 11, Paul sets his teaching on God's glory being displayed in his weakness by recounting the story of his vision and subsequent thorn. He himself tells the story of what took place, which then gives context to the main idea.

Additionally, the NT authors frequently reference the OT. The NT use of the OT can be a complex study which often requires a biblical theological perspective that sees the interconnectedness of all of Scripture. If those with oral preference have heard or memorized a large set of stories, they may already be able to understand how the NT message builds on the OT

---

21. Lovejoy, "Teaching the New Testament Epistles," 5.
22. Lovejoy, "Teaching the New Testament Epistles," 7.
23. Mirror-reading is the process of using the content of an Epistle to try and construct the historical situation (that is, the reason for writing the letter) that lays behind the letter.

story. Thus, as they learn, for example, that Peter in his first letter describes believers and their situation by using OT language like "a chosen race" and "royal priesthood" (2:9), they have a framework for understanding and interpreting such teaching.

In a similar way, since the chronological storying of the Bible provides those with oral preference with an understanding of biblical theology and the story of salvation history, they can place the Epistles within their proper canonical context. For example, much of the NT has an "already not yet" dynamic that looks back on the finished work of Christ was still awaiting its consummation when he returns. First Peter does this by pointing believers to a future grace with commands like "Set your hope fully on the grace that will be brought to you at the revelation of Jesus Christ" (1:13). Understanding such statements requires an understanding of the grand narrative of Scripture, which may actually be easier for non-literates.

Finally, many of Frost's internalization techniques can also be utilized to aid oral learners in interpreting the content of the Epistles. We already briefly looked at the example from Romans 12, but her principles also apply for understanding the structure of the letters as well. Sometimes this structure is a bit more logical, like in Ephesians, where Paul teaches on the gospel (chapters 1–3) and then builds on that foundation with practical guidelines (chapters 4–6). Other times, like in James or 1 John, the argumentation is more chiastic and circular, moving back and forth through several major themes. In both cases, understanding the structure may lead to more faithful interpretation and application, even among oral learners.

Conclusion

This chapter has considered the complex topic of interpreting the Bible alongside oral learners. Though complex, this topic is an important one given the abundance of people in the world today who either cannot or who prefer not to read. Though in previous chapters we focused more on evaluating how one's worldview and cultural framework both aids and hinders one's pursuit of the original author's meaning, in this chapter we provided more of a hybrid approach that seeks to provide understanding and insight into the biblical text.

We saw that many principles that literates used for interpreting Scripture can also be learned and implemented among oral learners. We also saw that having some literates who can go back to the text ensures greater faithfulness and understanding. At the same time, non-literates have something of an advantage at times because they have a strong biblical theological foundation that provides them with understanding of the Bible's grand narrative.

In conclusion, we can return to my experience I shared to start this chapter. When those brothers told me they didn't know how to teach oral learners in their churches how to interpret, we went back to the narratives we had already studied. Together we summarized what we thought was the main idea of the story and how it connected with the overall storyline of Acts. Then we discussed how they would tell the story in their context, and we followed that up with an additional question: "What would you do before or after the story to help others understand the main point?" In the end, their answer to that question looked very similar to the kinds of questions we asked each other as we engaged the text.

I taught them principles for interpreting and engaging *the text*, and they took the principles and repackaged them in a way that oral learners could engage *the story*. Thus, in many ways their preparation in the text looked different from the ways they planned to communicate the fruits of their studies with others, but in both situations the basic principles of interpretation led them to understand the original author's intention.

Conclusion

IMPORTANCE OF HERMENEUTICS IN MISSIONS CONTEXTS

IN THE INTRODUCTION WE considered Philip's encounter with the Ethiopian eunuch in Acts 8:26–40. In that text, Philip asked him if he understood a passage from Isaiah, and the eunuch responded by saying, "How can I unless someone guides me?" In some sense, this entire book has been a reflection on that question. How do missionaries come alongside national partners in a different cultural context and interpret Scripture with them? And how does the missionary do it in a way where his or her own cultural perspective and worldview doesn't dominate the process? Or, for the rest of us who live in a multicultural world, how do we consider the ways different cultural perspectives give us new insights into the texts? Or, how do we apply the truths of Scripture in a way that engages the key aspects of different worldviews?

Throughout the book we've seen that these are complicated questions. The first section, specifically, looks at key challenges as we seek to interpret Scripture in intercultural and multicultural contexts. The complexity of these questions was also explored in the second as we considered various proposals for doing cross-cultural hermeneutics. Finally, we explored it in this last section with some specific principles and applications of those principles. Along the same lines, we may also consider what these issues and the question of hermeneutics has to do with missions and those who are sent out to plant a church in places where few have heard the gospel before.

Importance of Hermeneutics in Missions Contexts

As we noted in the introduction, just like the Ethiopian eunuch, every church needs guides—guides who will lead the church to interpret Scripture in a way that is faithful to the original author's intent. This is the reason why Paul told Timothy his goal was "rightly handling the Word of truth" (2 Tim 2:14). With that goal in mind and in an attempt to tie much of this book to the broader missiological discussion, I am proposing five reasons why training in biblical interpretation should be an integral part of every missions strategy.

First, training in biblical interpretation benefits all believers, not just future leaders. While working on my MDiv some years ago, I led a short-term team to work with college students in a large city in Asia. Thankfully, the missionary already had a post-conversion discipleship plan in place for us to use if any students came to faith during our trip. Unfortunately, the lessons in this plan used the un-hermeneutically-sound approach of proof-texting to make their point. These new converts were confused why we would read one sentence from a place called "John" and then immediately be told to flip to a different page and read a completely separate sentence from a place called "Romans." Though literate, they didn't understand why we were not reading *sections* of the Bible but instead only reading a few *words* before turning somewhere else.

In response, our team made a slight adjustment to this plan in that instead of using twenty-six separate verses to teach about new life in Christ, we used only one text. I was amazed at what a change this small difference had on this discipleship process. This adjustment had zero impact on the *content* of the lesson, but it had a massive impact on what we *modeled* for these new believers. In addition to learning about their new life in Christ, they also learned about the importance of context and how one verse interacts with the verses around it. By the end of the first lesson, these brand-new believers could answer the question, "What is the main point of this passage?" with greater accuracy than many preachers!

Now, regardless of whether or not these new converts would become leaders in the years to come, our modeling of sound biblical interpretation equipped them with the tools to read and apply Scripture in their own devotional life. Hermeneutics is not just some class that people take in seminary. The ability to understand the meaning of the author in a way that leads to life-changing practical application is a skill that every believer needs.

A second reason why training in biblical interpretation should be a part of missions strategy is that such training equips future pastors to faithfully lead their churches. Unlike most seminaries in the West, the majority of students in our seminary training programs in Asia already have significant ministerial experience. What I hear most from these students, though, is that until they took our courses, they never really knew how to interpret Scripture. One student, in his early thirties and already preaching and teaching on a regular basis at a large and influential network of churches, told me, "Before, when I would preach, I would decide what I wanted to say, and then I would try to find a verse or two that said the same thing."

This dear brother, after learning some basic interpretation skills, went on to say, "Now I understand how to make the main point of the text the main point of my sermon." Such an admission should be encouraging to missionaries because it is easy to see what a difference this change will make in the life of newly planted church. Like Philip in Acts 8, this brother will be able to "guide" both believers in his church and unbelievers in his community for years to come through his application of the original author's meaning to their ever-changing cultural context.

Third, training in biblical interpretation equips leaders for appropriate contextualization. As we saw in chapter 4, discussions of contextualization often focus on the initial communication of the gospel to the target group, but, in reality, the process of contextualization goes far beyond this initial act of communication. After trusting in Christ, this group of people must work with the missionary to evaluate many of their cultural practices in light of biblical revelation. Paul Hiebert referred to this process as "critical contextualization."

The critical contextualization process is not easy to work though in that believers need to be able to exegete both their own cultural background and that of the biblical text. In chapter 11 we examined the issue of ancestor veneration among Chinese believers and saw that to navigate this issue believers need to examine both the cultural practice and relevant biblical texts. To do proper contextualization and think in biblical ways about the practice, they must have the exegetical ability to study those texts and apply the teachings in a way that leads to a new contextualized practice.

The previous example starts with the cultural practice and looks to Scripture for teaching that relates to such a practice, but the opposite is also true. In chapter 11 we considered several examples where we started with a specific text of Scripture and considered how the teaching of that text relates to a specific cultural practice. To consider one more example,

Importance of Hermeneutics in Missions Contexts

a preacher might start with 1 Peter 1:13–21, which commands believers to live a life a holiness and fear, while setting their hope on the return of Christ. His goal is to guide the church to better understand what a holy lifestyle looks like in their specific cultural context.

Good contextualization, then, goes far beyond the communication of the gospel. In fact, communication of the gospel is only the first step in the contextualization process. In some cases, the contextualization process starts with a specific cultural practice, but in others it starts with a specific biblical text. In both cases, though, if contextualization is to be done well, it is absolutely essential that believers in those churches, and especially the leaders of those churches, be trained to rightly handle the word.

A fourth reason for training in biblical interpretation is that it prepares missionaries for future service. While planting healthy churches among the target group is certainly the short-term goal of the missionary, the long-term goal is seeing those newly planted churches send out their own missionaries to other people groups. Just like the missionary who brought the gospel to his people group, this newly sent missionary will need to communicate the gospel, teach new believers, and lead the church he plants through the critical contextualization process—all tasks that require strong biblical interpretation skills.

Two years ago, I taught an NT exegesis course to a group of church leaders. Unbeknownst to me, one of the leaders in the group was preparing to spend six months sharing the gospel among a people group that is less than 0.5 percent evangelical Christian. Seven months later, I returned to the same city to teach another course, and I had a chance to reconnect with that brother. He shared with me some of the challenges he faced and then told me what best equipped him to communicate the gospel cross-culturally were the courses he'd taken on how to interpret Scripture. Training in biblical interpretation results in missionaries who are more effective at communicating and contextualizing the gospel message.

Fifth, and finally, training in biblical interpretation enables the planting of healthy churches. No one wants their work to be done in vain. The apostle Paul certainly didn't. As a result of persecution, he was only able to stay in Thessalonica for a few weeks. In time, these new believers also faced persecution, and Paul feared that some would turn away from the faith. He wrote in 1 Thessalonians 3:5 that such a result would mean "our labor would be in vain." If the churches Paul planted turned away from the faith or didn't stay faithful the gospel, his time and efforts were wasted.

Some missionaries emphasize the fact that Paul planted a church and then moved on as quickly as possible. In reality, though, Paul was frequently *forced* to leave quickly when persecution arose. The two exceptions were Corinth and Ephesus, where Paul stayed for eighteen months and three years, respectively. Paul not only cared about the existence of a church in these locations, he also cared deeply about the health of those churches. To put it another way, Paul not only cared about the birth of a church, he also cared about its longevity.

In considering Paul's example, we recognize that the question missionaries should be asking is not "How can we plant churches quickly?" The question we should be asking is "How can we plant churches that are healthy?" Certainly, one mark of a healthy church is that it is able to interpret Scripture and apply it to the local context. Training in biblical hermeneutics does not aim to answer every possible theological question, but, in contrast, it equips believers to find answers for themselves through their own faithful study of the Scriptures.

The foundation of healthy theology is healthy interpretation of Scripture. Christians in any culture look to Scripture to develop their theological convictions. How they handle Scripture affects how they work out their positions on key theological issues. It also impacts how they utilize Scripture in addressing critical issues of their context. If these new believers adopt healthy methods of interpretation, healthy theology—without a doubt a key mark of a healthy church—will follow.

Imagine for a moment that the Spirit never led Philip into the desert to cross paths with the eunuch. How different would this story have been if Philip had never led the eunuch to the correct interpretation of the passage? The sad truth is that believers in many parts of the world have had little training in biblical interpretation. Not only has no one "guided" them with good interpretational skills, but, as a result, now they are unable to guide others well. Missionaries would do well to heed the words of Peter, who wrote that Scripture both imparts new life (1 Pet 1:23) and engenders ongoing growth in Christ (1 Pet 2:2). If missionaries want their work to last, if they want to plant healthy churches, if they want local believers to know how to read Scripture and apply it to their lives, they must train them to rightly divide the word.

Bibliography

Abad-Santos, Alex. "Avengers: Endgame's 1.2 Billion Opening Weekend Is the Biggest in Movie History." https://www.vox.com/2019/4/29/18521581/avengers-endgame-box-office-1-2-billion.

Adamo, D. T. "Reading Psalm 23 in African Context." *Verbum et Ecclesia* 39.1 (2018). https://verbumetecclesia.org.za/index.php/ve/article/view/1783/3382#CIT0003_1783.

———. "The Task and Distinctiveness of African Biblical Hermeneutics." *Old Testament Essays* 28 (2015) 31–52.

Ajibade, Ezekiel A. *Expository Preaching in Africa: Engaging Orality for Effective Proclamation.* Carlisle, UK: Hippo, 2021.

Allen, Roland. *Missionary Methods: St. Paul's or Ours?* Grand Rapids: Eerdmans, 1962.

———. *The Spontaneous Expansion of the Church: And the Causes That Hinder It.* Eugene, OR: Wipf & Stock, 1997.

Allison, Gregg R. "Theological Interpretation of Scripture: An Introduction and Preliminary Evaluation." *The Southern Baptist Journal of Theology* 14 (2010) 28–37.

Ali, Shah, and J. Dudley Woodberry, "South Asia: Vegetables, Fish, and Messianic Mosques." In *Perspectives on the World Christian Movement.* edited by Ralph D. Winter and Steven C. Hawthorne, 680–82. 3rd ed. Pasadena: William Carey, 1999.

Anderson, Justice. "The Great Century and Beyond (1792–1910)." In *Missiology: An Introduction to the Foundations, History, and Strategies of World Missions,* edited by John Mark Terry, Ebbie Smith, and Justice Anderson, 199–218. Nashville: B & H, 1998.

———. *To Advance the Gospel: Basic Writings in the Theory and Practice of Missions.* Edited by R. Pierce Beaver. Grand Rapids: Eerdmans, 1967.

Anderson, Rufus. "Principles and Methods of Modern Missions." In *Classics of Christian Missions,* edited by Francis M. DuBose, 249–56. Nashville: Broadman, 1979.

Arnett, Randy. *Pentecostalization: The Evolution of Baptists in Africa.* Scotts Valley, CA: CreateSpace, 2017.

Arnold, Clinton E. *3 Crucial Questions about Spiritual Warfare.* Edited by Grant Osborne and Richard Jones. 3 Crucial Questions 12. Grand Rapids: Baker, 1997.

Atkins, Jackson. "Multiplying Disciples in an Oral Context." In *Beyond Literate Models: Contextualizing Theological Education in Oral Contexts,* edited by Samuel E. Chiang and Grant Lovejoy, 77–84. Hong Kong: International Orality Network, 2013.

Bailey, Kenneth E. *The Cross & the Prodigal: Luke 15 Through the Eyes of Middle Eastern Peasants.* 2nd ed. Downers Grove: IVP, 2005.

Bibliography

———. *Jesus through Middle Eastern Eyes: Cultural Studies in the Gospels*. Downers Grove: IVP Academic, 2008.

Barnes, Philip Wayne. "Missiology Meets Cultural Anthropology: The Life and Legacy of Paul G. Hiebert." PhD diss., The Southern Baptist Theological Seminary, 2011.

Barnes, Philip W., et al., eds. *The Abandoned Gospel: Confronting Neo-Pentecostalism and the Prosperity Gospel in Sub-Saharan Africa*. Africa: AB316, 2021.

Beale, G. K., and D. A. Carson, eds. *Commentary on the New Testament Use of the Old Testament*. Grand Rapids: Baker Academic, 2007.

Beaver, R. Pierce. "Introduction: Rufus Anderson, Grand Strategist of American Missions." In *To Advance the Gospel: Basic Writings in the Theory and Practice of Missions*, edited by R. Pierce Beaver, 9–44. Grand Rapids: Eerdmans, 1967.

Best, Ernest. *Second Corinthians*. Edited by James Luther Mays. Louisville: John Knox, 1987.

Blazyte, Agne. "Number of Starbucks Stores in China." *Statista*. https://www.statista.com/statistics/277795/number-of-starbucks-stores-in-china/.

Blue, Scott A. "The Hermeneutic of E. D. Hirsch Jr. and Its Impact on Expository Preaching: Friend or Foe?" *Journal of the Evangelical Theological Society* 44 (2001) 253–69.

Block, Daniel. *Judges, Ruth*. Edited by E. Ray Clendenen and Kenneth A. Matthews. New American Commentary 6. Nashville: B & H Academic, 1999.

Bock, Darrell L. *Luke 9:51—24:53*. Edited by Moisés Silva. Baker Exegetical Commentary on the New Testament. Grand Rapids: Baker, 1996.

Bosch, David J. *Transforming Mission: Paradigm Shifts in Theology of Mission*. Maryknoll, NY: Orbis, 2000.

Brock, Charles. *Indigenous Church Planting: A Practical Journey*. Neosho, MO: Church Growth International, 1994.

Brooks, Will. "Critiquing Ethnohermeneutics Theories: A Call to an Author-Oriented Approach to Cross-Cultural Biblical Interpretation." PhD diss., The Southern Baptist Theological Seminary, 2011.

———. "Grammatical-Historical Exegesis and World Mission." In *World Mission: Theology, Strategy, and Current Issues*, edited by Scott Callaham and Will Brooks, 239–67. Bellingham, WA: Lexham, 2019.

———. "Theological Education as an Integral Component of World Mission." In *World Mission: Theology, Strategy, and Current Issues*, edited by Scott Callaham and Will Brooks, 177–203. Bellingham, WA: Lexham, 2019.

Brown, Jeannine K. *Scripture as Communication: Introducing Biblical Hermeneutics*. 2nd ed. Grand Rapids: Baker, 2021. https://www.scribd.com/book/515479651/Scripture-as-Communication-Introducing-Biblical-Hermeneutics.

Caldwell, Larry. "Cross-cultural Bible Interpretation: A View from the Field." *Phronesis* 39 (1996) 13–35.

———. *Doing Bible Interpretation! Making the Bible Come Alive for Yourself and Your People*. Sioux Falls, SD: Lazy Oaks, 2016.

———. "Doing Theology across Cultures: A New Methodology for an Old Task." *International Journal of Frontier Missions* 4 (1987) 3–7.

———. "Part 1: Reconsidering Our Biblical Roots, Bible Interpretation, the Apostle Paul and Mission Today." *International Journal of Frontier Missiology* 29.2 (2012) 91–100.

———. "Part 2: Reconsidering Our Biblical Roots, Bible Interpretation, the Apostle Paul and Mission Today." *International Journal of Frontier Missiology* 29.3 (2012) 61–69.

———. "Receptor-Oriented Hermeneutics: Reclaiming the Hermeneutical Methodologies of the New Testament for Bible Interpreters in the Twenty-First Century." PhD diss., Fuller Theological Seminary, 1990.

———. "A Response to the Responses of Tappeiner and Whelchel to Ethnohermeneutics." *Journal of Asian Missions* 2 (2000) 135–45.

———. "Third Horizon Ethnohermeneutics: Re-Evaluating New Testament Hermeneutical Models for Intercultural Bible Interpreters Today." *Asia Journal of Theology* 1 (1987) 314–33.

———. "Toward Ethnohermeneutics Contextualization 2.0 and Beyond . . ." *Didaktikos Journal* (2018).

———. "Towards an Ethnohermeneutical Model for a Lowland Filipino Context." *Journal of Asian Mission* 7 (2005) 169–93.

———. "Towards the New Discipline of Ethnohermeneutics: Questioning the Relevancy of Western Hermeneutical Methods in the Asian Context." *Journal of Asian Mission* 1 (1999) 21–43.

Carson, D. A. "Church and Mission: Reflections on Contextualization and the Third Horizon." In *The Church in the Bible and the World: An International Study*. edited by D. A. Carson, 213–57. Grand Rapids: Baker, 1987.

———. *The Gospel According to John*. The Pillar New Testament Commentary. Grand Rapids: Eerdmans, 2001.

Carson, D. A., and Douglas J. Moo. *An Introduction to the New Testament*. 2nd ed. Grand Rapids: Zondervan, 2005.

Chan, Simon. *Grassroots Asian Theology: Thinking the Faith from the Ground Up*. Downers Grove: IVP Academic, 2014.

Chang, Jung, and Jon Halliday. *Mao: The Unknown Story*. New York: Anchor, 2005.

Chen, Kwang Yu. "The Book of Odes: A Case Study of the Chinese Hermeneutic Tradition." In *Interpretation and Intellectual Change: Chinese Hermeneutics in Historical Perspective*, edited by Ching-I Tu, 47–61. New Brunswick, NJ: Transaction, 2005.

Chiang, Samuel E., and Grant Lovejoy, eds. *Beyond Literate Models: Contextualizing Theological Education in Oral Contexts*. Hong Kong: International Orality Network, 2013.

———. *Beyond Literate Western Contexts: Honor & Shame and Assessment of Orality Preference*. Hong Kong: International Orality Network, 2015.

———. *Beyond Western Practices: Continuing Conversations in Orality and Theological Education*. Hong Kong: International Orality Network, 2014. https://orality.net/wp-content/uploads/2015/11/Beyond-Literate-Western-Practices.pdf.

"Chicago Statement on Biblical Hermeneutics." *Journal of Evangelical Theological Society* 25.4 (1984) 397–401. https://www.etsjets.org/files/JETS-PDFs/25/25-4/25-4-pp397-401_JETS.pdf.

Chou, Abner. *The Hermeneutics of the Biblical Writers: Learning to Interpret Scripture from the Prophets and Apostles*. Grand Rapids: Kregel, 2018. https://www.perlego.com/book/2998898/the-hermeneutics-of-the-biblical-writers-learning-to-interpret-scripture-from-the-prophets-and-apostles-pdf.

Chua, Daniel M. W. *Feeding on Ashes*. Petaling Jaya, Selangor, Malaysia: Kairos Research Centre, 1998.

Conn, Harvie M. *Eternal Word and Changing Worlds: Theology, Anthropology, and Mission in Trialogue*. Grand Rapids: Zondervan, 1984.

Bibliography

Corwin, Gary. "A Response to My Respondents: The Dialog Continues." *International Journal of Frontier Missiology* 24 (2007) 53–56.

Corwin, Gary, et al. "A Humble Appeal to C5/Insider Movement Muslim Ministry Advocates to Consider Ten Questions." *International Journal of Frontier Missiology* 24 (2007) 5–20.

Craigie, Peter C., and Marvin E. Tate. *Psalms 1–50*. Edited by Bruce M Metzger et al. World Biblical Commentary. 2nd edition. Grand Rapids: Zondervan, 2018. https://www.perlego.com/book/727793/psalms-150-volume-19-pdf.

Crain, Caleb. "Why We Don't Read, Revisited." *The New Yorker*, June 14, 2018. https://www.newyorker.com/culture/cultural-comment/why-we-dont-read-revisited.

Dever, Mark. *Nine Marks of a Healthy Church*. 3rd ed. Wheaton, IL: Crossway, 2013.

DuBose, Francis M. "John L. Nevius: Introduction." In *Classics of Christian Missions*, edited by Francis M. DuBose, 256–57. Nashville: Broadman, 1979.

Edmond, Charlotte. "Global Migration, by the Numbers: Who Migrates, Where They Go, and Why." *World Economic Forum*, January 10, 2020. https://www.weforum.org/agenda/2020/01/iom-global-migration-report-international-migrants-2020/.

Edwards, James R. *The Gospel According to Luke*. Edited by D. A. Carson. The Pillar New Testament Commentary. Grand Rapids: Eerdmans, 2015. https://www.perlego.com/book/1470287/the-gospel-according-to-luke-pdf.

Espiritu, Daniel L. "Ethnohermeneutics or Oikohermeneutics: Questioning the Necessity of Caldwell's Hermeneutics." *Journal of Asian Mission* 3 (2001) 272.

Etherington, Norman. "Introduction." In *Missions and Empire*, edited by Norman Etherington, 1–18. Oxford History of the British Empire, vol. 5. New York: Oxford University Press, 2005.

Friedman, Zack. "50% of Millennials Are Moving Back Home with Their Parents after College." *Forbes*, July 6, 2019. https://www.forbes.com/sites/zackfriedman/2019/06/06/millennials-move-back-home-college/?sh=6f787fd638ad.

Frost, Katie. "Non-Narrative Internalization." *Orality Landscape of Practice*. July 2021. https://sites.google.com/view/oralitylop/documents/hom/july-2021-non-narrative-internalization?authuser=0.

Gadamer, Hans-Georg. *Truth and Method: Elements of Philisophical Hermeneutics*. Translated by Joel Weinsheimer and Donald G. Marshall. 2nd ed. New York: Continuum, 1996.

Gaffin, Jr., Richard B. "The Redemptive-Historical View." In *Biblical Hermeneutics: Five Views*, edited by Stanley E. Porter and Beth M. Stovell, 89–110. Downers Grove: IVP Academic, 2012.

Garland, David E. *Luke*. Edited by Clinton A. Arnold. Zondervan Exegetical Commenary on the New Testament. Grand Rapids: Zondervan, 2011.

Green, Joel B. *The Gospel of Luke*. Edited by Ned Stonehouse et al. The New International Commentary on the New Testament. Grand Rapids: Eerdmans, 1997.

George, Timothy. *Faithful Witness: The Life and Mission of William Carey*. Worcester, PA: Church History Institute, 1998.

Georges, Jayson, and Mark D. Baker. *Ministering in Honor/shame Cultures: Biblical Foundations and Practical Essentials*. Downers Grove: IVP Academic, 2016.

Grunlan, Stephen A., and Marvin K. Mayers. *Cultural Anthropology: A Christian Perspective*. Grand Rapids: Zondervan, 1988.

Harris, Murray J. *The Second Epistle to the Corinthians*. The New International Greek Testament Commentary. Grand Rapids: Eerdmans, 2005.

Bibliography

Hesselgrave, David J. *10 Key Questions in Christian Missions Today.* Grand Rapids: Kregel, 2005.

———. *Communicating Christ Cross-Culturally: An Introduction to Missionary Communication.* 2nd ed. Grand Rapids: Zondervan, 1991.

———. "Contextualization and Revelational Epistemology." In *Hermeneutics, Inerrancy, & the Bible: Papers from ICBI Summit II*, edited by Earl D. Radmacher and Robert D. Preus, 691–738. Grand Rapids: Academie, 1984.

———. "Contextualization That Is Authentic and Relevant." *International Journal of Frontier Missions* 12 (1995) 115–19.

Hesselgrave, David J., and Edward Rommen. *Contextualization: Meanings, Methods, and Models.* Pasadena: William Carey, 1989.

Hiebert, Paul. *Anthropological Insights for Missionaries.* Grand Rapids: Baker, 1985.

———. *Anthropological Reflections on Missiological Issues.* Grand Rapids: Baker, 1994.

———. "Critical Contextualization." *International Bulletin of Missionary Research* 11 (1987) 104–12.

———. "The Flaw of the Excluded Middle." *Missiology.* 10.1 (1982) 35–47.

———. *The Gospel in Human Contexts: Anthropological Explorations for Contemporary Missions.* Grand Rapids: Baker, 2009.

———. "The Gospel in Human Contexts: Changing Perceptions of Contextualization." In *Missionshift: Global Mission Issues in the Third Millenium*, edited by David J. Hesselgrave and Ed Stetzer, 82–102. Nashville: B & H Academic, 2010.

———. "An Introduction to Mission Anthropology." In *Crucial Dimensions in World Evangelization*, edited by Arthur Glasser et al., 45–88. Pasadena: William Carey, 1976.

———. "The Missionary as Mediator of Global Theologizing." In *Globalizing Theology: Belief and Practice in an Era of World Christianity*, edited by Craig Ott and Harold A. Netland, 288–308. Grand Rapids: Baker, 2006.

Higgins, Kevin. "Acts 15 and Insider Movements among Muslims: Questions, Process, and Conclusions." *International Journal of Frontier Missiology* 24 (2007) 29–40.

———. "Diverse Voices: Hearing Scripture Speak in a Multicultural Environment." Paper presented to the Evangelical Missiological Society, Charlotte, NC, September 2010.

———. "The Key to Insider Movements: The 'Devoted's' of Acts: How Insider Movements Relate to the Nature of the Gospel Itself." *International Journal of Frontier Missiology* 21 (2004) 155–66.

Hinkle, Adrian. *Pedagogical Theory of Wisdom Literature: An Application of Educational Theory to Biblical Texts.* Eugene, OR: Wipf & Stock, 2017. https://www.perlego.com/book/881889/pedagogical-theory-of-wisdom-literature-pdf.

Hirsch, Jr., E. D. *The Aims of Interpretation.* Chicago: The University of Chicago Press, 1976.

———. "Meaning and Significance Reinterpreted." *Critical Inquiry* 11 (1984) 202–25.

———. *Validity in Interpretation.* New Haven: Yale University Press, 1967.

Hoefer, Herbert E. *Churchless Christianity.* Pasadena: William Carey, 2001.

Hodges, Melvin L. *The Indigenous Church: A Complete Handbook on How to Grow Young Churches.* Springfield, MO: Gospel, 1953.

———. "Why Indigenous Church Principles." In *Readings in Dynamic Indigeneity*, edited by Charles H. Kraft and Tom N. Wisley, 6–14. Pasadena: William Carey, 1979.

Holloman, Henry. "Response by Henry Holloman to Third Horizon Ethnohermeneutics: Re-Evaluating New Testament Hermeneutical Methods for Intercultural Bible

Interpreters Today by Larry W. Caldwell." Paper presented at the annual meeting of the Evangelical Missiological Society, Wheaton, IL, 1988.

Hwang, Jerry. "'How Long Will My Glory Be Reproach?' Honour and Shame in Old Testament Lament Traditions." Old Testamen Essays 30.3 (2017) 684–706. http://www.scielo.org.za/pdf/ote/v30n3/08.pdf.

International Orality Network. *Making Disciples of Oral Learners*. Edited by Grant Lovejoy et al. Bangalore, India: International Orality Network, 2005.

Jariya, Imum. "Western Cultural Values and Its Implications on Management Practices." *South East Asian Journal of Contemporary Business, Economics and Law* 1 (2012) 61–70. http://seajbel.com/wp-content/uploads/2014/07/Western-Cultural-Values-And-Its-Implications-On-Management-Practices-A.M.-Inun-Jariya.pdf.

Johnson, Elliott E. "Author's Intention and Biblical Interpretation." In *Hermeneutics, Inerrancy, & the Bible: Papers from ICBI Summit II*, edited by Earl D. Radmacher and Robert D. Preus, 407–30. Grand Rapids: Zondervan, 1984.

Kaiser, Walter C. *Toward an Exegetical Theology: Biblical Exegesis for Preaching & Teaching*. Grand Rapids: Baker Academic, 1981.

Kaiser Jr., Walter C. "The Single Intent of Scripture." In *Right Doctrine, Wrong Text: Essays on the Use of the Old Testament in the New*, edited by G. K. Beale, 55-69. Grand Rapids: Baker, 1994.

———. *The Uses of the Old Testament in the New*. Eugene, OR: Wipf & Stock, 2001.

Kaiser Jr., Walter C., and Moises Silva. *Introduction to Biblical Hermeneutics: The Search for Meaning*. Revised ed. Grand Rapids: Zondervan, 2007.

Kaptain, Steve. "Globalization Acculturation in Honor Shame Contexts: Competing Value Systems and Identity Confusion among Secondary Students in Kathmandu, Nepal." DMiss diss., Malaysia Baptist Theological Seminary, 2021.

Kato, Byang H. "The Gospel, Cultural Context, and Religious Syncretism." In *Let the Earth Hear His Voice: International Congress on World Evangelization, Lausanne, Switzerland*, edited by J. D. Douglas, 1216–28. Minneapolis: World Wide Publications, 1975.

Kim, Matthew, and Daniel Wong. *Finding Our Voice: A Vision for Asian North American Preaching*. Bellingham, WA: Lexham, 2020. https://www.perlego.com/book/2572310/finding-our-voice-pdf.

Köstenberger, Andreas J. *John*. Baker Exegetical Commentary on the New Testament. Grand Rapids: Baker, 2004.

———. *The Mission of Jesus and the Disciples According to the Fourth Gospel: With Implications for the Fourth Gospel's Purpose and the Mission of the Contemporary Church*. Grand Rapids: Eerdmans, 1998.

Kraft, Charles H. *Christianity in Culture: A Study in Biblical Theologizing in Cross-Cultural Perspective*. Revised ed. Maryknoll, NY: Orbis, 2005.

———. "Dynamic Equivalence Churches." *Missiology* 1 (1973) 39–57.

———. "Toward a Christian Ethnotheology." In *God, Man, and Church Growth*, edited by Alan Tippett, 109–26. Grand Rapids: Eerdmans, 1973.

Kristeva, Julia. "Word, Dialogue and Novel." In *The Kristeva Reader*, edited by Tori Moi and Julia Kristeva, 34–61. New York: Columbia University Press, 1986.

Kruse, Colin G. *The Second Epistle of Paul to the Corinthians: An Introduction and Commentary*. The Tyndale New Testament Commentaries. Grand Rapids: Eerdmans, 1987.

Bibliography

Kuruvilla, Abraham. *Judges: A Theological Commentary for Preachers.* Eugene, OR: Cascade, 2017. https://www.perlego.com/book/881840/judges-pdf.

Kwan, Simon Shui-man. "From Indigenization to Contextualization: A Change in Discursive Practice Rather than a Shift in Paradigm." *Studies in World Christianity* 11 (2005) 237–38.

Lanier, Sarah. *Foreign to Familiar: A Guide to Understanding Hot and Cold Climate Cultures.* Hagerstown, MD: McDougal, 2010.

Larkin, William J. *Cultural and Biblical Hermeneutics.* Grand Rapids: Baker, 1988.

Latourette, Kenneth Scott. *A History of the Expansion of Christianity.* New York: Harper & Brothers, 1937.

Lawless, Chuck. "Urgency and Healthy Church Planting." *The Great Commission Baptist Journal of Missions* 1.1 (2022). https://serials.atla.com/gcbjm/article/view/3101/4003.

Lee, Archie C. C. "The Chinese Creation Myth of Nu Kua and the Biblical Narrative in Genesis 1–11." *Biblical Interpretation* 2 (1994) 312–24.

———. "Cross-Textual Hermeneutics." In *Dictionary of Third World Theologies*, edited by Virginia Fabella and R. S. Sugirtharajah, 60–62. Maryknoll, NY: Orbis, 2000.

———. "Cross-Textual Hermeneutics on Gospel and Culture." *Asia Journal of Theology* 10 (1996) 38–48.

———. "Cross-Textual Interpretation and Its Implications for Biblical Studies." In *Teaching the Bible: The Discourses and Politics of Biblical Pedagogy*, edited by Fernando F. Segovia and Mary Ann Tolbert, 247–54. Maryknoll, NY: Orbis, 1998.

———. "Cross-Textual Reading Strategy: A Study of Late Ming and Early Qing Chinese Christian Writings." *Ching Feng* 4 (2004) 1–27.

———. "The David-Bathsheba Story and the Parable of Nathan." In *Voices from the Margin: Interpreting the Bible in the Third World*, edited by R. S. Sugirtharajah, 189–204. London: SPCK, 1991.

———. "The Dragon, the Deluge, and Creation Theology." In *Frontiers in Asian Christian Theology: Emerging Trends*, edited by R. S. Sugirtharajah, 97–108. Maryknoll, NY: Orbis, 1994.

———. "Doing Theology in the Chinese Context: The David-Bathsheba Story and the Parable of Nathan." *East Asia Journal of Theology* 3 (1985) 243–57.

———. "Returning to China: Biblical Interpretation in Postcolonial Hong Kong." *Biblical Interpretation* 7 (1999) 156–73.

———. "When the Flood Narrative of Genesis Meets Its Counterpart in China: Reception and Challenge in Cross-Textual Reading." In *Genesis*, edited by Athalya Brenner, Archie Chi Chung Lee, and Gale A. Yee, 81–97. Minneapolis, Fortress, 2010.

Lee, Peter K. H. "Two Stories of Loyalty." *Ching Feng* 32 (1989) 24–40.

Leeman, Jonathan. *Word Centered Church: How Scripture Brings Life and Growth to God's People.* Chicago: Moody, 2017.

Leschert, Dale. "A Change of Meaning, Not a Change of Mind: The Clarification of a Suspected Defection in the Hermeneutical Theory of E. D. Hirsch Jr." *Journal of the Evangelical Theological Society* 35 (1992) 183–87.

Lewis, Rebecca. "Promoting Movements to Christ within Natural Connections: A Proposed Definition of Insider Movements." *International Journal of Frontier Missiology* 24.2 (2007) 75–76.

Lim, David S. "Contextualizing Ancestor Veneration: An Historical Review." *International Journal of Frontier Missions* 32.3 (2015) 109–115. http://www.ijfm.org/PDFs_IJFM/32_3_PDFs/IJFM_32_3-Lim.pdf.

Bibliography

———. "Contextualizing Ancestor Veneration: A Theological Survey and Practical Steps for Implementation." *International Journal of Frontier Missions* 32.4 (2015) 183–194. http://www.ijfm.org/PDFs_IJFM/32_4_PDFs/IJFM_32_4-Lim.pdf.

Lingenfelter, Sherwood, and Marvin K. Mayers. *Ministering Cross-Culturally: A Model for Effective Personal Relationships*. 3rd ed. Grand Rapids: Baker, 2016.

Lo, Miki. "Using Narrative Analysis to Find the Author's Meaning: With Reference to Luke 2:41–52 as an Example." Unpublished paper.

Longenecker, Richard. *Biblical Exegesis in the Apostolic Period*. Grand Rapids: Eerdmans, 1975.

Lovejoy, Grant. "Teaching the New Testament Epistles Through Chronological Storying." Unpublished paper. https://orality.info/wp-content/uploads/2022/04/Teaching-Epistles-in-Oral-Contexts.pdf

Maxwell, David. "Decolonization." In *Missions and Empire*, edited by Norman Etherington, 285–306. Oxford History of the British Empire, vol. 5. New York: Oxford University Press, 2005.

Mburu, Elizabeth. *African Hermeneutics*. Langham Creative Projects. Carlisle, UK: Hippo, 2019. https://www.perlego.com/book/918430/.

McCaulley, Esau. *Reading While Black: African American Biblical Interpretation as an Exercise in Hope*. Downers Grove: IVP Academic, 2020.

Miles, Todd L. *A God of Many Understandings? The Gospel and a Theology of Religions*. Nashville: B & H, 2010.

Moberly, R. W. L. "What Is Theological Interpretation of Scripture?" *Journal of Theological Interpretation* 3.2 (2009) 161–78.

Musopole, A. C. "Witchcraft Terminology, The Bible, and African Christian Theology: An Exercise in Hermeneutics." *Journal of Religion in Africa* 23 (1993) 347–54.

Neill, Stephen. *A History of Christian Missions*. The Penguin History of the Church, vol. 6. 2nd ed. New York: Penguin, 1990.

Nevius, Helen S. Coan. *The Life of John Livingston Nevius: For Forty Years a Missionary in China*. New York: Fleming H. Revell, 1895.

Nida, Eugene. *Message and Mission: The Community of Christian Faith*. Pasadena: William Carey, 1990.

Nishioka, Yoshiyuki Billy. "Worldview Methodology in Mission Theology: A Comparison Between Kraft's and Hiebert's Approaches." *Missiology* 26 (1998) 468–69.

Ong, Walter. *Orality and Literacy: The Technologizing of the World*. Thirtieth Anniversary Edition. New York: Routledge, 2012.

Osborne, Grant R. *The Hermeneutical Spiral: A Comprehensive Introduction to Biblical Interpretation*. Revised ed. Downers Grove: Intervarsity, 2006.

Page, Sydney H. T. *Powers of Evil: A Biblical Study of Satan & Demons*. Grand Rapids: Baker, 1995.

Parshall, Phil. "Danger! New Directions in Contextualization." *Evangelical Missions Quarterly* 34 (1998) 405.

———. *Muslim Evangelism: Contemporary Approaches to Contextualization*. Revised ed. Waynesboro, GA: Gabriel, 2003.

Penner, Myron B. "Introduction." In *Christianity and the Postmodern Turn: Six Views*, edited by Myron B. Penner, 13–36. Grand Rapids: Brazos, 2005.

Pennington, Jonathan. *Reading the Gospels Wisely: A Narrative and Theological Introduction*. Grand Rapids: Baker, 2012.

Bibliography

Plummer, Robert L. *40 Questions about Interpreting the Bible.* Edited by Benjamin L. Merkle. 40 Questions Series. Grand Rapids: Kregel, 2010.

Poceski, Mario. *Introducing Chinese Religions.* Edited by Damien Keown and Charles S. Prebish. World Religions Series. New York: Routledge, 2009.

Porter, Andrew. "An Overview, 1700–1914." In *Missions and Empire*, edited by Norman Etherington, 40–63. Oxford History of the British Empire, vol. 5. New York: Oxford University Press, 2005.

Radmacher, Earl D. "Introduction." In *Hermeneutics, Inerrancy, & the Bible: Papers from ICBI Summit II*, edited by Earl D. Radmacher and Robert D. Preus, xi–xiii. Grand Rapids: Zondervan, 1984.

———. "A Response to Author's Intention and Biblical Interpretation." In *Hermeneutics, Inerrancy, & the Bible: Papers from ICBI Summit II*, edited by Earl D. Radmacher and Robert D. Preus, 431–38. Grand Rapids: Zondervan, 1984.

Richards, Randolph, and Brandon J. O'Brien. *Misreading Scripture with Western Eyes: Removing Cultural Barriers to Better Understand the Bible.* Downers Grove: IVP, 2012.

Ricoeur, Paul. *Interpretation Theory: Discourse and the Surplus of Meaning.* Fort Worth: Texas Christian University Press, 1967.

Ridgway, John. "Insider Movements in the Gospels and Acts: The Biblical Roots of 'Insider Movements.'" *International Journal of Frontier Missiology* 24 (2007) 77–86.

Rogers, Everett M., and Thomas M. Steinfatt. *Intercultural Communication.* Long Grove, IL: Waveland, 1999.

Sauter, Mark. "Theological Education for the Deaf." In *Beyond Western Practices: Continuing Conversations in Orality and Theological Education*, edited by Samuel E. Chiang and Grant Lovejoy, 63–72. Hong Kong: International Orality Network, 2014. https://orality.net/wp-content/uploads/2015/11/Beyond-Literate-Western-Practices.pdf.

Schleiermacher, Friedrich D. E. *Hermeneutics: The Handwritten Manuscripts.* Edited by Heinz Kimmerle, translated by James Duke and Jack Forstman. Atlanta: Scholars, 1977.

Schnabel, Eckhard J. *Paul the Missionary: Realities, Strategies and Methods.* Downers Grove: IVP Academic, 2008, 236–41.

Schreiner, Thomas R. *Paul, Apostle of God's Glory in Christ: A Pauline Theology.* Downers Grove: Intervarsity, 2001.

Steffen, Tom, and William Bjoraker. *The Return of Oral Hermeneutics: As Good Today as It Was for the Hebrew Bible and First-Century Christianity.* Eugene, OR: Wipf & Stock, 2020. https://www.perlego.com/book/1707046/the-return-of-oral-hermeneutics-pdf.

Stein, Robert H. *A Basic Guide to Interpreting the Bible: Playing by the Rules.* Grand Rapids: Baker, 1994.

———. "The Benefits of an Author-Oriented Approach to Hermeneutics." *Journal of the Evangelical Theological Society* 44 (2001) 451–66.

Stinson, Randy, and Dan Dumas. *A Guide to Biblical Manhood: How to Serve Your Wife, How to Mold Men through Baseball, How to Make Men in the Church, & More.* Louisville: SBTS, 2011.

Sugirtharajah, R. S. *Asian Biblical Hermeneutics and Postcolonialism: Contesting the Interpretations.* Maryknoll, NY: Orbis, 1999.

Bibliography

———. *The Bible and the Third World: Precolonial, Colonial, and Postcolonial Encounters*. New York: Cambridge University Press, 2003.

———. "Bible: Introduction." In *Dictionary of Third World Theology*. edited by Virginia Fabella and R. S. Sugirtharajah, 13–15. Maryknoll, NY: Orbis, 2000.

———. "Introduction." In *Frontiers in Asian Christian Theology: Emerging Trends*, edited by R. S. Sugirtharajah, 1–10. Maryknoll, NY: Orbis, 1994.

———. "Prologue and Perspective." In *Asian Faces of Jesus*, edited by R. S. Sugirtharajah, vii–xiii. Faith and Cultures Series. Maryknoll, NY: Orbis, 1993.

———. *Postcolonial Criticism and Biblical Interpretation*. New York: Oxford University Press, 2002.

———. *Troublesome Texts: The Bible in Colonial and Contemporary Culture*. Edited by J. Cheryl Exum, Jorunn Økland, and Stephen D. Moore. The Bible in the Modern World 17. Sheffield, UK: Sheffield Phoenix, 2008.

Sun, Wendel. "Biblical Theology and World Mission." In *World Mission: Theology, Strategy, and Current Issues*, edited by Scott Callaham and Will Brooks, 67–101. Bellingham, WA: Lexham, 2019.

Tappeiner, Daniel A. "A Response to Caldwell's Trumpet Call to Ethnohermeneutics." *Journal of Asian Mission* 1 (1999) 223–32.

Taylor, Howard. *Hudson Taylor's Spiritual Secret*. Chicago: Moody, 1989.

Tennent, Timothy C. *Theology in the Context of World Christianity: How the Global Church Is Influencing the Way We Think about and Discuss Theology*. Grand Rapids: Zondervan, 2007.

Thiselton, Anthony C. *Hermeneutics: An Introduction*. Grand Rapids: Eerdmans, 2009.

Thompsell, Angela. "Get the Definition of Ubuntu, a Nguni Word with Several Meanings." *ThoughtCo*. https://www.thoughtco.com/the-meaning-of-ubuntu-43307.

Travis, John. "The C1 to C6 Spectrum." *Evangelical Missions Quarterly* 34 (1998) 209–10.

———. "Must All Muslims Leave 'Islam' to Follow Jesus?" *Evangelical Missions Quarterly* 34 (1998). https://missionexus.org/must-all-muslims-leave-islam-to-follow-jesus/.

Treier, Daniel J. *Introducing Theological Interpretation of Scripture: Recovering a Christian Practice*. Grand Rapids: Baker, 2008.

Tucker, Ruth. *From Jerusalem to Irian Jaya: A Biographical History of Christian Mission*. Grand Rapids: Zondervan, 2004.

Vanhoozer, Kevin J. *Is There a Meaning in This Text? The Bible, the Reader, and the Morality of Literary Knowledge*. Grand Rapids: Zondervan, 1998.

———. "Pilgrim's Digress: Christian Thinking on and about the Post/Modern Way." In *Christianity and the Postmodern Turn: Six Views*, edited by Myron B. Penner, 71–104. Grand Rapids: Brazos, 2005.

Van Rheenen, Gailyn. *Communicating Christ in Animistic Contexts*. Pasadena: William Carey, 1991.

Venn, Henry. "On Steps Towards Helping a Native Church to Become Self-Supporting, Self-Governing, and Self-Extending." In *Classics of Christian Missions*, edited by Francis M. DuBose, 243–49. Nashville: Broadman, 1979.

———. *To Apply the Gospel: Selections from the Writing of Henry Venn*. Edited by Max Warren. Grand Rapids: Eerdmans, 1971.

———. "Three-Self Principles." In *Classic Texts in Mission & World Christianity: A Reader's Companion to David Bosch's Transforming Mission*, edited by Norman E. Thomas, 207–09. American Society of Missiology Series 20. Maryknoll, NY: Orbis, 1998.

Bibliography

Wu, Jackson. "Biblical Theology for Oral Cultures." In *World Mission: Theology, Strategy, and Current Issues*, edited by Scott Callaham and Will Brooks, 269–289. Bellingham, WA: Lexham, 2019.

———. *One Gospel For All Nations: A Practical Approach to Biblical Contextualization*. Pasadena: William Carey, 2015.

———. *Reading Romans with Eastern Eyes: Honor and Shame in Paul's Message and Mission*. Downers Grove: IVP Academic, 2019.

Wachowski, Larry, and Andy Wachowski, dirs. *The Matrix*. Burbank: Warner Bros., 1999.

Wan, Enoch. "Critiquing the Method of Traditional Western Theology and Calling for Sino-Theology." *Global Missiology* 1 (October 2003). http://ojs.globalmissiology.org/index.php/english/article/view/438.

———. "Ethnohermeneutics: Its Necessity and Difficulty for All Christians of All Times." *Global Missiology* (2004) 1.

Warren, Max. "Introduction: Henry Venn, the Man, His Thought and His Practice—An Interpretation." In *To Apply the Gospel: Selections from the Writings of Henry Venn*, 15–34. Grand Rapids: Eerdmans, 1971.

Waterman, L. D. "Do the Roots Affect the Fruits? Six Points to Consider." *International Journal of Frontier Missiology* 24 (2007) 57–64.

Weanzana, Nupanga, et al. "Psalms." In *Africa Bible Commentary*, edited by Tokunboh Adeyemo, 605–772. Grand Rapids: Zondervan, 2010. https://www.perlego.com/book/561417/africa-bible-commentary-pdf.

WhatCulture. "10 Movie Scenes Everyone Gets Wrong." *YouTube*, July 14, 2021. https://www.youtube.com/watch?v=hQka2D4ydpE.

Whelchel, James R. "Ethnohermeneutics: A Response." *Journal of Asian Mission* 2 (2000) 125–33.

Whiteman, Darrell L. "Anthropological Reflections on Contextualizing Theology in a Global World." In *Globalizaing Theology: Belief and Practice in an Era of World Christianity*, edited by Craig Ott and Harold A. Netland, 52–62. Grand Rapids: Baker, 2006.

Whitney, Donald S. *Praying the Bible*. Wheaton, IL: Crossway, 2015.

Wimsatt, William K., and Monroe C. Beardsley. "The Intentional Fallacy." In *The Verbal Icon: Studies in the Meaning of Poetry*, edited by W. K. Wimsatt, 3–18. Lexington, KY: University of Kentucky Press, 1954.

Winter, Ralph D. "Four Men, Three Eras, Two Transitions: Modern Missions." In *Perspectives on the World Christian Movement*, edited by Ralph D. Winter and Steven C. Hawthorne, 253–61. 3rd ed. Pasadena: William Carey, 1999.

———. "The Highest Priority: Cross-Cultural Evangelism." In *Let the Earth Hear His Voice: International Congress on World Evangelization Lausanne, Switzerland*, edited by J. D. Douglas, 213–41. Minneapolis: World Wide Publications, 1975.

Wolfe, J. Henry. "Insider Movements: An Assessment of the Viability of Retaining Socio-Religious Insider Identity in High-Religious Contexts." PhD diss., The Southern Baptist Theological Seminary, 2011.

Wong, Steven. *Exposing Chinese Ancestor Worship*. Petaling Jaya, Malaysia: Firstfruits, 2007.

Woodbery, J. Dudley. "To the Muslim I Became a Muslim? A Veteran Missionary and Scholar Weighs in on Muslim 'Insider Movements.'" *International Journal of Frontier Missiology* 24 (2007) 23–28.

Bibliography

World Council of Churches. "From Indigenization to Contextualization." In *Classic Texts in Mission & World Christianity: A Reader's Companion to David Bosch's Transforming Mission*, edited by Norman E. Thomas, 175–76. American Society of Missiology Series 20. Maryknoll, NY: Orbis, 1998.

Yan, Haiping. "Theatricality in Classical Chinese Drama." In *Theatricality: Theater and Performance Theory*, edited by Tracy C. Davis and Thomas Postlewait, 65–89. New York: Cambridge University Press, 2003.

Yeo, K. K. *Chairman Mao Meets the Apostle Paul: Christianity, Communism, and the Hope of China*. Grand Rapids: Brazos, 2002.

———. "Culture and Intersubjectivity as Criteria for Negotiating Meanings in Cross-Cultural Interpretations." In *The Meanings We Choose: Hermeneutical Ethics, Indeterminacy and the Conflict of Interpretations*, edited by Charles H. Cosgrove, 81–100. London: Continuum, T & T Clark International, 2004.

———. "Introduction." In *Navigating Romans Through Culture: Challenging Readings by Charting a New Course*, edited by K. K. Yeo, 1–30. Romans through History and Cultures. New York: T & T Clark International, 2004.

———. "Messianic Predestination in Romans 8 and Classical Confucianism." In *Navigating Romans through Culture: Challenging Readings by Charting a New Course*, edited by K. K. Yeo, 259–89. Romans through History and Cultures Series. New York: T & T Clark International, 2004.

———. *Musing with Confucius and Paul: Toward a Chinese Christian Theology*. Eugene, OR: Cascade, 2008.

———. "Paul's Theological Ethic and the Chinese Morality of Ren Ren." In *Cross-Cultural Paul: Journeys to Others, Journeys to Ourselves*, 104–40. Grand Rapids: Eerdmans, 2005.

———. *Rhetorical Interaction in 1 Corinthians 8 and 10: A Formal Analysis with Preliminary Suggestions for a Chinese Cross-Cultural Hermeneutic*. Edited by R. Alan Culpepper and Rolf Rendtorff. Biblical Interpretation 9. New York: Brill, 1995.

———. *What Has Jerusalem to Do with Beijing? Biblical Interpretation from a Chinese Perspective*. Harrisburg, PA: Trinity, 1998.

Yung, Hwa. *Mangoes or Bananas? The Quest for an Authentic Asian Christian Theology*. 2nd ed. Oxford: Regnum, 2014.

Zhang, Zhiyuan. "A Brief Account of Traditional Chinese Festival Customs." *Journal of Popular Culture* 27 (1993) 21.

黄柏和等。《基督徒与祭祖》。出头天神学丛书系列一。台北：雅歌出版社，1983。

曾昌发。《耶稣的比喻—从亚洲诠释学的角度研究路加福音中耶稣的比喻》。台北：永望文化事业有限公司，2018。